Everything Reminds Me of Tim

Dr. Tim Ball
PhD in Historical Climatology

Biography of Timothy Francis Ball

by Marty Ball and family, friends, and many others

Everything Reminds Me of Tim

Books by Dr. Tim Ball
Human-Caused Global Warming
The Deliberate Corruption of Climate Science
Slaying the Sky Dragon (with John O'Sullivan et al)
Eighteenth-Century Naturalists of Hudson Bay (with Stuart and Mary Houston)

©2024 Marty Ball—All Rights Reserved

ISBN 978-1-960405-26-5
eBook ISBN 978-1-960405-27-2

This book is sold subject to the condition that it shall not, by way of trade or otherwise, be lent, resold, hired out or otherwise circulated without the publisher's prior consent in any form of binding or cover other than that in which it is published and without a similar condition including this condition being imposed on the subsequent purchaser.

All cartoons and images come from personal collections, are in the public domain or are used with the kind permission of the copyright holder.

The title page illustration is created from a photo by Marg Trombley

Cover Design by Crystal Ball

STAIRWAY PRESS—Apache Junction

CAREFULLY SELECTED & EDITED BOOKS FOR DISCERNING AUDIENCES

www.StairwayPress.com
1000 West Apache Trail
Suite 126
Apache Junction, AZ 85120 USA

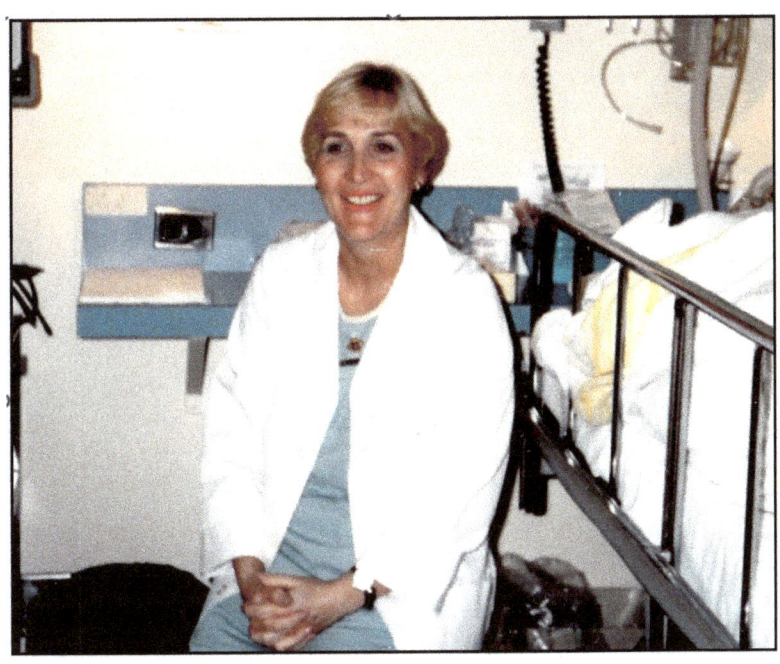

My nursing station, 1993

Introduction

By Marty Ball, Tim's Wife of 61 Years

MOST OF THE words in this book are what we retrieved from Tim while he was ill. His short-term memory deteriorated, but the long-term was clear.

David, Crystal, Tim Jr, Leann, and I wanted to explain what Tim's life has meant to us in book form. He was an extraordinary man. We don't know how to express our love and admiration for him in any other way.

We suggested many times over the years that he should write his own biography. The answer always was, "I would never do that. No one will even remember me two weeks after I am gone." We then asked him how he would like to be remembered, "I only want people to think of me as a kind person. If you really do write my biography, I would like you to make it humorous, as there is not enough humour in this world."

Altruism does not define him. I call him a mensch.

We hope he will be remembered forever with the publishing of this book. Please forgive the lack of continuity or repetitiveness. We have spent many loving hours doing this project. There were so many parts to Tim, and it was impossible to get it all into words. He wanted to be all things to all people. I called him a Triple A personality. Tad Anzai, our Japanese friend, called him a walking Encyclopaedia. We are sure he's in heaven with many people around him asking him questions. He was in his glory when able to pass on what knowledge he had. His brain would not allow him any rest.

Nothing was too much for him. He did many things, all overlapping in some way or another. Mary Campbell said he was a very complex man. She was right.

I am not an academic or intellectual. I am a bedside nurse, no more, no less. Tim often said I was a nurse first and a wife and mother second. I still don't know if that was a compliment. I must say here that Tim always treated me as his intellectual equal, but I daresay I didn't even come close. That meant more to me than he will ever, ever know.

I have tried to write this book in non-scientific jargon. I have included some of the articles he wrote for different websites or magazines. The scientific information is in Tim's books and his publishings, which are listed in his Curriculum Vitae at the end of this book. We were unable to keep his website going because of it being hacked so often. We managed to recover some of the material from his first and second sites with the help of very loyal and diligent friends.

Thank you!

Acknowledgements

TO OUR SONS, David and Tim Jr for their incredible remembrances of what their father taught and advised them, which I conveniently forgot over these many years. It was amazing to find how much they remembered.

Secondly, I owe an immeasurable amount to our twenty-five year computer guy, Andy Stewart. His incredible help, advice, expertise, loyalty, and knowledge were beyond expectation. In fact, he should be given the credit and compliment of being my co-author.

Next I would like to give credit to Bridget O'Reilly, my good friend, golfing partner and proofreader. I don't think many realize her exceptional talent and knowledge, which she very skillfully keeps under wraps.

The Ball family would like to thank everyone worldwide who contributed to Tim's legal and memorial funds. Without your help, Tim would not have been able to fight his lawsuits, and we would not have been able to publish this biography.

To those who have written the articles, letters and remembrances included in this book, we express our deep and heartfelt gratitude.

We are indebted to all of you.
—Marty, Dave and Tim Jr

Doug aged 3 and Dave aged 2

Table of Contents

CHAPTER ONE ... 7
The Ball Family—The Early Years ... 7
by Christopher Ball, Tim's Older Brother ... 7
An Addition to Chris' Contribution by Marty ... 14
Remembrance by Tim's Sister, Liz ... 14
My Brother Tim ... 14
Tim's Grammar School Friend, Mike Gough ... 16

CHAPTER TWO ... 17
Tim Arrives in Canada ... 17
Tim as a Student at the Universities—September 1968 to August 1972 ... 20

CHAPTER THREE ... 21
My Tim and Marty Ball Story—by Captain (Retired) Robert Ough CD ... 21
Over the Back Fence ... 23

CHAPTER FOUR ... 25
The Family ... 25
Douglas Richard Ball born April 7, 1962, in Summerside, PEI ... 25
David Christopher Ball, born July 20, 1963, in Summerside, PEI ... 25
Travelling to Winnipeg in November 1964 ... 26
Timothy Peter Ball, Jr was born in Winnipeg, MB, on June 20, 1967 ... 26
Miscellaneous Musings ... 28

CHAPTER FIVE ... 29
Search and Rescue Squadron—December 1964 to August 1968 ... 29
Miscellaneous Musings ... 30

CHAPTER SIX ... 31
The University of Winnipeg September 1972 to August 1996 ... 31
Miscellaneous Musings ... 33

CHAPTER SEVEN ... 34
Tim's Love of Art, Literature and Music ... 34
Miscellaneous Musings ... 35

CHAPTER EIGHT ... 36
THE EARLY YEARS by Dr Andrew Lockery, Geomorphology Professor, Colleague and Friend ... 36
The Professor ... 36
The Student ... 36
A Friendship Emerges ... 37
The Professor and the Graduate ... 37
The Professor and the Professor ... 38
Summary ... 38
Letter by Dr Jock Lehr, Geography Professor, Colleague and Friend ... 39

- Lessons Learned 39
- Letter from Dr. John Selwood, Geography Professor and Tim's Colleague 41
  - One of Many Criticisms of Tim came via a Manila Envelope to Tim's Office Marked Personal and Confidential on April 2, 1993 from Dr Geoff Scott 42
  - Letter written to Tim from Dr Geoff Scott. 1993 42
  - Miscellaneous Musings 43

CHAPTER NINE 44
- The Hudson Bay Company 44
  - Miscellaneous Musings 46

CHAPTER TEN 47
- Recollections by Dr Bruce Atkinson, Tim's PhD Supervisor at Queen Mary College, University of London England .. 47
  - Miscellaneous Musings 47

CHAPTER ELEVEN 49
- Tours for Credit Course Students 49
  - Day Trips and Weekend Tours for Credit Course Students in Tim's Physical Geography Class—1972 to 1996 49
  - Miscellaneous Musings 50
- Poem by One of Tim's Students 51
  - Tim Ball Speaks 51

CHAPTER TWELVE 52
- Three-Week Senior Citizen's Tours 1986 to 1996 52
- A Poem by May DeWet, 1986…a Long Tour Regular 54

CHAPTER THIRTEEN 56
- Building the Cottage at West Hawk Lake, Manitoba 56
  - Miscellaneous Musings 58

CHAPTER FOURTEEN 59
- Leaving Winnipeg and Moving to Victoria, BC 59
- 1996-2011 59

CHAPTER FIFTEEN 61
- Tim's Opinions on Universities: An Inside View, 1996 61
  - Miscellaneous Musings 63

CHAPTER SIXTEEN 64
- Letter from Joe and Mary Campbell, Winnipeg 64
  - Memories of Tim 64
  - Social and Family Life 64
  - Academic Life 64

CHAPTER SEVENTEEN 65
- Remediation at the Penninsula—The Leaky Condo Crisis 65

    During the First 18 years of Living at the Peninsula Condominium Units 65

    Marg Trombley Fellow Owner—Her Own Thoughts and Opinions (she was on the Strata Council with Tim) 65

    Letter from Mr. Val Dmiteryk—Caretaker at the Peninsula Condominiums 70

    Miscellaneous Musings 71

CHAPTER EIGHTEEN 72

    Tribute to Tim by Ian Jessop—Radio Talk Show host on CFAX in Victoria, BC from Jan 22, 2015 to July, 2016 72

CHAPTER NINETEEN 73

    Malcolm Roberts 73

        Celebrating Tim Ball 73

        Tim's Message is One of Hope in Humanity and, Thus, Hope for the Future 75

        I'm on Board with Tim and the Truth 75

        Miscellaneous Musings 76

CHAPTER TWENTY 77

    Tribute to Dr. Tim Ball, by Patrick Hunt, Tim's Friend April 2020 77

        IF by Rudyard Kipling 77

        A Tribute: An Inspiration, Mentor and Friend by Sheila Zilinsky—Author and Podcaster 78

        Tim Ball Remembered by James Corbett of the Corbett Report, Japan 80

        Thoughts and Opinions by Harv Chapple 80

        Ken Rowan—A Good Friend from Victoria Golf Club 81

        Miscellaneous Musings 82

CHAPTER TWENTY-ONE 83

    Mark Steyn's Article on his Website, September 26, 2022—'Ball's Bearing' 83

    Ave atque vale (hail and farewell : I salute you, and goodbye) 83

    Tim Ball Receives the Lifetime Achievement in Climate Science Award 84

    Tim's Thank You for the Achievement Award 84

    Publisher's Note by Ken Coffman—Stairway Press 84

    Dr Tim Ball, a Great Teacher who Deserved the Order of Canada 87

    by Tom Harris 87

    Miscellaneous Musings 89

CHAPTER TWENTY-TWO 90

    Letter by Susan Crockford, Assistant Prof at UVIC, Polar Bear Authority 90

    Losing my Adjunct Status at the University of Victoria 90

    Dr. Susan Crockford, 8 March 2023 90

    Excerpts from a Letter by Maggie Robinson, University of Winnipeg 92

CHAPTER TWENTY-THREE 94

    Tim's Article in *Country Guide Magazine*, March 2004 94

        Picture a World Without People 94

- The Rock 98.5 Radio Station in Yorkton, Saskatchewan by Jack Dawes 95
- Thoughts and Opinions by Andy Rowlands, Birmingham, England 96
- My Impressions of Dr Tim Ball 96
- Miscellaneous Musings 96

CHAPTER TWENTY-FOUR 97
- Should *Global Warming* Fraudsters Spend Time in the Clink? 97
  - Thoughts and Opinions from Pat Boone October 30, 2019 97
  - Miscellaneous Musings 99
  - Tim Ball's Student Exercises 99

CHAPTER TWENTY-FIVE 100
- Dedication by Kim Purdy, May 2023, Calgary, AB Canada—A Dear Friend of Tim's 100

CHAPTER TWENTY-SIX 101
- Dr Tim Ball Defeats Michael Mann's Climate Lawsuit! 101
  - Written by John O'Sullivan, Published on August 23, 2019 101
  - Hockey Stick—Discredited by Statisticians in 2003 102
  - Evidence in Legal Discovery and the Truth Defence 102
  - Have Skeptics Ever Proven that Mann's Graph was Deliberately Faked? 104
  - Putting Mann's Fraudulent Graph Under the Microscope 104
  - Victory that Comes at Great Personal Cost 105
  - Knowingly Fraudulent and Corrupt 106
  - Dr Ball Expresses Gratitude to Principia Scientific International 106
  - Dr Tim Ball: 106
  - As Jo Nova Reported on the joannenova.com.au Blog: 107
  - Two out of Two Major Court Wins by Ball Versus Junk IPCC Scientists 107
  - What is a 'Strategic Lawsuit Against Public Participation' (SLAPP Suit?) 108
  - Miscellaneous Musings 110
  - Tim Ball at the Heartland International Conference on Climate Change, 2014 110

CHAPTER TWENTY-SEVEN 111
- Canada Free Press 111
  - Judy McLeod's Apology for Tim on her Website 111

CHAPTER TWENTY-EIGHT 113
- Newspaper Articles 113
  - Tim's Letter of the Day—Times Colonist, July 13, 2005 113
  - Climate Studies have Basic Flaws 113
  - Opinion Pieces 113
  - Nurturing Doubt about Climate Change is Big Business. 113
  - *The National Post* Article, Refuting *The Globe and Mail* article, August 23, 2006 by Terence Corcoran 120

- Inside the Globe's 4,200-word Hatchet Job on Climate Skeptics 120
- The Background 120
- Hockey-Stick Science 121
- The Experts 122
- The Corporate Smear 123
- Chilling Debate 123
- The Suzuki Axis 124

CHAPTER TWENTY-NINE 125
- Radio Interview, One of Hundreds 125
  - Dr Tim Ball Interviewed on the Mike Rosen Radio Show on October 4, 2011 125
- Miscellaneous Musings 133

CHAPTER THIRTY 134
- Published Articles by Tim 134
  - Climate Change—Consensus vs. Science—Tim's article in Dialogue Magazine 134
  - Global Warming is not due to human contribution of Carbon Dioxide 134
  - Methods and Tricks Used to Create and Perpetuate the Human-Caused Global Warming Deception, as published on the *Watts Up with That* website 136

CHAPTER THIRTY-ONE 142
- 2007 to 2022 142

CHAPTER THIRTY-TWO 144
- Comments by our Oldest Son, David 144
  - "There He Was…Gone!" 144
  - Comments from David's wife, Crystal 145
  - Comments from Youngest Son, Tim Jr 146
  - Get on with it 146
  - A thought from Tim Jr's wife, Leann 148
  - Moon, Our Dog 148

CHAPTER THIRTY-THREE 149
- My Week in Oz with Tim Ball by Dr Tony Heller 149

CHAPTER THIRTY-FOUR 150

CHAPTER THIRTY-FIVE 171
- The Last Eleven Weeks 171
- Indispensable Advice 172
  - …inscribed on a beer mug that Tim had on his desk for many years. Unknown origin 172

CHAPTER THIRTY-SIX 173
- Curriculum Vitae—Dr Tim Ball 173
  - Education 173

- Career History 173
- Profile 173
- Books 173
- Contributions and/or Assistance 174
- Career Achievements 174
- Awards 175
- List of Publications for which he Wrote Regular Columns 176

CHAPTER ONE
The Ball Family—The Early Years
by Christopher Ball, Tim's Older Brother

MY BROTHER, TIMOTHY Francis Ball, was born on November 5, 1938 in Corsham Maternity home. Corsham is a village about 4 miles from our hometown of Chippenham, Wiltshire and although I myself was born in Chippenham, Corsham had one of only two maternity homes in the county at that time.

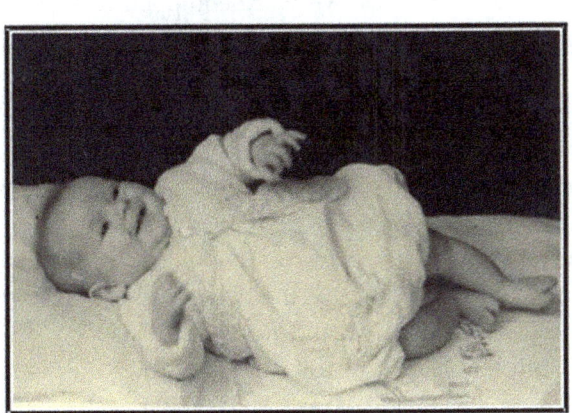
Tim, aged a few months, early 1939

Tim, aged about 1, early 1940

There is a lovely personal letter written by our Dad and sent to Mum in the home which suggests that Mum needed to be there for a few days for the birth. In the same letter Dad refers to the expected baby as either 'Timothy or Judith.' Our parents were Douglas V. Ball and Marjorie, nee King. They were Bristolians, from the east of the city in the Staple Hill and Downend districts. Their background is important because it explains the strengths and characteristics which they brought to us. I have always been grateful to them for the way they nurtured and supported us and so shaped our future.

I am sure Tim felt the same way as me.

Dad was the sixth of nine children of Alfred Herbert Ball and Kate Curtis. Although Alfred had been a soldier—he served in the Boer War in South Africa at the turn of the century in 1900—he was a tram driver and life was tough. Then Dad won a county scholarship and was able to attend Colston

TIM'S MUM, MARJORIE KING—2-YEARS-OLD

TIM'S DAD, DOUGLAS BALL IN 1927

School in Bristol, a prestigious fee-paying public school (in North America it would be called a private school). This was very important to us as a family because largely as a result of what he saw and learnt there, Dad became a socialist and a Catholic. We were raised as Catholics but he never forced his views onto us, believing passionately in the power of education.

This is why later he sent Tim and me to boarding school, and I think he was bitterly disappointed that circumstances meant that he could not do the same for Peter and Richard who came after us. He did manage to send Elizabeth to a convent school in Bath.

Mum was the older of two children of Arthur William King and Sarah Ann Eliza Hampson. She was only 4 feet and 11 inches tall (1.5 metres), but of very independent mind and a quirky sense of humour. This latter particularly she handed on to us. I have seen how Tim loves to use humour in his lectures and presentations. She opened a hairdressing salon in Staple Hill in the lean years of the 1920s and took over four years before agreeing to marry Dad.

Thus, although both sides of our family had come from modest agricultural and artisanal backgrounds in Norfolk and Somerset, Dad and Mum did so much to make sure we were equipped to make the most of what talents we had. After the birth, Tim was brought back to the family home at that time, 69, Rowden Hill, Chippenham.

[At this point, I am grateful that the extra research to write this has produced the likely solution to a puzzle which had arisen from my own birth. My birth certificate, and probably Tim's as well, gives the home address for Mum and Dad as 11, Rowden, and this is also the address used by Dad on the letter mentioned above. This address had never been mentioned by them and we had always assumed that they moved from their first house on Bristol Road straight to 69, Rowden Hill, taken by Tim and me to be our first childhood home. My wife Jacqui suggested that the street names could have been changed about this time and that the two addresses were the same house. A map dated 1938 shows the row of houses which includes No.69 and names the road on which they stand as Rowden. Counting the houses in odd numbers from the nearest to town as No.1, the sixth would be No.11 and this is the house I remember as No.69 when viewed on Google Maps. A year later we are recorded at No.69, Rowden Hill in the 1939 Census. Therefore, Jacqui is right and the address must have been changed between November, 1938 and the date of the census in September, 1939.]

TIM AND I, WITH DAD, OUTSIDE 69 ROWDEN HILL, FORMERLY 11 ROWDEN HILL, ABOUT 1942

69 ROWDEN HILL, AS IT IS NOW (COURTESY OF GOOGLE MAPS)

Everything Reminds Me of Tim

I have several memories of this time, which I relate to demonstrate the circumstances in which we grew up. This was, of course, the early days of WW2. Dad had not gone on to university like many of his contemporaries at Colston, I suspect for financial reasons, but he was doing well with large companies in Bristol before he lost his job due to the Depression. He became a sales rep with Huntley and Palmers Biscuits, but when the war broke out, he was obviously talented enough to be appointed as a senior security manager with the Ministry of Air Production (M.A.P.) He travelled all over the West of England checking the security arrangements in public buildings, factories and airfields. Therefore, he had a much bigger income than before, and also a petrol allowance. The war was thus a time of relative affluence for us, though we didn't know that at the time.

Nevertheless, most of my memories relate to the hardships of the time. I remember being carried one night out into the air raid shelter in the garden. It was only a pit in the ground, roofed over with curved corrugated iron sheeting and turf. The German bombers were on their way to bomb the docks in Bristol and South Wales. Only one bomb was ever dropped on Chippenham—a pilot who had got lost and was unloading for the journey back. It killed a lady living in a bungalow on the edge of town.

Food was always in short supply. Mum once queued for hours to get three or four oranges and was peeved with me when the unaccustomed citric acid brought me out in spots. My worst memory is the dreaded visits from the District Nurse who came at intervals to give Tim and me an enema to flush out tapeworms caused by the poor diet.

But as far as Tim is concerned there is this tale. He and I were playing in the garden one day when a lorryload of soldiers came charging past us on a training exercise. Tim threw his small spade at one of them, reportedly cutting the soldier's leg and causing the only casualty of the day.

I tell this tale because some years later when he and I were in our very early teens, we were walking back from town via a back path across the fields to our house in Cricketts Lane. We were confronted by 3 youths but it was Tim who shouted back at them so that they left us alone. These two incidents show an assertiveness in Tim which was certainly lacking in me. I have envied him this trait over the years—it must have been a factor in his later teaching and lecturing careers and his confidence in front of an audience.

In about 1943, we moved to a larger house called Langley Cottage in the village of Langley Burrell, about 2 or 3 miles out of Chippenham.

This house had a paddock to the right of the house as viewed above. We had a collie type mongrel dog called Buster who wore a path across the grass of the paddock chasing planes. We also kept sheep in it. One day Dad was bending to pick horseradish roots when the ram butted him rather hard. Dad had to eat standing up for a day or two.

Although the house was next door to the village pub at the front, the paddock was separated by a wall at the back, beyond which was the garden of the Payne family in Old Brewery House. The wall had been part of a building at one time and had the remains of a window in it. We would squeeze through the bars and spend many hours playing with Payne children, Mark, Anne and Judith. The family became good friends—Mark was best man for me when I married my first wife Dorrie. As a child, Mark had a problem with his legs. He wore leg callipers and we played in their garden for the most part.

Behind the cottage were wheat fields. We would help in the harvest, stacking the stooks of wheat to be thrown onto the horse and cart. Most years there was an old threshing machine, belt driven by the tractor. I vividly remember that in one field the wheat was cut from the outside in towards the centre. When there was only a small square left, dogs would be sent in to flush out the rabbits onto the guns of the farmers.

Tim and I would also go with the other children to the fence surrounding a camp at one end of the village, occupied by American soldiers. They would throw us sweets (candies) and respond to the popular phrase at the time... "Got any gum, chum?"

There was a small shop and post office in the village run by Mrs. Bryant, but Mum would walk us all to Chippenham regularly to do more shopping and visit her hairdressing shop (though for the most part Dad ran it). This was a round trip of four or five miles, pushing a pram which must have held two children because Pete and Richard were only four and two at the most. I have no idea how she managed it but that was what you did in those days, you just got on with it—there were no buses or taxis.

Langley Cottage was a good time in my memory. The picture above is of a party organized by Dad to mark VE Day (Victory in Europe Day), when the war ended. VE Day was May 8, 1945 so the picture must have been in that summer. (Dad is standing on the left with Tim in front of him and I am the boy running back toward the house.) Dad also organized a magician in the Village Hall who caused great amusement by producing an egg from the bosom of Lady Scott, wife of the Lord of the Manor.

I have other memories too. Spending some time up a tree where Mum had chased me because I had dropped and broken a jar of jam (remember that this one jar would be a month's supply!!). And Pete, aged three, being found drunk because Mum had left a part bottle of stout open on the kitchen table.

Soon after the end of the war, we moved to a large house in East Tytherton, another two or three miles out from town beyond Langley Burrell.

As can be seen from the photograph it had originally been a Moravian Girls Boarding School, though with only about 20 boarders. (Interestingly, I found out later that Mark Payne's mother, Renee, had been a pupil there at one time.)

VE Day party outside Langley Cottage, May 8, 1945—Langley Cottage as it is today

The house came with some of the trappings of the former school's 'still' used to make alcohol, which made it a paradise for us children. To the left of the photo was a tennis court, and to the right four or five classrooms. The whole top floor of the house was one room, a dormitory—the smaller 'windows' at the top are false—where we played football on rainy days with a large woolen pom-pom which Mum made for us.

At the rear of the house was a wooden gym, which we hired out to the local primary school. We built dens in the grounds, one across a small stream, and again it is remembered as a happy time.

After a while, Dad's younger brother Len and his wife Auntie Rita and our cousin Michael, came to live with us—the house was quite large enough. Uncle Len was an officer in the Royal Air Force, at nearby Compton Bassett, I think. For a while we had two German POWs (prisoners of war), called, if memory

Our house in East Tytherton, formerly a Moravian Girls Boarding School

serves, Wilhelm and Josef, who were dropped off from a lorry each day from their camp near Melksham to work in the garden. They were given one of the classrooms for use on a rainy day and must have quite enjoyed the time with us as a 'cushy' number. They carved things from wood for us, most notably a beautiful crib and figures which we used at Christmas for many years. Dad kept in touch with Wilhelm for some time after the war. Since the war was officially over by August, 1945 with VJ (Victory over Japan) Day, this must have been in the winding down period when arrangements were being made for their repatriation.

This was in 1946, when Elizabeth was born, an event I remember vividly because I was crushed behind the bedroom door when Dad came rushing upstairs excitedly to announce her birth.

We then moved again about 1947/1948 to a beautiful Georgian house, No. 19, St. Mary Street, behind the parish church in the middle of town. I think that at this time Dad was still earning the better salary from his M.A.P. job because it was a large house with a library and according to the brochure when it later came to be sold, two Adams fireplaces, which would now be worth a lot of money.

19, ST. MARY STREET, CHIPPENHAM, AS SHOWN ON THE ESTATE AGENTS BROCHURE AT THE TIME OF ITS SALE

Uncle Len and Rita also came to live there before Len was sent to Germany, from where they moved to Canada. We had a servant, Mary, who helped Mum in all sorts of ways, and was almost one of the family.

As with the other houses, No. 19 had a large garden, mainly a large lawn surrounded by flower beds. Tim and I must have played in the garden a great deal, because my main memory is of one day deciding to help Dad by painting a wooden summerhouse with bright green paint, helped by Tim's friend, Michael Gough. Unfortunately, I at least, and probably Tim too, were wearing brand new brogue shoes, possibly purchased for our move to Belmont Abbey, which got covered in the paint. I remember vividly lying in bed waiting for Dad to come home that evening. However, the anticipation must have been worse than his punishment which I do not remember at all.

This leads nicely to a significant next stage in our lives. It was decided to send Tim and me to a small Catholic boarding school near Hereford. Belmont Abbey School was run by the Benedictine monks of the monastery there. We were taken to a specialist outfitters in Cheltenham one day and kitted out with all the clothes and equipment which we would need, including a wooden-bound trunk inscribed C.J. and T.F. Ball.

It was in the house for many years later. There is a photograph of us children in the library at No. 19 in which Tim and I are wearing our new school uniform. Barely visible on the blazer breast pockets are a lion and a tiger, signifying which schoolhouse we were to be in, although I have forgotten which was which. I think mine was the tiger.

We spent four years at the school from 1948 to 1952. I did well academically because I had passed the 11+ grammar school entrance exam the previous year and most of my classmates had not, which was usually why they were sent to Belmont.

Tim also did well but after two years he was sent north to the preparatory school for Belmont called Alderwasley Hall in Derbyshire. I remember many aspects of boarding life—the dormitories, Sunday afternoons spent collectively writing letters home, sitting in a draughty church and serving at Mass, and many memories of friends and acquaintances. Funnily enough I enjoyed at least one year being a 'fag' for a school prefect called McLoughlin. I was in effect an unpaid servant, cleaning his room and polishing his rugby boots among other chores.

But it also brought benefits. McLoughlin was in charge of the school tuck-shop so he got me extra sweets from time to time (sweets were still rationed at the time) and allowed me to keep the penny deposit on his lemonade bottles when they were returned. I could also use him as an excuse when I was late for something. I only had to say "I was just doing something for McLoughlin..."

There were only about 70 boys in the school, so I was usually thrown into rugby and cricket games with boys who were much bigger. That and other aspects of boarding school life meant that I was never really happy there, so I was not too disappointed when Dad and Mum had to take us away from the school.

Nevertheless I did learn politeness and good manners there which have stood me in good stead subsequently.

Meanwhile Tim was thoroughly enjoying the experience, especially at Alderwasley, and was very disappointed when we left. I think at the time that he blamed me and my unhappiness, but we now know that we had to leave because Dad and Mum realized that they could not afford to send Peter and Richard there as well, so it was a case of one out, so all out.

However, that is not the whole story. Much later in life, whilst I was tracing the family history, I was told that at about this time, Dad had loaned a friend a pretty large sum of money but the 'friend' had reneged on the debt. If this is true it would make every sense, because we were taken away from Belmont and moved from St. Mary Street to a modest dormer bungalow about a mile out of the town off London Road at 2, Cricketts Lane. I remember a friend from Belmont coming to stay at Cricketts Lane so we had sold St. Mary Street before we left the school.

Either way Tim and I were sent to the local Chippenham grammar school to be followed by Pete and Richard. I remember Tim and I playing in the garden at Cricketts Lane. We played football on the lawn with the constant danger that the ball would go into the field next door which was used by a gaggle of unfriendly geese. Whoever had kicked the ball would have to leap the fence and make a dash to retrieve it while the rest of us tried to divert the geese. We could roam off into the countryside beyond the garden—Mum had an old school bell which she would ring to call us for meals.

But my main memory of the time here was an awareness of how tough life had become for Dad and Mum. Seven of us were crammed into a small house and money clearly short. I had to sleep on a small landing at the top of the stairs and I will never forget the sound of Dad coming up the steps reciting prayers on his rosary beads. Mum was very ill at one time and had to spend weeks in hospital in Bath. Our Auntie Ethel came to run the

Belmont Abbey School, 1948-1949, Front row: CJB second from right, TFB second from left

No.2 Cricketts Lane, Chippenham
(courtesy of Google Maps)

household for a while.

Within a year or two I had moved into the Sixth Form and my life revolved selfishly around my gang of mates. We played sport (rugby, hockey and cricket) for the school on a Saturday morning and in the afternoon played cards at one of our houses. I had a series of part-time jobs, filling sacks of coal at the railway yard, tidying up and delivering cloth for a tailor on the High Street, delivering the post at Christmas, and then every holiday working for a wholesale grocery firm.

I have to be honest and say that I was so wrapped up in my own life that I have little idea what Tim was doing during these years. He had his own group of friends, but I could not now name a single one of them.

About 1954 we moved yet again, this time to a larger house nearer the centre of town, No.12 Marshfield Road, almost opposite the house where I was born. We boys slept in the attic bedrooms behind the dormer windows seen in the photo on the right.

In 1956, despite not working as well as I should, I won a County Scholarship and went off to Bristol University. In the meantime, Tim was articled to an architect in the town and helped design buildings which can still be seen down by the bridge over the River Avon.

I was told he was doing well but things went wrong in his second year—I think the architect was not a good man to work for—so he left the firm. But this meant he became liable for National Service which was in existence at this time, and being Tim, he immediately decided to take advantage of a scheme helping people to emigrate to Canada. A factor in this may well have been that Uncle Len and Auntie Rita had moved to Canada some years before. This all took place so quickly that I was summoned home from University one weekend to bid him farewell.

If I have not related these events correctly, I apologize, but this is how I was led to believe it all happened. Remember that I was away in Bristol at University, wrapped up in my own existence. All of you in Canada must pick up the story from this point.

Inevitably, this account of our early life is filled with my own anecdotes and memories. I have tried to make it a record of the conditions under which we all grew up as a family and the love and support our parents endeavoured to give us.

We were influenced by the tough conditions under which they themselves grew up and the enormous devotion they gave us and the determination that we should have as good a start in life as possible. I never underestimate the sacrifices they made.

12 Marshfield Road, Chippenham
(courtesy of Google Maps)

**THE BALL FAMILY—OCTOBER 1980
CHRIS, RICHARD, MOTHER BALL, PETER, LIZ
AND TIM**

For me, this account has served two purposes. First, it is a more personal record of the early years, not found in the basic sources of census and parish records. This was also true in the spoken and written records that Mum left.

Second, it is information for the future generations which will not be found elsewhere—information which makes the people concerned into real people. For example, recently Kirsten Perrault, granddaughter of Len and Rita, has used the family history to travel around Britain visiting all the houses where her ancestors lived.

So I hope this is of interest and that the information can be of use to the coming generations in the future.
—*Christopher J Ball.* **May 2020**

An Addition to Chris' Contribution by Marty

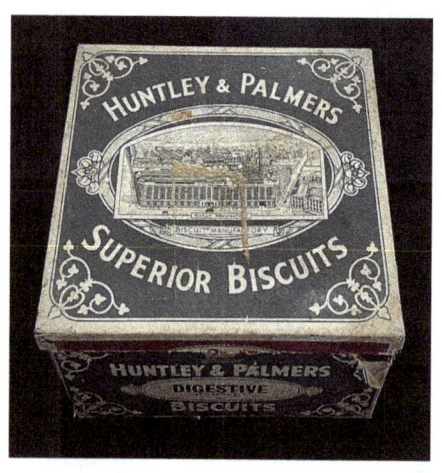

Douglas Sr, (Tim's father) got a salesman's job with Huntley and Palmers Biscuits after the war. He was eternally grateful to them even though he disliked the job. A car was a benefit, essential to him and his growing family. He felt much gratitude and loyalty to them. He did that job for 36 years to support his family.

He also managed the three beauty salons that Marjorie owned when they married. (Married women did not work in those days.) That could have worked out better. Tim's Dad was not a businessman. He was overly generous with his staff. The Swinden Salon, and Bristol, were the first to go out of business, then the Chippenham shop. In later chapters, you will realize this part of Tim's character was genetic.

Douglas Sr delivered biscuits to a particular residential home weekly and never knew who lived there or what function it had. He finally learned that it held soldiers so badly maimed during the war that they had themselves declared deceased. They didn't want their families to see them ever again.

Very, very sad!

After retiring from Huntley and Palmers, Douglas Sr became a registrar for a community college in Chippenham. He loved that job and the students, and they loved him.

They planted a tree on the campus in his honour when he died. (Tim would have liked to see if the tree was still there in later years.)

Tim's father died suddenly in March 1972 at the age of 64.

Remembrance by Tim's Sister, Liz

My Brother Tim

I ONCE ATTENDED one of Tim's speaking engagements in Dauphin, Manitoba. He was speaking to one of his favourite groups—farmers. He had enormous respect for the farming community, feeling they were generally misunderstood or ignored by the general population until, through circumstances beyond their control, there were empty shelves in the supermarket! Equally, most of the farmers respected Tim as they appreciated that he was one of their greatest champions and was in awe of what they did and how hard they worked.

After his speech, people were milling around talking and

TIM WITH HIS SISTER, LIZ MUIR NOVEMBER, 2018

catching up with friends when one lady, obviously not recognizing me as a local, asked who I was. When I replied that I was Tim's sister visiting from the UK, she said, "You must be so proud of him and all he does."

It was the first time I had considered being proud of my big brother, but it made me realize that I was and always had been, very happy to be his sister. But of course, as the little sister, I would never say that to him! I always told him that amongst all the accolades he received, my job was to keep his feet firmly on the ground, but, as it turned out, my 'job' was never a busy one, as Tim's feet were always very firmly planted.

Because of the age gap and Tim away at boarding school in my early years, we didn't know each other very well before he left to live in Canada when I was eleven. And yet, somehow, we were always close.

My family and I moved to Canada in the early 1990s. Finally, I could spend time with Tim and get to know him. I quickly learned that he was an open book who loved to talk and interact with people. We spent many happy hours in Winnipeg, and then when we had all moved to Vancouver Island, we got together 'to set the world to rights.'

Of course, we never achieved our goal, but it was fun trying.

Tim had a quick wit, often teasing in a kindly way. He could put people at ease with just a few words and appreciated every day, unassuming people, calling them 'the salt of the earth.' The janitors, wait staff, retail workers, etc., quietly went about their work without acknowledging their essential contribution to society.

Tim's sense of humour was legendary in my own family, and it is the one thing my three sons will mention when asked what they remember of their Uncle Tim.

He had a sense of fun and a love for life that was second to none. Walking around Victoria, rather than take the same streets each day, he would make a game of it by letting the changing traffic lights dictate which way he would go. Spending time with him was always a pleasure, as his joy was infectious.

The letters and references to his wife, Marty, have included showing how people admired Tim. Many loved him, especially those whose cause he championed so fervently.

His beliefs on the climate change issue brought a sense of sadness to his latter years, but he never lost his positivity, regardless of how many criticisms came.

He would not be silenced, never wanting anyone to be able to say, "I never knew that!"

Tim firmly believed knowledge was power. People armed with both sides of an argument could then draw their own conclusions.

Unfortunately, those beliefs brought about a lot of hate and jealousy. He received many death threats and was subject to many published lies regarding his academic credentials and achievements, which sadly followed him to his grave and are still on the internet for all to see. As a family, we tried desperately to counteract these lies, but quickly learned that it is tough to disprove a negative. What's the saying about "mud sticking?" This is more true than ever now, with the World Wide Web absorbing good and bad information and spreading it to all corners of the globe in seconds.

But at least we know Tim's words will never be lost, thanks to the internet. Anyone who knew Tim knew he was one of the most humble, gentle and unassuming people you could ever meet. He was generous to a fault, especially with his time and loved sharing his knowledge, but always left the person to decide.

He had the most fantastic memory of the climate, among many other subjects, and loved to discuss and share that knowledge. And his thirst for knowledge never left him!

There was never a dull moment around Tim, and certainly never any awkward silences or lulls in the conversation!

He was an amazing teacher who loved all his students, both young and old.

I know this is how he would love to be remembered.

Thank you, Tim, for all you gave me and my family.

And yes, I was, I am, and always will be very proud to call you my big brother.

Love you, Tim.

—*Liz Muir*

Tim's Grammar School Friend, Mike Gough

The Ball and the Gough families were good friends in Chippenham, Wiltshire, UK, mainly because they belonged to the same Catholic church. Mike and Tim became good friends in grammar school as well.

Tim went to Canada, and Mike entered the Metropolitan Police in London. They only occasionally communicated until Tim started his doctorate at Queen Mary College at the University of London. He and Mike rekindled their old friendship each summer, which was very important to them. They would tour and walk along London streets. Mike would look for impending crime, and Tim would look at the architecture and history—two different worlds and how they were perceived.

Mike was working his way up in the ranks at Scotland Yard and made it to commander, but further promotions did not happen because he didn't have the 'right school tie.'

When Tim graduated with his doctorate, Mike arranged a lovely hotel near the Royal Albert Hall where they held Tim's convocation. Tim's mother, Marjorie and I sat proudly for over four hours. Tim was given his PhD scroll after over 2,000 graduates filed before the chancellor. Mother and I wandered amongst the crowd looking for Tim following the ceremony. Finally, we decided to wait at the front door until Tim found us. We were exhausted, and rather than take the bus provided to escort us to the reception, we returned to our hotel and the three of us had dinner with Mike Gough.

TIM WITH MIKE AND MAUREEN GOUGH AT TOWER OF LONDON, 1983

Mike updated us on his years of police work. He travelled two hours daily to and from work, taking his car from home to the train station, which he rode via the Underground to Scotland Yard. The same scenario was going home. He rarely saw his children growing up as they were asleep when he left home and when he returned.

Tim asked Mike what his worst experience was as a policeman. Without hesitation, he said it was the bombing of the Horse Guards by the IRA (Irish Republican Army) in London on July 20, 1982. As a nurse, my first question was whether he had used CPR on the victims. Mike answered, "Marty, my concern was a second bomb," which did happen two miles away two hours later.

Many of our tours with senior citizens started in London. The four of us met regularly. Mike and Maureen took us to various sites. We stood on the steps of Buckingham Palace for the changing of the guards. We also had a personal tour of the Black Museum at Scotland Yard. The journey between Mike and Maureen's home to various sites seemed endless. I wonder how they ever found their way.

Mike and Maureen visited us in Winnipeg and again in Victoria. Mike retired from the police force and got the job as head of security for Tescos, a grocery chain in Britain.

Sadly, Mike died in 2018. I am still in touch with Maureen.

CHAPTER TWO

Tim Arrives in Canada

TIM'S BROTHER CHRIS wanted to emigrate to Canada but decided at the last minute that he couldn't leave England. Tim said, "I'll use the ticket." In October 1957, Tim flew from London to New York to Toronto with only $48 in his pocket.

He had an uncle in Toronto and stayed with their family until he got settled in a job. After a few dead-end jobs, the last being in Sudbury, Ontario, he hitchhiked to North Bay, Ontario and joined the Air Force. We know little of his time in Ontario. Things could be more specific between entering Canada in 1957 and ending in Winnipeg in 1960. Tim never looked back. He never thought it was necessary. He didn't write home for over a year after arriving in Canada. His parents must have been worried? Maybe not!

After writing the RCAF entrance exams, he was transferred to Winnipeg for aircrew training as a radio operator. Tim had some reason he could not train as a pilot, which I still don't know. He had to master 'Morse Code,' a challenge for Tim and his flight cadet classmates.

My class of student nurses went to the Cadet's Mess for dances on Saturday nights. Two cadets picked us up and promised to return us to the nurse's residence. Tim was driving an MG, and I jumped in his car. We chatted happily during the half-hour drive to the cadet's mess. We danced until eleven when I had to report for night duty. Tim was a great dancer and I was thrilled to be his partner. Tim asked if he could phone me on the following Wednesday at 7 PM and arrange another date. I never thought he would keep his promise, but he did, and we ended up courting from August 1960 to June 1961, during which time he asked me to marry him.

Our wedding day was a sweltering day on June 5, 1961 in Estevan, Saskatchewan. We danced all afternoon and evening. (Tim always said he got married so he wouldn't have to dance anymore. He kept that promise for years until our son David and Crystal married in July 2003. One dance only, of course.)

There were only morning weddings in the Catholic church at that

time. My mom got up at 6 AM each day the week before the wedding to bake buns. It was so hot during the day. No electric stove, only an oil-burning kitchen type. She had to make, bake and serve lunch at noon and again in the late evening. We had dinner catered for 65 guests. None of Tim's family were there, of course. We did have a phone call from Douglas Sr and Marjorie. We could hardly hear them above the noise of the wedding guests. The time difference was seven hours.

We danced all afternoon and evening. At midnight a few of my family were shedding tears as we loaded the car with our gifts and started on the long trek from Estevan to Summerside, PEI, in the beastly 88 Oldsmobile.

We drove south through the USA via Chicago and refuelled and refuelled. We went to Niagara Falls and refuelled and refuelled. We drove through Ontario and refuelled and refuelled, then Quebec and refuelled and refuelled, then through the Gaspé Penninsula and New Brunswick, to Cape Tormentine. We then boarded the ferry to Prince Edward Island. The journey seemed endless.

MARTY AT HER GRADUATION, MAY 1961, AND HER MOM KATHERINE (KATIE) MARTIN GISI

After booking a hotel in Summerside, we realized we had little money and no place to live. (We each thought the other had all the money when neither of us had any. We never discussed money while we were courting…bad planning.) All we had was a carload of dishes, sheets and towel sets. Thank goodness for HFC (Household Finance Company.) They were our saviour. They loaned us $300 which we used to settle into a furnished basement apartment which we were fortunate to find, even though the military were moving in and out of Summerside all the time.

Tim reported for duty at the air force base, a twenty-minute commute from Summerside. I went to Prince County Hospital looking for a job as a registered nurse and was hired immediately. There has always been a need for trained nurses. I reported for orientation the following Monday morning.

In a small town, I could walk to work. My rotation was to work eleven days, 7 AM to 3 PM, then off three days—then eleven evenings, 3 PM to 11 PM, and off three days—then eleven nights, 11 PM to 7 AM, and off three days. By the third set of nights, I was pregnant, sick and exhausted. I resigned and worked part-time as a private-duty nurse until our son, Douglas was born.

TIM'S RCAF GRADUATING CLASS

ARGUS AIRCRAFT OF 415 SQUADRON

Everything Reminds Me of Tim

Tim was part of the 415 Squadron doing Russian submarine patrol for 18 to 20 hours. During these hours, the plane was only 50 feet over the water during the day and 200 feet at night. They used Magnetic Anomaly Detection (MAD) devices to locate Russian submarines. Tim often said, "I don't know what we would have done if we had found one." They encountered many whales, but no Russian submarines.

During almost four years in Summerside, Tim took various military training trips to places like Northern Ireland, Iceland, Britain, Bermuda, and the Azores.

In 1962, the commanding officer, Mike Lewis, transferred Tim to the Operations Department as the operations officer in Summerside. It was a desk job, and Tim loved it—regular hours and no long flights.

We made longtime friends in the RCAF. Bob and Marg Ough, John and June Kirby, Ron and Estelle Lorenz, Liz and Jim Katsikas, Peter Gilchrist and Roberta Shaw, Perry and Sharon McKinnon, Bob and Shirley Hopper and many, many more. So many are gone now. Our fondest remembrances were of our air force days.

1963 was an anxious time. In October, there was the 13-day Cuban Missile Crisis. The RCAF was part of NORAD (North American Air Defence) and NATO (North Atlantic Treaty Organization). The 415 Squadron were on a two-minute alert and could not leave the base.

In November 1963, they were again on alert after U.S. President John Kennedy's assassination in Dallas, Texas.

Just after son number two, David's birth on July 20, 1963, Tim drove to Montreal to pick up his mother and sister. They were arriving by Cunard liner to Montreal from England to stay with us for six weeks. It was my first meeting with Mother Ball, Marjorie, and Tim's sister, Liz, who was sixteen years old and very excited to have her first long holiday with her mom.

I was still in the hospital with David when they arrived.

This period was high on my stress meter. The food Tim and I cooked was not English food, and that didn't please Marjorie. I was in tears a few times. Dougie was only fifteen months old and still in diapers and I was breastfeeding David.

When it was time for Mom and Liz to return to England, Tim drove them to Moncton, New Brunswick, and they took the bus from there to Montreal. They said later that the cruise was the best part of their holiday. We understood.

Tim's claim to fame was being the longest-ranking flight lieutenant in the RCAF before getting promoted to captain. Tim regularly made protests about things he thought were unfair. The social committee fund subsidized alcohol at every social event but not the food. Tim didn't drink much, so he thought this was unfair.

Another incident happened while Tim was picking up his paycheck. There was a sergeant in front of him in the line. The payroll sergeant was to serve the officers before the airmen. Tim said that "first come, first served" was fairer. The squadron leader summoned Tim and charged him with insubordination. Tim took off his stripes from his summer uniform shirt, laid them on the table before the squadron leader and said, "I will no longer need these," and walked out. Hence, promotion was a long time coming.

1967 and 68 were difficult times for Tim. The hearing damage from the aircraft noise during the long flights in the Argus meant he could barely hear a thing while waiting for corrective surgeries. For example, he could not hear Doug and Dave cry. The first operation, a stapidectomy, was performed on Tim's left ear in Toronto in 1967 followed by the right ear in Winnipeg in 1968. What a wonderful thing to have this intricate surgery. When Tim returned home from the Winnipeg hospital, he kept waking up during the night with the noise of the furnace starting—it was so loud for Tim. It took a while to get used to hearing again. This was a turning point in our lives since he could no longer fly as a radio operator.

As an interesting side issue, Tim tried for 40 years to get a military pension for the hearing damage. It was continually refused. The Department of Veterans Affairs suggested the deafness was caused by congenital otosclerosis and only aggravated by the noise of the Argus aircraft. With the help of doctors and lawyers, Tim finally managed to receive his disability pension in 2008—$352 per month. We learned along the way that many aircrew had similar hearing problems, and dealing with these was a great expense to the Department of Veteran Affairs.

Tim as a Student at the Universities—September 1968 to August 1972

During his last years serving in the RCAF, Tim went to night school. He amassed the credit courses necessary for Grade 12, plus many of the first- and second-year courses for his BA degree. When he was released from the nine years on his short service commission, he enrolled at the University of Winnipeg full time. I began full-time evenings at the Grace Hospital when Dougie was two and one half and Tim Jr was one year old.

One of us was always home with the children. Tim would go to university in the morning after giving the boys their breakfast and getting Dave off to school. He arranged his classes so he could be home before I went to work. Tim was always waiting at the window when I came home from work at midnight to make sure I was safe, where he had a snack ready for me. He never missed, even the many times I was late because of the need to work overtime.

These years were not our most exciting. It seemed we were between social groups but couldn't afford much in that direction anyway. With a son that was ill and two other young children we were fully occupied.

It was a happy day when Tim was hired by the University of Winnipeg as an instructor in the geography department in September 1972.

CHAPTER THREE

My Tim and Marty Ball Story—by Captain (Retired) Robert Ough CD

I ORIGINALLY MET Tim Ball in the first quarter of 1960. My situation was as follows…I had applied because of an RCAF effort to allow ground crew personnel of certain electronic trades to re-muster to the aircrew trades. I took advantage of this situation and passed the appropriate Personnel Selection Unit (Officer) PSU(O) testing at Centralia in the fall of 1959. At this time, I was stationed at RCAF Namao (Edmonton) with 435 Transport Squadron. Subsequently I was transferred east to start training.

In February of 1960 at RCAF Station Centralia, we were enrolled at the pre-flight training school (PFTS) and commenced a 16-week course of intensive training on course 6003. We were given the subordinate officer rank of Flight Cadet. Several weeks later a new intake of flight cadets arrived and started as Course 6004…<u>Tim Ball was on that course</u>. Dudley (D'Arcy) Thornton who had been with me in Clinton on the electronic courses was also on the same intake.

It was the beginning of some of the most valuable friendships I have ever had…Bob Robert, Yvan Giroux, Denis Gauthier, John Kirby, Hank Morris, Paddy Devlin, Mike Leigh, Ron Lorenz and Peter Gilchrist to name just a few.

After PFTS the pilots were sent off to Penhold and the Observer (Nav Trade) were sent to Winnipeg…this was one of the CNR train rides I will never forget. John Kirby and I had so much fun on that trip.

In Winnipeg, we settled into our routine in Barrack Block 89 and began a year-long training program at the Air Observer School (AOS).

Our commanding officer on the base was Group Captain Mitchell (a highly decorated pilot for his WWII service.) The Officer Commanding of Air Observer School was Wing Commander Keith Greenaway—one of the most distinguished air navigators in the world…inventor of the R-Theta computer and a specialist in grid navigation in the Arctic. He also was asked by the US Government to be part of the crew as Lead Navigator on a blimp flying to the Arctic area. He said he much enjoyed the challenge and the trip.

Not long after our arrival in Winnipeg, we were introduced to the dances that were held in the flight cadet's mess. It did not happen every Saturday night but at least once a month a group of nurses or other ladies who worked for such companies as the Great West Life Insurance Company would show up for our dance. It was on these occasions that I met Meryl, Katey, and Bernadette Deschenes.

As well, our pal John Kirby met June Hawthorne who later became his wife.

On one of those nights, Tim Ball met a student nurse in her final year of training at St. Boniface Hospital…Martha Gisi. Tim and Marty fell in love and were married after we finished our training and received our wings. They both were great pals of mine and rank as great friends to this day.

I had just arrived at RCAF Station Summerside on June 15, 1961 when I was advised that my kid brother Alvin had been killed by a car while he had been delivering papers for the Toronto Star. I flew home for the funeral with the help of my new Officer Commanding of the Operational Training Unit

BOB AND MARG OUGH

(OTU), Wing Commander Mike Lewis. Mike had been a bomber pilot in WWII and won the Distinguished Flying Cross for mine laying, being shot down and taken as a prisoner of war. More important, he was from Port Hope as I was, and Mike knew my father pre-war.

Tim and Marty's house became a safe haven for me to visit off-base and Marty was a great cook as well as being the hostess for many of our fellow students on the Operational Training Unit course. This also brought about a great opportunity for Marty to learn to play bridge, which was the card game of choice in the RCAF. We also would attend the many serenades at the George R. Pearkes, Victoria Cross (for gallantry) Branch of the Royal Canadian Legion…local talent was also included.

When the OTU was completed, we went to RCAF Greenwood for the Argus Conversion Unit, then returned to Summerside to take up duties with 415 (Maritime Patrol) Squadron. I was assigned to Crew 2 under Flight Lieutenant Bob Connell and Tim was on Crew 4 with F/L Stew Mohr. Our officer commanding of 415 was Wing Commander S.S. Mitchell who we called 'Sub Sinker' Sid. A term of endearment.

Tim and Marty were thrilled when Dougie was born, and I was his god father…an absolute honour only to be cut short some few years later by his passing.

June and John Kirby were blessed with the birth of two daughters—Elaine and Janet. Both of them were like daughters to me, and I have never let those relationships drift away.

It was while in Summerside that I married Marg. We moved back to my hometown of Port Hope and shortly after that started our family. Both Michael and Kevin were born in PEI. Kelly came along eight years later when I was flying out of Arnprior, Ontario.

Tim and Marty moved on to Winnipeg where Tim began his wonderful career at university along with earning a PhD in climatology. In 1965, I transferred to the Reserve list, moved out of Summerside and back to Ontario.

I did my commercial helicopter pilot license and took up my career in rotary wing flying which saw me through the next fifty years of my life earning a living in that field.

It took me on numerous trips through Winnipeg where I was able to visit with Tim and Marty. These were precious times that I cherish. Our many long conversations on climate change—which were novel to me—were quite inspiring and these were supplanted by many conversations on the history of the Hudson's Bay Company. Tim and I would visit the HBC archives where there existed the 20 tons of recorded history (stories and maps) that were so fascinating to see. The HBC and the CPR to me are the greatest duo that helped to make Canada the country it is today. I have devoured books on the history of the HBC and this was under the informal tutelage of Dr Tim Ball. He and Marty would talk of their annual travels to Britain with groups of seniors visiting such places as Orkney and the HBC history that included the windswept northern islands. My interest in that area of the world included the upbringing of my favourite Arctic explorer, Dr. John Rae.

With my past personal contact with many of the HBC posts, some of which I lived in, it was now allowing me to be more of a participant in my conversations with Tim about the history of that fabulous organization.

We talked at length about the remote possibility of flying in a

BOB OUGH AND TIM, 1977, HUDSON BAY COMPANY ARCHIVES

relatively inexpensive fixed wing (whatever that means when one speaks of aircraft prices) to the sites of some of the arctic aircraft accidents. This was a lofty aim that will now go away due to the vagaries of ageing.

Ah, the memories, some of which grow dimmer with the advancing years. I will always have in my heart the thoughts about the battles that Tim fought with 'climatologists' on an ongoing basis…regardless of who was right or wrong, he always stood up for his viewpoints on this matter of global interest.

Marty, Tim and family, I will say in closing that this friendship of sixty-two years has flown by and will end only when someone in the Great Beyond decides on the timing. Until that time…Cheers!!

With love and respect,
—*Bob and Marg Ough and family*
….Marg passed away January 2, 2023

Over the Back Fence

On December 1, 1964, we moved into a new house on Danbury Bay in St. James, a suburb of Winnipeg. The Federal Government had a program that allowed new home buyers to purchase a home for $500 down with a 6.25% mortgage for 25 years. It was a gift from heaven. The location was perfect for Tim because it was near the RCAF base for the Search and Rescue Squadron.

Our next-door neighbours were Harry and Rita Schmidt. Harry was a builder. It never ceased to amaze us that he could work at his job and build a house. He sometimes worked until three AM. We could faintly hear the hammering at any hour.

We became the best of friends. We were the same age and raised our children side-by-side for 9 years. Tim and Harry chatted over the back fence regularly while Rita and I were doing those wifely and motherly duties inside.

When their first son was two months old, Tim asked Harry, "Is the baby sleeping through the night?" Harry's answer "As far as I know, he is."

I went into labour with our third son, Tim, Jr at 2 AM on June 20, 1967 (Canada's 100th Anniversary.) Tim could not get our Volkswagen Beetle started. We naturally called Harry, who offered to drive me to Grace Hospital in his car. Tim would not have it. Harry had to push our car until it started. Tim was at the wheel, and I was in the back seat counting the time between contractions.

Rita was so impatient for spring to arrive each year. Winnipeg had long, cold winters. As soon as the snow melted, she planted plastic flowers in their front garden. We would all watch the cars slow down to admire the early flowers and roar with laughter.

We partied plenty and made fast friends with Hank and Hilda Plenert along with Vern and Annita Giesbrecht. Annita and Hilda were sisters and also Harry's first cousins. I also worked with Hilda in the emergency department at Grace Hospital.

HARRY AND RITA SCHMIDT

Hank died suddenly in September 1989 at the age of 47.

We regularly visited Falcon Lake, Manitoba (Harry and Rita's cottage), very near our place at West Hawk Lake, Manitoba. We owe Harry so much for helping Tim put up our cottage walls. Tim needed Harry's expertise and help. Harry was a gift from God. To this day, we don't know how we would have coped. We needed so many hands. Mine and our boys were not enough.

Sadly, Rita lost her battle with cancer in November 2018. We miss her very much. She requested all those attending her funeral to bring a toque and mittens for the needy of the church congregation.

Rita was such a giving person.

Miss her so much.

CHAPTER FOUR

The Family

Douglas Richard Ball born April 7, 1962, in Summerside, PEI

David Christopher Ball, born July 20, 1963, in Summerside, PEI

WE KNEW NOTHING about raising children. One set of grandparents was 3,000 miles to the west, and the other was 3,000 miles to the east in England. It is only possible to pass on values and cultures when the teachers are close at hand, often the grandparents' duty.

At two and a half years old, Douglas started falling, and his eyes began to cross. We saw our family doctor, who sent us immediately to an eye specialist in Charlottetown, a 45-minute drive from Summerside. That doctor insisted that Doug had been crossing his eyes from birth, which was not true.

Any parent would have noticed!

The eye doctor put corrective lenses on Doug, but that just aggravated his situation. He continued to fall and would cry when the wind blew strongly rattling the windows. We think he suffered severe headaches and was unable to tell us.

I kept telling Tim and friends that I thought he had something wrong with his brain. At the time, Ben Casey was a popular TV neurosurgeon. Tim suggested I had seen too much of the series.

We rationalized and struggled with looking after our lovely boys, being so young, trying to hold our jobs and raise our children.

In July of 1964, we decided a holiday was in order and decided to visit my family in Estevan, Saskatchewan. It was three days and three nights by train from Moncton, NB, to Regina, Saskatchewan. I won't go into the horrors of that journey. Two young boys in diapers, in two tiny roomettes. Tim and Dave were in one roomette, and Doug and I were across the aisle in another. We called it the train ride from hell. There were no facilities for young children, such as play areas and soft food.

During the first few days of our stay in Estevan, Douglas and David came down with German Measles with super high temperatures. A young general practitioner, Dr Squires, who lived across the street from my parents came to our aid on a hot Sunday afternoon. He wondered why Douglas wore glasses and why his skull sutures had not melded.

The doctor admitted both boys to the Estevan hospital and X-rayed Doug's skull the following day. After informing us of his suspicions, he immediately sent us to Regina to have Dougie examined by a Neurosurgeon, Dr. James.

Douglas was isolated for a week in Regina Grey Nuns Hospital until the measles had run its course. After a few days, the neurosurgeon did a craniotomy, and found a slow-growing occipital malignant type tumour near the base of the skull near the spine. He removed part of the tumour and inserted a shunt to keep the spinal fluid moving and not collecting in the brain. Doug was blind for a few months, so I could not leave his side. I slept, or should I say, I tried to sleep on a chair beside his hospital crib. He kept calling to make sure I was still there. He could not understand why it was night-time all the time and I was not in my own bed. No McDonald's House then.

Tim had to return to his job in Summerside, so we again went to Household Finance Company to borrow enough money to fly back to PEI instead of the long train ride again. Tim flew home with David, and I stayed in Saskatchewan until Douglas was well enough to be released from Dr. James' care. I had him wear a hat so no one would see his scar and shaved head. He was heavy to carry and still could not see. It was a long flight from Regina to Montreal, then to Halifax, and the short hop to Summerside. I was so happy to get home to see Dave and Tim Sr that I could hardly contain myself.

It had been two weeks since I had seen David or Tim, and David did not recognize me. My heart felt like it would break. It took a few days before he would let me hold him again.

We arranged an appointment with a radiologist in Halifax, as suggested by Dr. James. During the visit, the radiologist advised that he had never done radiation on a child before. Tim said he wasn't going to practice on our son. We all left his office in a hurry.

After this setback, Tim immediately applied for a transfer to the Search and Rescue Squadron in Winnipeg. Why Winnipeg? Because we were familiar with the city and its doctors. Many thanks to the Summerside senior officer, Wing Commander Mike Lewis. He went out of his way to get us transferred to a city that could take care of our ill son.

Travelling to Winnipeg in November 1964

This time, we travelled across Canada in a Volkswagen Beetle. We put the back seat down and covered it with blankets and pillows. I would turn around in my passenger seat and care for both children in diapers. There were no seatbelts in those days, or disposable diapers!

We took the Trans Canada Highway over the northern route, the same as the train, but for us this was a far more suitable means of travel. There were still trees, rocks and water, but it was more appealing and comfortable. We even got a speeding ticket as we passed Port Arthur and Fort William (now Thunder Bay). Imagine that! We were in a bit of a hurry because we wanted to beat the snow, which usually arrives in Winnipeg by late October.

We arrived in a thankfully snowless Winnipeg in November 1964, and stayed with Theresa and Erhardt Meier. (Theresa was my roommate in residence while in nurses training). They had three sons at the time and with our two, they were a handful. We spent a very energetic and stressful two weeks, waiting for our house in the suburb of St. James to be ready.

**Terry Meier, Tim and Erhardt
(this photo was taken in August 2007, two months after Tim's quintuple cardiac bypass surgery)**

We were and are the best of friends to this day. Such a kind and generous couple. Erhardt was a baker and a good one as well as being a businessman. He took a big risk when buying the Donut House on Selkirk Avenue, but did very, very well. Every visit we paid to them in the north end of Winnipeg was a treat. He gave us all sorts of bread and pastry on each visit, so our boys were always very happy to accept their hospitality.

Erhardt died very suddenly of a heart attack on July 6, 2020. He was finally going back to work at his bakery after the six-week COVID shutdown, but never quite got over having to close his business and lay off all his workers, one of whom was his son. We were very saddened by his death.

Timothy Peter Ball, Jr was born in Winnipeg, MB, on June 20, 1967

Doug and Dave called Tim Jr our centennial project. (He was only a few days old when the older two boys looked into the crib and asked if he had any teeth.)

Douglas died after having a second craniotomy by Dr Dwight Parkinson in Winnipeg in October 1969. He never regained consciousness. He passed away quietly on January 17, 1970, at age almost 8 at the St. Amant Ward for retarded children.

David and Tim Jr. had a reasonably normal growing-up period. After Tim retired from the RCAF in September 1968, I started working from four to twelve at The Grace Salvation Army Hospital. Tim would arrive home from classes and leave the car running. Then I would leave for work without restarting the vehicle—a real advantage in the cold Winnipeg winters. Tim would get up with the boys in the morning and give them breakfast before he went to classes so I could sleep a little longer.

The boys wanted to be rich rock stars and skiing bachelors from the time they were in first grade. We, of course, wanted them to get their education, take piano lessons and go from there. This was a no-go. In their early teen years, they each had to play the guitar. The piano we bought just collected dust. Guitar lessons followed, as it was the only instrument they would play.

They are still playing and writing music in their late fifties and still have the same goal, but they could never afford to quit their day jobs. We were neighbours and friends of Brad and Dan Roberts of 'The Crash Test Dummies' and their parents. (In 1996, the Roberts family bought our cottage when Tim and I decided to move to Victoria, BC.)

Dave and Tim Jr practised their music in our recreation room, each with their separate bands, promising it would end if we got noise complaints from the neighbours.

They each had one day a week. Both boys had different styles and bands. We never got one noise complaint. Tim Sr could not bear the noise from 7 to 10 PM, so he had to leave the house and visit his friend, Larry Anderson. I stayed upstairs in our bedroom until 10 PM when I asked them to go home. We had our jobs in the morning, and they had to go to school.

Tim Jr travelled with his band, 'The Shivers,' for over seven years but brilliantly managed to get his BA during that time.

He decided to move to Hawaii in 1997 and ended up working for MAC cosmetics while earning his MBA at night school at the University of Hawaii. He met his lovely wife, Leann, twenty-three years ago in Honolulu. In June of 2022, they transferred to Phoenix, Arizona where Tim is the district manager for The Guitar Center music store.

TIM JR. BA GRADUATION, 1995 UNIVERSITY OF WINNIPEG, WHERE TIM WAS TEACHING

They kept their property in Honolulu where they will retire in ten or fifteen years to be close to Leann's daughter, Carly, along with Carly's husband, Aaron and three sons, Liam, Nash and Owen.

Dave met Crystal in Calgary. On meeting and finding out her name, Dave said "Oh, that means we can't ever be married with a name like Crystal." That started the romance and they married in 2003. A son Devon was born April 28, 2004 and daughter Ainsley April 3, 2007. Our lovely daughter-in-law and grandchildren made us very happy.

They lived in Calgary until March, 2016 when they sold their property and moved to Sooke, BC to be nearer to us. That was so good of them as they had a struggle at first.

Crystal bought a candy store in downtown Sooke. When the COVID-19 pandemic happened, she was forced to close the door and walk away. However, in a short time she was hired to work in a homeless shelter, which was her wish, as she had worked in the same field in Calgary.

Dave was unable to continue in carpentry because of his health so took the Class 1 truck driver's course. In 2018 they bought a house in downtown Sooke and are continually renovating it. They have chickens and a big garden plus two dogs. A busy household.

The Family Enjoyed Ten Days in Honolulu for Tim Jr's MBA Graduation

Miscellaneous Musings

The problem then was—and still is now—that people are educated in the false philosophy of uniformitarianism: the misguided belief that conditions always were and always will be as they are now, and any natural changes will occur over long periods of time.

Consequently, most people did not understand that the cooling was part of the natural cycle of climate variability, or that changes are often huge and sudden. Just 18,000 years ago we were at the peak of an Ice Age. Then, most of the ice melted and sea levels rose 150 meters (490 feet), because it was warmer for almost all of the last 10,000 years than it is today.

This misunderstanding, combined with the new paradigm of environmentalism (it is illogical and wrong to soil your own nest) created the belief that perfectly ordinary changes must be manmade, and thus had to be corrected by us as well.

From *Geo-Engineering: Ignoring the Consequences* by Tim Ball and Tom Harris

CHAPTER FIVE

Search and Rescue Squadron—December 1964 to August 1968

TIM REALLY LIKED Search and Rescue in Winnipeg. He would be called in at short notice, but could be away for weeks at a time. It was an interesting part of his Air Force career and it was here that he became interested in climate. His unit covered the four western provinces, plus North Western Ontario and the North West Territories.

SEARCH AND RESCUE AIRCRAFT—EXPEDITOR HERCULES CC130. TIM FLEW IN THIS AIRCRAFT AS A RADIO OPERATOR FROM 1964 TO 1968. ACCORDING TO TIM, IT WAS TWO INCHES LONGER THAN ITS ORIGINAL LENGTH WHEN IT WAS RETIRED

The northern half of each province was nothing but dense forest, and further north it was snow and permafrost. Trying to find a downed plane or a missing person was next to impossible.

This is when Tim saw the tree line from the air. Many times they searched from Yellowknife in unimaginable cold, as low as -70 degrees Fahrenheit (around -57 Celsius). The crew were issued parkas that were super warm with the hoods trimmed with wolf or wolverine fur. This fur was special because the humidity from exhaled breath did not form icicles on the fur. I have not been able to find the scientific reason for this phenomena. Most interesting!

If one's face was exposed to the wind, it froze in seconds. In winter, the engines of the aircraft had to have fires under them to get them warm enough to start.

On one occasion an American couple were lost and two of their relatives wanted to help look for them. They helped search with Tim's crew all day. When they landed at the end of a long day, the couple accused them of going around in circles. They were shown the map and the exact route that was covered. The comment made was, "We will never say again that the world is overpopulated."

Another search that created much interest was for a person who wanted to fly his Cessna from Anchorage, Alaska, nonstop, to Tallahassee, Florida, in order to break records. He emptied the aircraft of all non-essentials such as seats and supplies. All that remained were numerous containers of gasoline. The airport staff had to push his plane onto the runway and also help by pushing it along the runway in order to take off. Unfortunately, he could not get over the mountains. It took him two hours to get to 8,000 feet, after which he crashed into a mountainside in a ball of fire. It didn't take too long to find that crash site. He was an American who never received approval from the Canadian government or any authority. He was never held to account. He had made many attempts to do this flight. Tim said he must have had a death wish.

The star of all the many searches was a bush pilot, named Bob Goshy. He was lost at least five times. It seemed he wanted to make a name for himself, like many others. This time he was in the snowy part of the north when

Tim's crew made radio contact with him.

He was north of Yellowknife.

He didn't know where he was but he had set down his plane somewhere in the whiteness. They asked him if he could see the sun? Answer,"Yes." "Where is the sun from you?" The only place the sun could be is south. Turns out, he was flying in the wrong direction. When they did pick him up, he had frozen feet and fingers which had to be amputated. He apparently had 10 empty Vodka bottles in his gear. He made it into 'Life' magazine and was paid $5,000 for his story. Not sure what happened to Bob after this, but Tim was sure his flying days were over.

As the famous saying goes, "There are old bush pilots and bold bush pilots, but no old, bold bush pilots."

Many such searches ended in tragedy, but it was a celebration if any were found alive. One lone survivor had built himself a lean-to, and did very well in keeping himself alive, but in the end committed suicide. The insects were driving him out of his mind. Mosquitos and black flies are relentless in the north.

The North fascinated Tim. He plotted his own treeline for his doctorate and found it had moved fairly far north from the late 1700's map by explorer and map maker, Peter Fidler who was in the employ of the Hudson Bay Company. Fidler had an amazing career and became one of Tim's heroes.

Approximately 12,000 years ago, the warming climate caused the melting of the glaciers resulting in the land rising. The land is still rising. The many lakes in Manitoba, Ontario, and Quebec will decrease and also become shallower as time passes.

The 'all day' nights and the 'all day' days were unbelievable to Tim. The aurora borealis was beautiful beyond belief.

The residents of the north survived the hard conditions in extraordinary ways. Food was very expensive, but alcohol was the same price as in Winnipeg. The cost of shipping was mind boggling. One person wanted to build a house, so he ordered cinder blocks to be delivered. However, the cost was unmanageable, so he decided to have the blocks mailed, which cost him far less. Good old Canada Post.

There are many more unbelievable stories of their searches in Northern Canada.

Too many to relate here.

Miscellaneous Musings

Pope Francis advocates the global warming agenda of the UN Intergovernmental Panel on Climate Change (IPCC), with the help of the Obama White House. Apparently, he doesn't know their ultimate objective of reducing and controlling population generally contradicts Catholic doctrine.

…

But the Pope doesn't need to worry; Italy, France, and other European nations are offsetting the decline with Muslim immigrants with higher TFRs. [Total Fertility Rates]

Apparently, the Pope could learn from the French philosopher Montesquieu. He reportedly said, whenever he was tempted to talk about something on which he had little knowledge, he remembered his personal guideline. Never talk to other men about his wife, because they might be more knowledgeable on the subject than he was. Maybe the problem for perspective is that the Pope doesn't have a wife.

From *Pope Francis Apparently Doesn't Know IPCC Climate Objective Contradicts Catholic Doctrine* by Tim Ball

CHAPTER SIX
The University of Winnipeg September 1972 to August 1996

TIM WAS HIRED by The University of Winnipeg (former United College) as an instructor in the Geography department. Where else would you put a climatology major? It has yet to be determined whether it was an art or science. (The University of London has it as a science.) Tim's starting salary was $7,900 per year. In 1972, we were happy to get that.

Tim knew he was where he wanted to be, in the classroom. It showed because he had a significant enrolment in each class. He regularly had a line-up of students outside his office waiting to see him. Some weren't even registered in any of his courses.

He was nominated three times for the Clifford Robson Award for excellence in teaching. A block of students threatened to go public the third time if he did not receive it. Tim was the first to receive the award without his PhD.

UNIVERSITY OF WINNIPEG

TIM RECEIVING THE CLIFFORD J. ROBSON AWARD IN 1976 AND THE CLARENCE ATCHISON AWARD FOR COMMUNITY SERVICE IN 1988

Tim worked on the PhD for almost ten years part-time. He travelled to Queen Mary College at the University of London, England, most summers to meet with his supervisor, Bruce Atkinson—(this book includes a separate chapter by Bruce). They travelled once to the University of East Anglia, where the Climate Research Centre is located and where he met Hubert Lamb, the founder and director at the time. Tim had high praise for Dr. Lamb and his work.

Tim taught Physical Geography, which included Climatology, Water Resources and Political Geography. He always marked his own exams and term papers, using the money allowed for markers to hire a student to manage his office, clean it, do his filing and answer his phone.

He employed many students during his twenty-five years, but the main one that I remember is Jane E. Curtis.

She was loyal to Tim and remained so for 20 years after we retired to Victoria, writing long handwritten letters until 2018. We tried to find out what happened to her but were never able to connect with anyone else that knew her.

Betty Harder was a loyal, devoted, professional and efficient secretary in the geography department. Tim could not say enough good things about her and did so many times, especially in his last days. He wanted me to tell her how valuable she was to the department, which I did regularly via emails.

The first 15 years at the university were great. We became friends with most of the members of the department of geography. We went to parties and dinners. We had Halloween costume parties for five years in a row at our home. They were such fun.

We made special friends with Andy and Val Lockery.

Allen and Deb Hosey were also dear to us. Tim was the best man when they married in December 1968 at the University of Winnipeg chapel.

Debbie died very suddenly on July 20, 2019.

Tim went to work early each day to prepare for his classes. He liked early classes since most of the other profs preferred later times. He always carried a large, rolled-up world map into the classroom and hung it at the side of the podium. I still have that map, but it is pretty worn.

His colleagues accused Tim of giving 'Mickey Mouse' courses. According to them, he had large class enrolments and easy exams.

Tim's subsequent claim to fame came when he became the longest-ranking associate professor before being promoted to full professor. There were many reasons for this.

ALLEN AND DEB HOSEY 1998

He rarely attended department meetings. According to Tim, they spent hours discussing unimportant issues. He felt he was more productive doing other things. Tim's colleagues stopped discussing topics with him because he talked too fast. Things became increasingly difficult for Tim as the climate issue became more and more political.

Tim always took the part of the student or underdog rather than the professor or administrators. A large problem began when Tim was appointed to the Sexual Harassment Committee. It was an unpopular appointment and avoided by all the other professors.

After a short time, we knew why.

However, Tim regarded it as another challenge. One particular case involved two girls who accused the same professor of sexual harassment. Tim interviewed both girls separately. They did not know each other and Tim found they had similar stories. Naturally, Tim took their side. The Professor was found guilty, and the only punishment was denial of a merit increase that year. Tim went to the president and asked why the professor got off so lightly. She said she was afraid of the repercussions from the faculty union.

Tim went public on local TV and radio. This got him into even more trouble with the faculty. He said justice must not only be done but seen to be done. It was treasonous to the faculty, and they made that apparent to Tim. They shunned Tim at every turn, even turning their heads when passing in the hallway.

Hence, there were no promotions or merit increases for Tim. Not sure if he still holds the record for being the longest acting professor before being promoted.

In what other profession does your peer group decide on merit and promotions?

When Tim questioned them for denying him a merit increase, part of their reasoning was he had a wife who worked as a nurse and lived in a big house in St James. (It wasn't any bigger than anyone else's in the department.) It was a disappointing end to socializing within the Department of Geography.

His favourite year was 1980, during which he was the acting Dean of Students. He could counsel students all day and every day, and also organize his time at the Winnipeg Archives more efficiently. The administration was pressuring him to finish his doctorate. He was continuously harassed to the point where he finally told an administrator that he had scrapped it altogether. This caused an over-reaction, but they stopped bugging him.

I remember the dining room table always being covered with exam papers. The students very much appreciated that Tim did all his own marking.

While Tim did his share of research, it seemed to be the 'wrong' research or apparently 'not enough' to get his merit increase, plus they were already ostracizing him for his views on Global Warming.

When did Tim start giving talks outside the University? He spoke to any group at any age, from kindergarten to senior citizens. There isn't a road he hasn't driven on in the prairie provinces, and I loved going with him when I could.

He never missed a class and was never late.

Tim often tells the story of talking to a grade 4 class. He was introduced as a Climatologist when a boy raised his hand to ask a question. "How many mountains have you climbed anyway?" Tim tried not to laugh, answering his question as best he could without embarrassing the lad.

Tim gave many lectures to grade 12 students as he felt the transition from high school to university was a much bigger step than many realized. Helping them understand this by providing the right information was extremely important.

Tim's last year of teaching was almost too much for him. He gave 150 public talks apart from his regular classes. He also taught a summer course to provide us with extra money. He went from the university to the airport and from the airport to the university.

The non-credit course for senior citizens was too large to hold in the largest classroom, which had 250 seats. There were over 600 enrolled the last year, so Tim held this same class three times each week in 1995-96.

Tim felt like he was on a treadmill and couldn't get off. He found it impossible to say no to anyone. He thought he should be all things to all people. I called him a triple A personality and even though I helped him as much as possible, I was afraid of another cardiac incident.

Tim retired eight years early, taking a hefty penalty on his pension income. Virtually everyone around him told him he was insane to do this. Some never forgave him for 'deserting' them or their agenda.

We finally discussed moving to Victoria, BC.

Where else in Canada would a climatologist choose to live?

Miscellaneous Musings

It's not that long ago that in the universities, the old professors had the prevailing wisdom and the young professors came in and challenged it. Now the young ones are coming in with the indoctrinated views, and it's the old people that are saying, 'hey, hang on a minute.' People like me, and Fred Singer at 92, and Bill Gray at 86. They've completely flipped the whole process of the education approach upside down because of what they're doing in the schools with the indoctrination."

From a speech called *Global Warming Is the Biggest Deception in History* at Freedom Force International's Third Congress, December 3, 2016

CHAPTER SEVEN
Tim's Love of Art, Literature and Music

TIM OFTEN SAID that if he were the last man on earth, he would need only a library of books, music, and art. Later, he humorously added the need for eyeglasses and hearing aids.

There was always music of some sort playing in our house. Sometimes on the radio or long-playing records, then 45s and later cassettes, then DVDs, iPods, computers and iPads. An ever-changing scenario.

Tim's love of music was unlimited. He listened to every type, from Slim Whitman's Country and Western to Opera. Ella Fitzgerald was the voice with the broadest range. Tim listened to her for hours at a time, along with Kathleen Ferrier, a favourite contralto and Joan Sutherland, his favourite opera star.

Wagner was Tim's favourite composer. Tim would load his iPod with over 200 musical pieces for road trips. He could name virtually everyone by the time we reached our destination, which was usually Calgary from Victoria or the return. Tim remembered his father listening to Vera Lynn during the Second World War. Douglas Sr. called her, 'Moaning Minnie.

Tim often cried while listening to music. He said, "Music is one thing the politicians couldn't politicize. Not yet, anyway." (There is rap music, of course.)

Tim thought Caravaggio was the greatest artist in the world. The impressionists wowed Tim by using a unique technique to show the pollution in the bright yellow skies they painted. He often showed the work of Turner and Gainsborough in his lectures.

Queen Elizabeth I was one of Tim's heroines. He considers her the greatest Monarch and leader of all time, followed by Katherine the Great of Russia. Tim has every book ever published about Queen Elizabeth I and loved to talk about her during his lectures.

He also read and studied everything he could find about Charles Darwin's life and writings and was happy to discuss him with anyone who was interested.

Tim believed that Shakespeare wasn't Shakespeare but was the 17th earl of Oxford, Edward de'Vere. This is still being argued, but Tim was firm in his belief.

Tim had immense admiration for Dr John Rae who, among other exploits, led an expedition investigating the fate of John Franklin's Arctic voyage which set out to find the Northwest Passage. Dr Rae is buried in St Magnus Cathedral in Kirkwall, on the Orkney Islands.

The Spectator magazine was always at Tim's bedside throughout our marriage. His mother,

TIM KEPT THIS TINY FIGURINE OF ELIZABETH 1 ON HIS DESK

TIM BOUGHT THIS STONE, WHICH QUOTES SHAKESPEARE, IN DOWNTOWN VICTORIA AND CARRIED IT HOME IN HIS BACKPACK. IT WEIGHS FIFTY POUNDS, AND LIVES ON OUR PATIO.

Marjorie, was also a voracious reader. She went to the library in Chippenham every Monday morning, returned five books and took out another five. One of these was for Douglas Sr. who would only manage the first chapter before falling asleep and never finishing (according to Tim).

Marjorie told the family, "You are never alone if you have a book." It was a habit Tim carried throughout his life and he taught our children and grandchildren to do the same. There was always a book or magazine in his briefcase or backpack.

Tim amassed every book on history he could pack on our bookshelves. We sold, gave away or donated over three thousand books from his university office and our Winnipeg home before moving to Victoria, and since arriving added many more.

While history was the most common theme, there was Shakespeare, Royalty, all of Samuel Pepys' Diaries, the history of most countries and many historical figures.

What intrigued Tim the most was how time never seemed to matter in long ago days. You could not phone to tell someone you planned to visit. One just went regardless of what you might find. It mattered not if you stayed up all night because you didn't have to punch a clock for your workday.

Captain Bligh of the Bounty was a hero to Tim, not a heartless Captain as Hollywood tends to portray him. When Bligh was forced to sea with 18 men in a small 23-foot boat, he had to navigate from the island of Tofua, across the South Seas approximately 3,600 miles first to Timor, then to Jakarta, in the Dutch East Indies, from where they were able to arrange passage to England. It was an incredible feat, with limited food rations (one of their members was killed during a stop on a nearby island where they attempted to land for provisions) and severe sailing dangers. Fletcher Christian's brother subsequently sued Bligh for the mutiny on the Bounty.

Bligh won.

Benjamin Franklin was also one of Tim's heroes, who, along with his long and unequalled history of accomplishments, had several kidney and bladder stones painfully pass during his lifetime. Bizarre things like this amused Tim.

He particularly liked biographies, those of famous or infamous men and women, wanting to know why they were notorious. Much of it was surprising and unexpected, reminding Tim continuously that, "Power corrupts, and absolute power corrupts absolutely. Most great men are bad men." Voltaire.

Our library, no surprise, is filled with climate books. Hundreds of them, even those by David Suzuki, along with Al Gore's *Inconvenient Truth*.

Go figure?

Someone asked Tim to do a critique of Al Gore's book, which he did. All the post-it notes are still in place. When finished, he said, "What am I doing? Someone will just sue me again."

So, he put it aside. If anyone cares to write this critique, all the legwork is complete. Sir Christopher Moncton found 37 errors.

Tim found 54.

Miscellaneous Musings

As a Geophysicist I am fully aware of how the fabricated climate models were used to create a crisis where none was physically possible but to explain this to the public requires that public has knowledge which is generally not the case. After a quarter century of this global warming fraud (the Earth has actually been cooling since 2002) Tim Ball has finally done what to date no scientist has been able to do and expose climate change for the fraud that it is in a way that resonates with the public by detailing the political machinations of the principals involved in creating the climate change issue to serve their ideologically driven self-serving political agenda.

Climate change is an environmentalist fabricated fraud claiming to save the planet when in fact *The Deliberate Corruption of Climate Science* is the scientific truth aimed at saving the planet from this environmentalist fabricated fraud. It is Dr. Tim Ball and not Al Gore who deserves the Nobel Prize for warning the world about the true nature of climate change.

—Norm Kalmanovitch

CHAPTER EIGHT

THE EARLY YEARS by Dr Andrew Lockery, Geomorphology Professor, Colleague and Friend

The Professor

ANDY LOCKERY AND his wife Val arrived in Winnipeg in 1968. Unlike most university professors he had a multi-disciplinary background. A BA honours degree in the departments of anthropology, archaeology and geography, with a double major in geology.

York Factory Manitoba

His PhD in the faculty of science was titled Sea Level Change as a result of glacier melt in the past 19,000 years. It involved research in Iceland, underwater research in the North Sea and the use of the electron microscope to identify whether sediments were coastal, fluvial or aeolian in origin, as well as archaeological analyses of artefacts and C14 dating. Geophysics, geology, glaciology, oceanography, marine zoology, palynology (pollen analyses,) geography, archaeology were all represented in the Thesis supervision and the chief examiner was the head of environmental studies at the university of East Anglia.

The PhD simply states that it was awarded in 'science.'

The Student

Tim and Andy met when Tim registered for a course in geomorphology. Tim, unlike European university students, was a mature student, having emigrated to Canada and spent time working in mining towns, (Elliot Lake comes to mind), but for most of his time in Canada he had been a radio operator in the RCAF before being pensioned out after experiencing hearing damage from the engine noise, with the resultant surgery ending his career.

Tim was not alone in the class as it is quite common in Canada for students to work part time to fund their education. In fact, I keep in touch with 11 students from that class and at 24 years of age I was probably close to the average age of that group with Tim being at the upper end.

The lecture that stands out in my mind as the one that had the most influence upon Tim was one that looked at the 475-foot increase in world sea levels since the end of the last ice age some 19,000 years ago. The intriguing part being that there is still 214 foot of potential future sea level rise in the remaining ice sheets and glaciers. There was a clear need to understand both what had happened in the past, and more to the point, what was going to happen in the future.

Tim, of course, like all RCAF members, had a solid base of knowledge in both meteorology and climatology. A very stimulating discussion arose, and the lecture evolved into an explanation for what might explain the changes in climate that might cause an ice age and what might cause it to end.

Two scientists stand out. The first, Milankovich, a theoretical mathematician in Yugoslavia, applied his skills to calculate the variability of solar radiation reaching the earth. His calculations produced a graph of alternating warm and cold periods anywhere from 18,000 to 30,000 years apart.

He published his results in 1927 and sadly nobody recognized the value of his work until Cesare Emiliani, a microbiologist at Florida State University, obtained permission to study the deep ocean cores taken in the Atlantic Ocean in the 1960s. I had met Cesare at an oceanographic conference and was able to share with my class the nature of his work, which was published a year later. He checked the cores for the presence or absence of a particular zoo-plankton called foraminifera, which was so sensitive to temperature that it would die if ocean temperature were to change by as little as one degree Centigrade. His comprehensive study proved that Milankovich's theoretical work was absolutely accurate. Both scientists confirmed that there were 36 ice ages during the Pleistocene glaciation, and not four as the glaciologists, geologists and others had claimed.

Eventually Emiliani analysed the deep ocean sediments one kilometre off the Hawaiian coast with senior earth scientists in attendance and finally they accepted that he had confirmed what Milankovich had calculated 43 years earlier.

The effect of these discussions in the classroom was fascinating, with one student in particular, Tim, exhibiting a curiosity bordering on a level of enthusiasm that impressed not just me, but all of the other students in the class, that here was a climatologist in the making.

A Friendship Emerges

It was six to eight weeks after we met that I realized I not only had a truly remarkable student in my class, but also that I and Val had made a special friend. In addition to our lengthy after-class discussions, Tim decided we needed help adjusting to living in Canada.

Tim drove us around the city when we started looking for a home, and also invited us to supper at his home where we met his wife Marty, a farm girl from southeast Saskatchewan who was a very highly regarded nurse at the Grace Hospital. We also met two of their three children, Tim Jr, a highly energetic preschooler, and their middle son Dave, a quieter, more thoughtful youngster.

It was at this time that Val and I realized just what a sacrifice the family were making to get Tim his education. Marty worked nights as a nurse and Tim looked after the boys during the night and got them ready for school so Marty could get some sleep before he headed to the university for his classes.

We had some wonderful times together and got to know both youngsters. (Our first memory of Young Tim was a blonde youngster in a diaper sprinting up to the fridge yelling MEEP! MEEP! Marty producing a glass of orange juice (I believe Beep was its name.) Young Dave was quieter but showed a maturity and careful thought before he spoke, a trait he has maintained throughout his life. I think we met him at a time when he was adjusting to the absence of Dougie, the eldest of the three boys, who had a brain tumour, and was at that time, in the St Amant Centre.

This brief diversion from (educating Tim) was necessary because it shows what a difficult time it was in their family life and also explains why our lifelong friendship was so special.

The Professor and the Graduate

Tim proceeded to ace all of his courses and graduated as an A student. Immediately upon graduation, Tim applied for a master's degree at the University of Manitoba. I was appointed as external examiner and his thesis was an excellent piece of work! (In conversations with his supervisor I got the impression that Tim's knowledge of the subject exceeded that of his supervisor.)

The Professor and the Professor

Upon graduation, Tim was immediately hired as a professor in the geography department at the University of Winnipeg. In a matter of just a few years Tim had progressed from a first-year student to a valued colleague.

His teaching skills quickly became apparent and Tim was nominated for the Robson Award, an award presented to the University's best teacher. This is not an easy award to win as the University had always emphasized the importance of teaching. Tim's nomination was in the second year of it being offered and he won it with ease.

You could only win it once, which is a good job as Tim would have won it every year. After several years of finishing second, I finally matched Tim and won the award.

Not content with having only a Masters degree, Tim decided he needed a PhD. Upon reading his thesis that was completed at the University of London England, I found it to be one of the most exceptional pieces of work that I have read.

Tim had to keep working as a professor, he had to find time to help Marty raise the family, and he had to complete the research for his PhD. He chose a most interesting topic in that it provided a new insight into climate change in a large area of Canada where no formal records exist. He basically studied the 'Hudson Bay Company Archives' and recorded the date of any event that related to the climate in all of the sites of year-round trading posts.

Examples would include the date a river or lake froze, the date when geese left or returned, the dates when the mercury froze in barometers or thermometers.

The end result was a PhD for Tim, and it was the first document to provide detailed evidence that confirmed that Northern Canada (between the 16th century and the 20th century) had a pattern of warmer and cooler periods that matched Europe.

It was the first document to confirm that climate change was global and not regional.

**ON THE RIGHT, ANDY LOCKERY AND HIS WIFE VALERIE
FROM THE LEFT, NILA SCOTT, JIM RICHTIK, ELAINE AND BILL RANNIE**

Summary

Tim went on to become a world-famous climatologist, travelling widely to speak at international conferences and presenting research matching the predictive works of Milankovitch and Emiliani.

When Tim and I first met the world's climatologists, they held their review of current research in climate in Stockholm, Sweden in 1949 and had voted 99% in favour of global cooling. In 1999 at their most recent meeting they voted 99% in favour of global warming.

Tim has steadfastly claimed that the popular view of global warming as a result of increased levels of CO_2 is incorrect. There is a strange dichotomy between the Western Hemisphere and Asia, Russia, and Eastern Europe. Western climatologists do not usually have as strong a background in science as their eastern, Asian and Russian counterparts. Astronomy, astro physics, oceanography and geophysics are the common qualifications in Asia, Russia and China.

The result is that the Western Hemisphere climatologists favour global warming and the east favours an approaching cool period or mini ice age.

In concluding my thoughts regarding Tim and me, they tell me that the measure of a teacher is that a good teacher's pupils surpass that teacher!

There is no doubt in my mind that Tim has done that. And his insistence that global warming is not caused by CO_2 is 100% correct. In fact, global warming is the precursor of an ice age. Think about it…an ice age requires heavy snowfall in parts of the world that currently are deserts.

Canada's Arctic, for example is a desert in terms of precipitation. The only way an ice age can occur is if all the sea ice in the Arctic and around Antarctica were to melt and so provide more snow than can melt in the short high latitude summers. Remember an ice age is really a pluvial period triggered by heavy precipitation globally. How else could woolly mammoths that eat tree leaves and grasses survive and dominate ice age fauna. How else can the Sahara Desert be the granary of the Roman Empire.

When a man-made gas, sulfur hexafluoride, is 235,500 times more efficient than CO_2 as a greenhouse gas, one kilogram of that gas in the earth's atmosphere equals the greenhouse gas entering the atmosphere of 1.3 million vehicles driven for one year. Sulfur hexafluoride is used as an insulating material in wind farms and solar panel farms.

We as humans are clearly doing our best to hasten the return of the next ice age. As Vladimir Putin said when asked what he thought of Greta Thunberg, "She's a lovely young girl; pity she's been so badly misinformed."

In conclusion, Tim Ball is correct—just as Milankovitch and Emiliani are correct.

—*Andy Lockery* (Andy passed away on September 2, 2023)

Letter by Dr Jock Lehr, Geography Professor, Colleague and Friend

Lessons Learned

As the bus full of senior citizens pulled away from the bus terminal adjacent to the University of Winnipeg for a day trip, something did not seem right. I turned to Tim and asked him if the engine sounded weird. He shrugged and said, "It sounds OK to me." Twenty minutes later, it became increasingly clear that we had a problem, and our driver, who was now having difficulty keeping up a reasonable speed, blurted out, "We'll have to stop at Ste Agathe and call for a new bus; they'll get another down to us in about half an hour."

So, we rolled into the Ste Agathe service station and shuddered to a halt. As luck would have it, we had planned a coffee break there, so I announced that everyone should go into the coffee shop and pick up a coffee and muffin, for which we would pick up the tab, and take a half-hour break. As all 46 senior citizens trooped off the bus, the driver approached and reassured us that there would be a replacement bus arriving in 30 minutes. I felt a flood of relief.

Right on time, the relief bus arrived. By this time all the seniors had finished their coffee and snack and were waiting by our broken-down bus. The replacement bus looked a bit different though. Maybe a tad smaller. I asked the new driver how many passengers it held? "Thirty-six," he said, I could scarcely believe my ears. When told there were 48 of us, counting Tim and myself, he wasn't much fazed. "I'll get another bus sent out. It should be here in half an hour or so." This had all the makings of a disaster.

"They've already had coffee, so what do we do now?" I asked Tim. "We're screwed."

I first met Tim shortly after I joined the Department of Geography at the University of Winnipeg in September 1976. By then he had a reputation as an excellent teacher who was very popular with students. I was not exactly new to teaching as I had taken a one-year post-degree teaching certificate at the University of Liverpool, and I had previously taught at a College of Technology in the UK for a couple of years and had two years teaching as an instructor at the University of Victoria in BC. Nevertheless, I asked Tim for some tips to help me improve in the classroom, and he was generous enough to give me some practical advice, the kind of advice based on experience not textbook learning, and which I used throughout my teaching career.

Early on, Tim suggested that I do as he was doing and volunteer to give an extension course for the University's over 55-year-old students. It was an attractive proposition because, as Tim pointed out, there was no marking involved, the mature students all wanted to be there, and we received a stipend for our efforts. So, I did, and never regretted taking his advice.

It was during one of these seniors' classes, when I was lecturing on the making of the prairie landscape, that I casually remarked that it was all very well for me to show images of Mennonite and Ukrainian settlements, but there was nothing like being in the field and experiencing the real thing. "Well, why don't we do that?" said one elderly gentleman. It was a bit of a rhetorical question that was greeted with approval by almost everyone there. So, I approached the administration and they were keen on the idea and gave the go-ahead. I knew I did not want to do this alone, so I asked Tim if he was interested. He was. So, here we were in Ste Agathe, with a broken-down bus and at least half an hour to kill before a proper-size bus would arrive. I was cursing myself for undertaking the project.

Tim motioned for all the seniors to gather round and pointed upwards, towards the west. "Do you see those high wispy clouds? They're cirrus clouds and are about four or five miles up, certainly over 20,000 feet. It's very cold at that altitude, so they are composed mostly of ice crystals. That makes them thin and wispy. Cirrus clouds usually indicate the approach of a warm front." He went on to explain the process of the passage of a warm and cold front, pressure and temperature changes, and so forth, explaining which clouds produced what kind and what intensity of precipitation, how the wind shifted as a front passed and the various cloud types associated with each phase of a front's passage. Half an hour passed quickly and Tim was still answering a barrage of questions when our new bus, a 48-seater this time, drew up and parked.

The theme of the trip was supposed to be the cultural landscapes of southeastern Manitoba, but the participants spent most of the trip looking at the sky, rather than at the landscape I was trying to explain. It was a valuable lesson, mostly for me. I realized that a good teacher can do a lot with very little and it is possible to make the ordinary fascinating, provided the audience can relate to the subject, and the teacher is passionate about it. That incident at Ste Agathe changed the way I approached field trips and the way I taught geography thereafter.

Tim and I led many one-day field trips around southern Manitoba for those enrolled in the University's 'seniors' program, and I watched Tim use the same teaching strategy when we passed through long stretches of flat, unremarkable prairie. He would use something as unremarkable as a prairie slough to launch out on a mini-lecture on continental glaciation, or a shelter-belt to spark a discussion about micro-climates. The participants lapped it up, and so did I.

After we had been running day-trips for a couple of years, we were asked if we could take a longer overnight trip to the Duck Mountains. We had no trouble filling a tour bus. After a long day of guiding and talking we stayed overnight at a hotel in Swan River. When everyone had been assigned their rooms and had settled down for the night, Tim and I went to the hotel's bar to talk things over and plan our schedule for the next day. While we were sitting in a booth having a beer, I noticed the only other person in the bar constantly sneaking furtive views of us. Eventually, Tim left to go to the washroom and the other patron immediately came over and asked what we were doing in Swan River. I explained that we were guiding a field trip for senior citizens and we were both professors at the University of Winnipeg.

"Do you know Professor Ball?" he asked. I said I did. He then went on to tell how Professor Ball had given a lecture to a local farmers' group in Swan River about a year ago, and it was a fantastic presentation. "The best I have ever heard," he declared. He was in the midst of telling me how marvellous Tim was as a speaker, when Tim came back into the bar. I told him that rather than tell me, he could tell Tim, who was then in the act of sitting down.

What happened next is indelibly impressed on my memory. The guy introduced himself to Tim and mentioned that he was in the audience when Tim had spoken to his farmers group a year previously. Without missing a beat, Tim asked him whether his daughter had decided as to whether she would attend the University of Manitoba or the University of Winnipeg and told him that he remembered discussing her dilemma with him. I was astonished, and so was the farmer, who was both amazed and delighted to have Tim remember him. At that point,

I am sure, had Tim asked him for a thousand-dollar loan, he would have got it.

Before we turned in for the night, and after the farmer had left, I asked Tim how he did it. He admitted he always showed up for a presentation very early and sat down with the first arrivals and chatted, he always asked their opinions of local issues and, in the case of an agricultural audience, sought information as to how the crops were doing, the problems local farmers were facing, and so forth. Then, during his presentation, he would be sure to refer to the information given to him, place issues in a local context and, most importantly, refer to the people with whom he had spoken for verification of his facts and the points he was making. That way, Tim explained, the audience is on his side and more likely to accept arguments, even if they run counter to their opinion. I always considered this a very effective strategy and one that I confess to using later on more than a few occasions.

Developing a close rapport with students was always important to Tim. Whereas I always struggled to recall my students' names, Tim did so effortlessly, or at least it appeared to be effortless, though I am pretty sure he put a lot of work into it. Tim was a popular teacher. In 1976, he was one of the earliest recipients of the Clifford Robson Award for Excellence in Teaching. Not surprisingly, his classes were always full. And introductory classes at the University of Winnipeg could accommodate as many as 225 students.

So, why were his classes so popular? Firstly, he knew his students as individuals. He knew everyone's name and a bit about them. Secondly, he was always a bit of an iconoclast and rebel. Tim and authority did not always get along, and I think that most students could relate to that. Thirdly, he was enthusiastic and passionate about his subject and that comes across to the audience. Lastly, and most importantly, he placed the material he was discussing in a frame of reference to which his students could relate. Material becomes a lot more relevant and easier to recall if it is placed in a context that is meaningful, rather than being just an abstract concept without any immediate application.

I remember Tim invariably used current news reports to establish the significance of the material he was explaining. This is far easier said than done. An obligation to keep abreast of current events sufficiently well to be able to expound upon them at the drop of a hat requires a great deal of diligence and considerable effort.

They say that imitation is the sincerest form of flattery. When it comes to my teaching style, Tim should consider himself flattered. I learned a lot from watching him in operation both in the classroom and, especially, on field trips. He probably never thought of it that way, since I never took a class from him, but I was also one of his students.

—*Jock Lehr*

Letter from Dr. John Selwood, Geography Professor and Tim's Colleague

Dear Marty:

Turning now to your request: forget about getting a chapter from me. I have never been able to spin out a story containing so little substance, of which Tim is a master.

However, for what they are worth, here are some comments that might contribute to your biography.

I first met Tim when he was a student of mine taking a class on the geography of Africa, and it was there that I first came to appreciate the skill to which I earlier referred.

It was a class with only a handful of students and I ran it as a seminar class. At the time, I was a novice lecturer and I was quite tentative in my approach to the class, because I had not had much experience at the time in spinning out my material and larding it with irrelevant anecdotes, interspersed with jokes.

I will always be grateful to Tim in helping me through that class in that he was able to volunteer remarks that extended for minutes that quite lacked in substance, which drew heavily on his general knowledge but made it quite clear on the other hand that he had not read the prescribed material. I don't know if Tim will be able to recall that class, but I have continued to smile at his audacity and ability to BS. Nevertheless, he is a consummate entertainer who has inspired countless numbers of students to become engaged in their studies.

Having said that, I do appreciate that he has a wealth of general knowledge and substantial awareness of the material in his doctoral field of speciality. I am not myself particularly knowledgeable in that field and hesitate to judge Tim and his stated position on global warming. I do, however, agree with him in his argument that the great majority of his adversaries have not studied the subject with the same level of intensity that not more than a large handful of scholars have.

I also subscribe to the position that it is very necessary that there be some contrarians who are able to mount an argument that runs counter to conventional wisdoms.

I also get pissed off by those who resort to ad hominem arguments in support of their claims. Tim copped a lot of flak through his career in charges of this nature. It is interesting to see how he is condemned because of being financed by industries with a vested interest in getting his support, (not true of course) while those who are making those charges have likewise been granted large amounts of money and support from governments and those who are condemning the pollution generating industries.

I am afraid however, that Tim does have a reputation for bad mouthing his colleagues.

For all that, I still find Tim to be a likeable fellow. I hope that you'll find these remarks of some value.

I hope too, Marty, that this finds you and your family in good health. Cheers and a hello to Tim.

—*John Selwood, February 2020.* (Sadly, John died on August 31, 2020)

One of Many Criticisms of Tim came via a Manila Envelope to Tim's Office Marked Personal and Confidential on April 2, 1993 from Dr Geoff Scott

Geoff's PHD was in Cultural Geography

I will only include the first two chapters of the pages because it continues with more reasons why Tim's views are wrong and everyone else's must be right. Geoff had many peer-reviewed articles to prove his point at the end of his letter. Tim also knew most peer reviewers were biased, believing in Anthropogenic Global Warming. Geoff never knew that Tim's doctorate was in the Faculty of Science from the University of London, England (nor would he care).

Letter written to Tim from Dr Geoff Scott. 1993

Dear Tim:

This letter is written without malice or prejudice and will not be discussed with or shown to anyone else unless you initiate a third-party discussion of it first. I have just read a comment attributed to you in the Interlake Agri-News. It amazed me that I am compelled to correct you on it and point out how some of your other recent media comments are inaccurate, misleading, or simply wrong.

I am writing instead of talking because I find you very easily irritated when you hear an opposing opinion or something you might interpret as being negative about yourself. You are also rarely around to talk to anyway and are always in too much of a hurry or never seem to get to departmental meetings or Physical Geography committee meetings where we could chat. I have often been impressed by your willingness to speak out on issues, but with that comes the responsibility of at least a rational argument and the correct quoting of information (such as Jager, last October, quoting you on Winnipeg's coldest winter and the coldest temperatures in Winnipeg and Canada. Between you, all three answers were wrong!)

I am surprised that you see only one picture—that is, that all climatic changes must be environmentally produced. Convinced by your archival studies that climatic changes are natural and ongoing (point on which no one disagrees with you!), you have therefore concluded that climatic forcing is somehow wrong! I know you do not have a science background.

Still, with your comprehensive reading, you must comprehend that these are two issues, not one.

Yes, they are related issues, but one should be distinct. You rarely attempt to clarify why you disagree with climatic models that predict global warming, you say they are wrong! (Tim said then that the climate models don't work, a position he maintained until his death, and which has been extensively proven.)

Then you say, about the people that do modelling research on the topic, that "when you go public, there is another whole social responsibility that kicks in." But you go public with your seemingly unsubstantiated opinions and predictions and trust people to believe you! How can you demand such purity of others when you fail to live up to your professed standards? I find this double standard troublesome.
—*Dr Geoff Scott, University of Winnipeg*

Geoff elaborates on other articles and data that prove Tim is wrong. (In Geoff's opinion.)

Boat Full of Tim's Tour Group going from Churchill Manitoba to Fort Prince of Wales

Miscellaneous Musings

Regardless, recent [temperature] changes have been too small to even notice and are often less than the government's estimates of uncertainty in the measurements. In fact, we lack the data to properly compare today's climate with the past.

This is because, until the 1960s, temperature data was collected using mercury thermometers located at weather stations situated mostly in the United States, Japan, the UK, and eastern Australia. Most of the rest of the planet had very few temperature sensing stations. And none of the Earth's oceans, which constitute 70% of the planet's surface area, had more than the occasional station separated from its neighbor by thousands of kilometers.

The data collected at the weather stations in this sparse grid had, at best, an accuracy of ±0.5 degrees Celsius. In most cases, the real-world accuracy was no better than ±1 deg C. Averaging such poor data in an attempt to determine global conditions cannot yield anything meaningful. Displaying average temperature to tenths or even hundreds of a degree, as is done in the graphs by NOAA and NASA, clearly defies common sense.

Modern weather station surface temperature data is now collected using precision thermocouples. But, starting in the 1970s, less and less ground surface temperature data was used for plots such as those by NOAA and NASA. This was done initially because governments believed that satellite monitoring could take over from most of the ground surface data collection. But the satellites did not show the warming forecast by computer models. So, bureaucrats closed most of the colder rural surface temperature sensing stations, thereby yielding the warming desired for political purposes.

Today, there is virtually no data for approximately 85% of the Earth's surface. Indeed, there are fewer weather stations in operation now than there were in 1960.

So, the surface temperature computations by NOAA and NASA after about 1980 are meaningless. Combining this with the problems with the early data, the conclusion is unavoidable: it is not possible to know how the Earth's so-called average temperature has varied over the past century and a half.
—From *Overheated Claims on Temperature Records* by Tim Ball and Tom Harris

CHAPTER NINE
The Hudson Bay Company

THE HUDSON BAY COMPANY originated in London, England. They employed men mainly from the Orkney Islands since they sailed by the islands on the northern route to Hudson Bay, Canada. The men signed up for five years with a salary of five pounds a year. Twenty-five pounds was enough to buy a piece of land in the Orkneys on which they could make a modest living for the rest of their lives.

YORK FACTORY SETTLEMENT—1870S AND 1930S

YORK FACTORY SETTLEMENT—MAIN QUADRANGLE

The Hudson Bay Company, created by Royal Charter in May of 1670, was granted wide powers, including exclusive trading rights in the territory traversed by rivers flowing into Hudson Bay. This vast region was named Rupert's Land. The original commodity was beaver pelts due to the European demand for felt hats made from beaver fur. They set up Fort Churchill and York Factory (roughly 125 miles south).

After trapping during the fall and winter when beaver pelts were of the highest quality, Indigenous peoples travelled in the summer months to these trading posts to barter furs for manufactured goods such as metal tools, guns, textiles and foodstuffs. The now-iconic point blanket was one such item bartered for furs.

The journals were maintained meticulously and continuously for most of those years.

The 'keepers of the archives' in Winnipeg were of tremendous help as Tim waded through the journals of the Hudson Bay Company Archives looking for weather-related data, beginning in 1714.

Tim recorded more than 3 million digits of data, including wind direction, when the geese arrived and left each year, amounts of snow or rain, and temperatures. Mercury thermometers in the 1800s made the temperature records more accurate. Before that, they determined the severity of the cold by how near the fire the brandy froze.

In the early 1970s, Tim entered all the data he had amassed from the journals into the computer with cards. Roger Kingsley was the guy at the University of Winnipeg who helped him. The computer was the size of a room. Now, all that data can be done with a handheld device.

Tim came across many interesting stories, one of which follows. These could fill another book independently, but I will tell only the one that intrigued my sons and myself the most.

KEEPERS OF THE ARCHIVES
MAUREEN DOLYNIUK, JUDY VALENZUELA STANDING, SHIRLEE ANNE SMITH SEATED WITH ARTHUR RAY, DEC 2018

FORT PRINCE OF WALES, NEAR CHURCHILL, MANITOBA—CONSTRUCTED BETWEEN 1731 AND 1771

In early spring (April I think) one year, I don't know which, three HBC employees set out to walk the 125 miles from Churchill to the York factor. Walking along the shore was very difficult, so they decided to walk on the ice, which was beginning to break. The wind pushed the piece they were on out into the bay, and they could not get back to shore for many days. Two men succumbed to the elements, but one named Ross was still alive when the wind finally changed direction, and the ice floe was blown to shore again.

Ross's hands and feet were frozen solid, so he crawled on his elbows and knees the remaining distance of 12 miles, and made it to the York Factory.

The other employees didn't think he would survive, but he did. The limbs were turning gangrenous, so the staff decided to amputate them. They sharpened some knives, as best they could, and amputated Ross's hands the first day. Brandy was the only anaesthetic. A few days later, they amputated his feet. He survived! He got better and better each day. The HBC executives had to return him to the Orkney Islands, as he was not earning his £5 a year salary. The rest of the employees agreed to give £1 of their salaries for his passage home.

Can you imagine giving one-fifth of your salary to another employee?

Tim made three trips to the Orkney Islands where he tried to find some record of Ross, but never did. The £52 they collected would have lasted him a lifetime in those days.

Tim's Tour Group Bus, Tim on the Right

Miscellaneous Musings

Education was always about indoctrinating children to think the way the powerful in society wanted. This was done openly and primarily centered on a religious belief. Now the indoctrination is denied because they claim education is not about religion. In fact, it is about the new religion of environmentalism that is being used to create equally, if not more indoctrinated, young minds. Few parents have any idea what their children are learning in the schools. It is not the wide ranging, free thinking, investigative experience they think.

One way this is apparent is in the movement of young people through the education system. Historically they entered university and challenged the prevailing wisdoms. Now they come fully indoctrinated with environmentalism that ignores facts, manufactures false information and blames humans for everything. It is significant that challenges come from much older people who know and understand the fallacies. Everyone knows that information is power, but it's exploitation of power that has allowed a few to control and manipulate people.

Throughout my career I've worked to help people learn and understand climate and how it changes. The contradiction amused me when I was dubbed a climate change denier. So much information in today's world is couched in jargon or terminology alien to most. This is expanding with the change from generalist to specialist understanding. It means abandonment of general rules and even forbids generalizations. The chances of understanding are diminished as each specialist only knows one small piece of any complex system.

Climatology is a generalist discipline in a world of specialization. Even a basic understanding requires integration of almost everything from cosmic radiation from space to volcanic heat on the bottom of the ocean and everything in between. It is almost impossible to leave anything out as those who try to produce simulations through climate models understand or ignore depending upon their objective.

Knowledge is valuable but only if it improves the human condition. As a consequence, beyond understanding the generalist nature of climate I am especially interested in how it affects all aspects of human existence. This website will examine a wide variety of topics about the way the environment affects humans and the way humans affect the environment.

We're in an information revolution because the Internet is democratizing information.

—Tim Ball

CHAPTER TEN

Recollections by Dr Bruce Atkinson, Tim's PhD Supervisor at Queen Mary College, University of London England

I FIRST MET Tim in the early 1970s when he was seeking to start studies for a PhD. He visited me at the Department of Geography, Queen Mary College, University of London. He was, of course, a "mature student" and had a clear idea of what he hoped to do.

He knew of records containing the meteorological observations taken at stations on Hudson's Bay over long periods in the eighteenth and nineteenth centuries. These are held in the Hudson Bay Company Archives. Analysis is these observations would enable climatic variations in that area to be elucidated on a scale of many decades.

As a result of our discussions, he became registered as a PhD. student at the University of London.

At the time he was on the academic staff of the Department of Geography at the University of Winnipeg, so this meant that supervision, such as was required, was obviously at a distance. This was in the days before the internet and widespread email. In 1976, I visited Winnipeg to see the original records in the archives and have more detailed discussions about the project.

DR. BRUCE ATKINSON—2010

On returning to the UK, I started to receive chapters of the thesis and the story of the climate at two stations on the Hudson Bay began to emerge, complemented by the atmospheric changes that underlie the weather variations. The PhD was awarded in 1983 and published papers based on the thesis appeared soon after.

I hope my recollections are accurate. It was a long time ago! I also hope that you are able to cope in the demanding times to come.

Best wishes.

—*Bruce*

Miscellaneous Musings

"When we allow science to become political then we are lost. We will enter the internet version of the Dark Ages, an era of stifling fears and wild prejudices, transmitted to people who don't know any better."
—Michael Crichton

"When people learn no tools of judgment and merely follow their hopes, the seeds of political manipulation are sown."
—Stephen Jay Gould

UNIVERSITY OF LONDON

Queen Mary College

Timothy Francis Ball

having completed the approved course of study and passed the examinations has this day been admitted by the Senate to the University of London Degree of

DOCTOR OF PHILOSOPHY

Vice-Chancellor

26 October 1983

CHAPTER ELEVEN

Tours for Credit Course Students

Day Trips and Weekend Tours for Credit Course Students in Tim's Physical Geography Class—1972 to 1996

TIM'S STUDENTS LOVED these educational journeys. Many said after taking the tours they never looked at the landscape the same way again.

He started with city tours, then provincial tours, including Churchill, including combining two with The Rupertsland Research Centre conferences. (Tim was the founder and director of this organization with an office in the University of Winnipeg.) These RRC conferences were held in Churchill in 1988 and the Orkney Island in 1990. While there was much work involved, they were very successful and enjoyed by all from around the world.

On the Churchill trips the group would take the CN train from Winnipeg to the town of Hudson Bay, Saskatchewan, then back into Manitoba through the tundra (perma-frost) to Churchill, enduring a very bumpy and tedious trip that took nearly twenty-four hours. Tim kept everyone amused with his lecturing.

Two days were spent in Churchill with visits to the Fort Prince of Wales and Sloops Cove. A highlight was riding in the tundra buggies hoping to see polar bears in the wild. It was very disappointing if none were found. Tundra buggies were high off the ground, having huge tires for the rough terrain, keeping the riders as far from the polar bears teeth and claws as possible. Many of the students and tourists were reckless and had to be reminded to stay clear of the bears.

There were, however, often a few polar bears in captivity that had been spoiled by eating at the garbage dump. They were, rather sadly, waiting to be shipped off to Zoos all around the world.

Tim and the students always flew back to Winnipeg to avoid another long train ride.

A few of these shorter tours were also organized for the Manitoba Historical Society, The Ruperstland Research Centre, and other similar organizations. Tim loved doing them.

JOHN SELWOOD, TIM AND JOCK LEHR MAY 15, 1985

TIM AT FORT PRINCE OF WALES 1988

Tundra Buggy, Churchill Manitoba
Miscellaneous Musings

Most people live in the world they perceive. For example, the Inuit tradition is the Earth is saucer-shaped because there is a mirage effect in the arctic called looming. A thin layer of warm air close to the surface that makes the horizon 'rise up' creates it. The visual evidence for most people is that the Earth is flat with a surrounding rim.

There are few places where you can be high enough with a flat surrounding to see the Earth's curvature. That doesn't mean they don't know the Earth is round, it is simply their experience. It also means they rarely think about things in a 3-D way, which brings us back to the Mercator projection and its influence on spatial perceptions of the Earth.

Benjamin Franklin (1706-1790) was one of the most perceptive and aware people in history. He was, by all measures, a legitimate polymath. However, he also spanned the onset of the Renaissance. As the first joint postmaster general for the American colonies, he increased the speed of mail between America and France. This was especially important during the US Revolution. He provided thermometers to postal ships, so they could stay in the warm, strong North Atlantic Drift going east and avoid it going west.

Despite this, and his experiments with kites and lightning, Franklin could not understand the wind patterns associated with mid-latitude cyclones. This was a spinning motion around a low-pressure center that moved across the country. It wasn't until 1857 that Dutch meteorologist Buys Ballot established the relationship between wind direction and the horizontal pressure pattern. As part of my instructions for Canadian farmers on how to track weather systems, I taught the simple method based on Buys Ballot's Law for tracking the movement for the center of a low-pressure system. In the Northern hemisphere with the wind at your back, the low is on your left. They combine with this with a barometer to determine the direction and movement of the system. They can calculate when it will pass and allow them to plan to get chores done.

The public lack of 3-D perception continues. Most are unable to imagine or even explain how the moon orbits the Earth. People look at weather maps but are unable to visualize the 3-D atmosphere. Few know the Troposphere that effectively marks the top of the atmosphere in which weather occurs is twice as high over the Equator with an extreme difference between 20 km at the equator in summer and 7 km over the Poles in winter. For most people, the weather is 1-D, while climate is 3-D.

—Tim Ball

Everything Reminds Me of Tim

Poem by One of Tim's Students

Composed by Jean Gregory, April 1993.
The senior citizens class at the University of Winnipeg.

Tim Ball Speaks

The Excitement mounts
The crowd's at its peak,
The word has gone out,
Tim Ball's going to speak.

His enthusiasm is infectious,
He has so much to relate,
Encyclopedic memory
and his humour's just great.

"Environmental panic",
Was his topic that day,
But he just gets started
When it's "by the way"

However we enjoy,
All his little diversions
For they take us on such
interesting excursions.

His interests and subjects,
range far and wide
His elation with learning
He can't keep inside.

He talked of the law,
medicine, anthropology,
science and religion
and some on psychology.

There were robins and cowpies,
"your grandmother's a gorilla"
The odd study the id,
naval gazing and global villages.

He talked of Darwin, Suzuki,
Einstein and Von Braun,
Jim Baker, MaDonald,
Copernicus and on.

The weather, the gulf war,
prisoners and their vote
oil slicks, free trade
Most anything of note.

Lawyers and loop holes,
Meech Lake, GST,
privies and water
"Oh, that reminds me"

Indians, Norwegians,
Our Canadian winters,
each of his topics,
divides and splinters.

Friars Balsam, salt peter,
Riparian Laws,
the facts keep on coming,
with narry a pause.

So from all of us here,
and those who are not,
we love your talks,
and thanks a whole lot.

CHAPTER TWELVE
Three-Week Senior Citizen's Tours 1986 to 1996

THESE BEGAN AS a result of Tim teaching a non-credit course for retirees as a part of the continuing education series at the university. I never knew whether Tim or one of these seniors suggested taking overseas tours. It doesn't matter now. He taught this class for 12 years and had over 600 registered during the last year. He had to repeat that class thrice weekly because the largest classroom only held 225. He, of course, taught his credit course students with priority. Tim's colleagues thought Tim should spend more time on promoting his own career since he received no academic credit for teaching non-credit courses.

Our first extensive tour was to the UK. (I took my holidays at this time each year so I could go and help as much as I could, only as a nurse, of course.) We generally travelled in May to miss the primary tourist season. We got better rates on flights and hotels. On our first tour, we took 49 people plus Tim and me. The bus held 50 with an extra stool for Tim at the front with his microphone in hand. Tim used to say that having a 'captive' audience was always favourable.

TOUR BOAT ON LAKE WINDERMERE

Tim surrounded himself with numerous books for reference. He talked about the history, architecture, trees, flowers, landscape, climate and everything else interesting along the way.

It was lovely for all of us to sit higher in the coach. We could see over the hedgerows and the stone walls. The many coach drivers we had were exciting and engaging themselves. A favourite was Bunny Austin, with whom we felt safe in the heavy traffic on the British Isles, which always made me a tad nervous.

Tim worked constantly to make each tour the best experience possible, striving to make it better than anyone's prior travel tours. Each tour always had a theme, mostly art, music and literature. We also rotated our hotels from city ones to country inns. Many of the seniors were seasoned travellers and, in some cases, knew more about the countries than Tim because of previous visits. Every minute was a challenge, and Tim loved it.

SCOTLAND, HEADING TO THE ORKNEYS

He hovered over each and every one in the group like a mother hen.

We wish we had kept the itinerary of each trip, but unfortunately, we lost them all along the way. However, a few names of the regulars come to mind: Rod and Dorothy Steinbart, Enid and Russ Jordan, Helen Moroy, Olga Cormilo and the Cowsun sisters. So many others were regulars, including Ed and Mary Curtis, who often said, "We have that follow Tim Ball disease."

We also have fond memories of the people who made it all possible, with a special shout-out to Max Johnson and Carolyn Pirani. These two did much of the leg work before departure, ensuring each tour was the absolute best, including pre-checking each hotel to ensure it was up to the standard we expected.

Not long after dismantling the Berlin Wall and Checkpoint Charley, we toured most of Europe, even the eastern part. Whole villages would come into the streets to see people from Canada. They wondered why we were there.

When we toured countries where English wasn't the first language, we had an interpreter travel with us. Her name was Alina Peretti, and she spoke seven languages. During a dinner in Berlin, she invited some of her friends to meet Tim and me. Each was from a different country, and Alina carried on a conversation and changed languages as she talked to each of us. We could not believe anyone could do that so brilliantly.

Alina's life story was also fascinating. She was born in Poland, where she married and had two children. They had difficulty making a living after WW2, so she decided to emigrate to England. She advertised in the English press for a husband who would marry her on the promise of divorce as soon as she obtained British citizenship. She then divorced her Polish husband and married an Englishman.

After a sufficient time, Alina fell in love with the Englishman and couldn't divorce him. She told us she loved both her men. There were no children by Mr Perretti. Alina was so uninhibited. On one occasion, she hugged Russ Jordan and he almost fainted. But Alina said, "You are a good man, but don't worry, I already have two husbands!"

She worked with us for years as a tour guide and interpreter, mainly in Europe. On one occasion with her leading, we visited the Auschwitz prisoner-of-war camp. She picked up some flowers, not telling us why. In the camp, she stopped by a shrine, where she laid the flowers, crying for a long while. Later in the coach, she told us her sister was shot at that spot during the war.

MARTY AND ALINA IN ITALY

The tour groups loved Alina, as did Tim and I. We kept in contact with her for many years following the tours. She remained in London, only occasionally returning to Poland to visit her first husband and children.

We gave two gifts at the final dinner on each of our tours. One was for the person who had paid the most attention to what we saw. The second was for the one who had retained the most information passed on by Tim along the way. Rod Steinbart made two lovely little walnut wooden boxes as prizes. The winners were thrilled with these very special mementoes.

Learning from our first tour, we limited the number of travellers to 25 for the subsequent 11 tours. Everyone was more comfortable. They could

HOLDING UP THE LEANING TOWER OF PISA

sit alone or not, and getting on and off was much easier since it took far less time. I was responsible for counting heads to ensure all were on board. I was counting heads in my sleep. Tim told them he would never leave anyone behind, but there was one who tried to sabotage a tour, and that was our pink lady. She wore a pink jumpsuit during the three-week tour, and we waited for her each time we met at the place of departure.

But on one occasion, we lost this lady at the Tower of London. Tim raced through the whole complex while our coach was double-parked during rush hour traffic. We finally gave up and returned to the hotel, only to find the lady had returned by taxi without telling anyone in our group. What a relief to see her safe. She phoned and apologized, and Tim replied, "That's okay, as long as you are safe." I would have had words with her had Tim allowed.

(This was shortly after Tim's heart attack in Oxford, which we didn't know about then.) I kept telling him his vomiting and cold sweats were likely a gallbladder attack due to eating too many fatty English breakfasts (which he loved). What a good nurse I was.

The chest pain had eased somewhat when we arrived back in Winnipeg three days later, but his description of feeling like he was wearing a tight shirt rang a bell and I called the doctor, who immediately placed him in Grace Hospital. However, after twelve days, two Cardiologists could not agree on the diagnosis and treatment, so they sent him home. He was only forty-six at the time. Tim was very fortunate! The doctors told us that many have massive cardiac arrests after these relatively minor myocardial infarctions, indicative of partial blocking of the coronary arteries.

Tim was fine until June 2007 when Dr Lynn Fedoruk did a quintuple bypass at the Royal Jubilee Hospital in Victoria. The blockage of 1986 had already formed collateral circulation. This worked well until February 2017. More later on that experience.

In 1991, because of the first Gulf War, we went to the Yukon and Alaska and returned by cruise ship to Vancouver.

Over the 11 years and 12 tours, we naturally had a few minor incidents health-wise, but mostly colds and gastrointestinal problems. However, on the last tour of the Maritimes, Nova Scotia, Newfoundland and Labrador, one of our senior ladies broke her ankle on the Sunday of a long weekend. She tripped on a rock despite having good walking shoes. We had a difficult time getting her a flight back to Winnipeg. She was in such pain and all we had were ice and analgesics. We learned all went well with her surgery the following Tuesday morning.

We visited England, Scotland, Ireland, Wales, the Orkney Islands, France, Germany, Poland, Hungary, Czechoslovakia, Austria, Spain, Portugal, Italy, the Channel Islands, Brittany, Normandy, Newfoundland and Labrador, Yukon, Alaska and British Columbia.

Tim and I always cherished the wonderful times and experiences we had. Thank you to those who helped make them so memorable.

A Poem by May DeWet, 1986…a Long Tour Regular

We drove the roads of England
and looked at many things
for stones, tors, birds and things
and cabbages and Kings.

Arundel's, a chilly place
with portcullis and maces
Stern Howards look down from the walls
no smiles e'er cross their faces.

Farringfords, a lovely place
and a bonus for us all,
was to meet the poet's descendent
visiting the Hall.

He told us of his childhood there,
how the famous came to dine.
On New Years eve at midnight
Jenny Lind sang Auld Lang Syne.

Lily Hobbs proved she's no coward
by ascending in the chair
to view the famous Needles,
did she do it on a dare?

In Exeter Cathedral
we Canadians read with pride
the plaque to John Graves Simcoe,
erected when he died.

Everything Reminds Me of Tim

We saw a play at Chichester,
it really was quite odd
all the people seemed quite batty
I swear it, honest to God.

The Barbican at Plymouth
is a fascinating place,
we also went to Helston
where the dancers set the pace.

The roof of the Old Post Office
is like a nursery rhyme.
You'd bump your head on the twisty stairs
if you didn't duck in time.

On Lands End rocky headland,
while gazing out to sea,
Doris, Edna and Lily
enjoyed a pot of tea.

In years gone by the wool trade
made Devon very wealthy.
Fine sheep still run the meadows
and they certainly look healthy.

A place of infinite beauty
Wells Cathedral is the fairest,
the fan vaulting the statues
are surely the country's rarest.

The mysterious spell of Stonehenge
seen on mid-summer eve,
gave rise to many stories
that the Druids used to weave.

And then we had our bad day, the 25th a
Sunday.
Everything had been well planned,
to give us a super day.
But the fog drifted in along with the rain,
so we had to forego our ride on the train.

Then traffic of monstrous proportions
caused a line-up of cars on the path,
the program got changed from what had been
arranged.
But the Lord was still dishing out wrath.

I'm sure we thought of tragic Charles
when we climbed at Carisbrooke,
the glorious view from atop the Keep,
demands a lengthy look.

We drove straight to the Castle
to find the time had been changed.
They said "come at eight for your Mead and
your meat"
not seven o'clock as arranged.

But the feast was a smashing success
with minstrels and harpist and wenches.
The tables were loaded with marvellous food,
and we sat on traditional benches.

Chester has half-timbered houses,
it's a city of infinite charm.
If anyone changes a building,
the citizens sent an alarm.

Inevitably at Stoke-on-Trent,
we shopped to our hearts delight.
Old Josiah would indeed be pleased
when the coaches came in sight.

We soberly remembered
the bombings of the war,
and the terrible pain and tragedy
that Coventry bore.

And now we have the town of the Bard
and dear London to explore.
The bits of knowledge we've acquired
will serve us evermore.

Bunny was adept
at managing the bus.
The way he got around corners,
without a bit of fuss.

Tim and his lovely lady,
were our shepherds all the way,
their thoughtfulness and kindness
we never can repay.

CHAPTER THIRTEEN

Building the Cottage at West Hawk Lake, Manitoba

TIM ALWAYS SAID he would move mountains for me and he almost did.

We bought the lot, sight unseen, in January of 1978. It was located on Indian Bay on West Hawk Lake, 100 miles east of Winnipeg. There was no road access, so we had to purchase a boat, motor, two paddles and four life jackets.

We would leave the 12-foot aluminum boat at McDougall's landing, which was very near the number one highway, and carried the motor and equipment back and forth from the city. We stayed with our friends, Pat and John Scott in their log cabin (which was about a half mile away by boat from our location.) and very close to McDougall's landing. We were and still are very grateful to them for being so kind, letting us stay with them during the initial days of building our place. Otherwise, we would have needed to set up a tent with thousands of mosquitoes to cope with day and night. Their cottage was fairly large and all eight of us (4 parents, 4 children) slept very comfortably.

We fell in love with West Hawk, which is a crater lake about four miles by four miles, deeper and colder than most in this area. Our family still talks about the happy times there. Looking back now, we don't know how Tim did this almost single-handedly.

There was no road, no dock, no path. Tim attached the boat and trailer to the hitch, loaded with all the equipment and started on his own as soon as the lake was ice-free, usually in May. Our next-door neighbour at the lake, Bob Armstrong (Armo), was accommodating when Tim contacted him. Tim borrowed a transit from the University and began marking the support pad spots. He used the Armo dock and hauled everything through the brush and incline to our lot. We can only imagine how many trips were made. A path was carved between the Armo dock and our cottage, and we purchased the longest extension cord in Christendom. Then the fun began for Tim.

All he had was a used stepladder and a skill saw to start, given to him by Larry Anderson. Larry was Tim's best friend and luckily, he was a carpenter/renovator.

A nearby lumberyard delivered the lumber in small amounts. Tim arranged for it to be delivered to McDougall's landing and prearranged the exact time so Tim could meet them when they arrived to save unloading it and reloading it into the boat.

That was a busy summer on weekends. Tim was working at the HBC archives in Winnipeg during the week recording the data for his doctorate. We stayed with the Scotts most of the time even when they weren't there. In 1979 we bought a huge Mercury Marquis station wagon. It allowed us to haul more lumber and supplies from the city. If it rained, I had to ride under the dash so the wood would fit inside the car. Lucky me! Not very comfortable.

Maybe that was when my arthritic problems started?

By the September long weekend that year we were finally able to stay at our own cottage, missing only one window. We covered it with plastic until Tim and the boys installed the window the next day.

**LARRY ANDERSON
OUR VERY GOOD FRIEND**

That first night, we set up temporary beds in the living area and covered our faces with mosquito repellent. We managed to sleep fairly well, probably because we were so tired. All four of us worked like beavers that weekend, getting the cottage ready to inhabit.

OUR COTTAGE ON INDIAN BAY, WEST HAWK LAKE, MANITOBA

Tim got up early and made a makeshift table on which to put the food to make a cold breakfast. We purchased many necessities at garage sales and were also given things that other cottagers didn't need anymore. What a windfall! How Tim put up the beams for the roof still befuddles us. He said he carved out a two by eight with a chisel to fit on his head. Then he fitted the beam on this piece balancing it as he climbed the ladder and pounded the nail that held it in place. It's difficult to explain, but I think you get the idea.

Larry helped wire the cottage for electricity. This was a big step forward as we no longer needed the extension cord. Then the plumbing was installed with the help of John Scott. He and Tim installed and connected the water pump at the water's edge to the cottage. Each weekend we were thrilled with another luxury. A stove and then a refrigerator. Hauling those up this steep path was a sight to behold. Our sons and I helped as much as we could. The waterworks and shower were especially rewarding, as we no longer had to bathe in the lake.

Then the dock was built, first setting in two cribs which Tim had to fill with stones to secure the planks. Tim dove to the bottom of the lake hundreds of times to collect the rocks. He even found a matching pair of white men's leather shoes. We dried them out and presented them to Armo. "Armo, are these your shoes?" Armo answered, "Yes, I was wondering where those were?" We still laugh about this to this day.

The toilet was our biggest problem. Tim built an outhouse first. By law he had to find a spot that had at least three feet of sand to filter the waste. That was our 'Big John'. Then we purchased an electric toilet called an 'Incinolet.' That worked very well for fifteen years. It burned the waste until only ashes remained, which we threw in the outdoor john. And of course, it was called the 'electric chair' making it one of the more hilarious topics of conversation when friends visited.

Tim named the cottage 'Sisyphus,' the son of Aeolus, punished in Hades for his misdeeds in life by being condemned to the eternal task of rolling a large stone to the top of a hill from which it always rolled down again.

Our boys got an education like never before. What do two neighbouring bachelors do on the weekends at a lovely lakeside? Ha! They would come on Friday evenings (sometimes with their girlfriends) with two plastic bags of groceries and four cases of (24 in each) beer. They partied till the early hours each Friday and Saturday. We were always invited, and while we didn't always go, it was go or listen to the noise.

Each morning after, both Bob Armstrong (Armo) and Ralph Linden would jump in the lake in the nude. Dave and Tim Jr could not believe their eyes. It was the event of the day for them as young teenagers. "Look, Mom and Dad. Ralph and Armo don't have any bathing suits."

On Saturdays, we would have barbecues at the Scotts' or our place. The four children would water-ski until dinner. Tim drove the boat while John spotted. Pat and I sat on the dock, watching, gossiping, and drinking wine. I occasionally water-skied, and I couldn't even swim. I didn't even get my hair wet. Tim said it was sheer fright that kept me upright. The Thanksgiving weekend was usually our last for the year. We closed the cottage and never saw it again until the next May long weekend.

There was a period when our boys were a little older when they wanted to party on their own at the cottage. On the weekends, when we went to the lake, the boys would revel in the city. The empty beer cases and full garbage bags at each place told us they had a good time. What we didn't know didn't hurt us.

When Pat and John Scott separated, Tim wasn't keen on going to the lake anymore. He did manage to get a road built from the Ontario border, which was only one-quarter of a mile from our bay. All seven of the cottage owners shared the cost. Tim never got to travel this road. So sad. The boys and I used the cottage as much as we could, but the upkeep became more than we could manage. Dave and Tim Jr were very disappointed when we sold in 1996 to Norm and Eunice Roberts, the parents of Brad and Dan Roberts of the Crash Test Dummies musical band. I've been asked many times what I did to help during the build. I took care of the food and held the boards while Tim sawed them.

We cannot thank Larry enough times for all his advice each week when Tim visited him on Monday evenings. They talked for hours and hours over many cups of coffee. The topic was mostly about what Tim would be doing to the cottage next weekend.

Sadly, Larry died in May 2006.

Douglas and Marjorie Ball on the right with Rich and Liz in the 1960s

Miscellaneous Musings

"The idea of a differing angle of the sun is critical to understanding climate and climate change. This is why the word climate derives from the Greek word for inclination. It is also why the Greeks were able to identify three climate zones: the Torrid, Temperate, and Frigid."

—Tim Ball

CHAPTER FOURTEEN
Leaving Winnipeg and Moving to Victoria, BC
1996-2011

TIM REALIZED HE was on a never-ending treadmill during the academic year, 1995 and 1996.

Speaking engagements were many, especially on the prairies with primarily farmers and farm groups, since weather is incredibly important to them. There wasn't a road on the prairies that Tim hadn't travelled. He spoke far and wide, primarily in Canada and the USA with media interviews from all over the world as well. Tim was known as the Weatherman.

Peter Warren of CJOB radio in Winnipeg interviewed Tim regularly for many years. Peter took questions from his audience and never tolerated small talk. Immediately after Peter got the usual question: "How are you?", he would reply, "Get on with it." (He and his wife Gabi also retired to Victoria about the same time as we did). Peter continued to broadcast from Vancouver on weekends for Corus Radio and interviewed Tim even when many considered Tim a heretic.

Tim felt indebted to Peter for being brave enough to give him airtime.

Thank you, Peter.

In April 1996, we finally started to talk about retirement. It was eight years before Tim's no-penalty pension retirement age but felt he could not carry on at this pace. We determined what our combined retirement income would be and decided we could live on it if we didn't have a mortgage.

We sold the house and cottage. The cabin sold immediately, but the house took seven months, from April to October 1996. There were better times to sell, but we wanted to avoid another Winnipeg winter. (During our last two winters, we had a -19C high for the day, 11 days in a row.)

Most thought we were out of our minds, and sometimes we felt that too. Dave and Tim Jr, living in Winnipeg, were naturally disappointed with selling the cottage. Neither could afford to maintain the cabin, let alone buy it.

We had a garage sale and gave away as much household stuff as possible. Between Tim's office and our home, we had over 3,000 books, most of which went to family and friends. We put my car on the train to be transported to Nanaimo on Vancouver Island and drove west leisurely and comfortably in Tim's Camry. Travelling across the prairies and through the mountains was most enjoyable this time of year. The scenery was breathtaking. This journey was a holiday in itself. No one could interrupt us, although, again, we wanted to 'beat the snow'.

We stayed at The Royal Scott Hotel in Victoria for two weeks while looking for a permanent home. Our real estate person drove us everywhere on the island until we realized we wanted to live in downtown Victoria. Staying at this hotel made us realize how privileged we could be and thus decided on a condo in a part of Victoria known as the Songhees. We also wanted to be near a hotel with a shuttle bus and taxi service so Tim could easily access the airport and ferry for his speaking engagements.

Neither of us liked gardening, so the condo idea was something we agreed would be adequate for many years. We also decided we never wanted to move again and loved the idea of no stairs! This proved to be an excellent plan. Twenty-seven years later, I am still here and very happy we made this decision.

We could walk downtown, do most of our errands, have lunch, and shop. A five-star hotel was next-door, where we could book our children and friends for a beautiful harbour view experience.

Now that Tim had far less to do, he golfed three times each week when he wasn't lecturing somewhere.

I joined several women's clubs, golf and bridge groups.

TIM ON THE 8ᵀᴴ HOLE AT VICTORIA GOLF CLUB

On non-golfing days, Tim did a long walk every day he could with his backpack on board. He walked and learned about the city and its history. The outline of the Hudson Bay Company fort on Government Street intrigued him, and he went over it inch by inch. Our many visitors received an escorted tour by Tim of downtown Victoria, including the history of the Hudson Bay Company.

Very soon after we settled in, Tim decided, while exploring, to talk to downtown shopkeepers, looking for individuals that might need help, either setting up, or with their businesses. The first was his barber. Tim gave him $2,000 so he could set up his own barbershop. He went bankrupt. Then a Cafe owner in Bastion Square was in trouble financially. Tim gave him $2,000. He also went bankrupt and closed his business. Next, a waitress in a cafe wanted to set up her own tearoom. Tim gave her $800. We never saw her again. I think Tim thought he was Santa Claus, but it was likely his way of "adding value" which was always his mantra, but very soon decided that giving away our money didn't have the desired results.

Tim and I regularly went to our condo Strata Council meetings. Tim periodically offered his advice on matters concerning our buildings. There were 97 units in our complex, including townhouses. He was encouraged to run for council and was subsequently elected and soon after became president.

Following Tim's first two years on the committee, they decided to do an 'envelope study' on our buildings to see if they were sweaty or leaky. Most condos around us did have this problem because of a vapour barrier policy set in place by the BC government. While these barriers are necessary in dry, cold climates, they are hazardous in damp environments. The wooden or metal framing has a tendency to rot or rust after a few years. This devastating result arose from environmentalists lobbying with misinformed demands and solutions.

Our condo was only 2 years old when it was declared 'leaky'.

Details of these remediation years are covered in a separate chapter by Marg Trombley.

The years 1996 to 2011 were some of our happiest. We golfed, socialized and went to the theatre and symphony regularly. We went out for dinner and played regular Saturday evening bridge with Howard and Sheena Guest. We also did some low-level holidaying with the Guests. We visited Tofino, the Tigh-Na-Mara Resort in Parksville, Kelowna, and Harrison Hot Springs.

Tim's speaking engagements gave us plenty of extra income, and we never looked back.

CHAPTER FIFTEEN

Tim's Opinions on Universities: An Inside View, 1996

RECENTLY, THE CHAIRPERSON of the board of the University of Manitoba asked to meet with me after hearing my comments about the failure of universities on CJOB Winnipeg radio.

After a public relations message on the great things being done at universities, warning shots were fired.

"You need to have all the facts about some issues. You have a great deal of influence in this province and could harm at a time when some people are beginning to question what is happening in universities."

Harm to whom? Why are people asking questions? It is time I used up some of my credibility to force change in institutions that vehemently resist change from within.

Frankly, it is time someone asked questions and demanded real answers. Of course, I am not the first and will not be the last to assault the ivory tower. I will be beaten back by those inside who only use their considerable intellectual skills to defend the indefensible. They will offer spacious examples of success, trot forward students who thoroughly enjoyed their university years and others who genuinely benefited from the precious few who genuinely stimulate learning.

Yes, universities offer some benefits, but the cost of people and money should be lowered.

If all is well, why have so many perceptive people made such devastating comments over the years?

Thomas Jefferson said of universities that "they commit their pupils to the theatre of the world with just enough learning to be alienated from industrious pursuits, and not enough to do service in the ranks of science."

Thomas Merton wrote, "I am willing to admit that some people might live there for years, or even a lifetime, so protected that they never sense the sweet stench of corruption that is all around them—the keen, thin scent of decay that pervades everything and accuses with a terrible accusation the superficial youthfulness, the abounding undergraduate noise that fills the buildings."

Camille Paglia believes, "Our major universities are now stuck with an army of pedestrian, toadying careerists; fifties types who wave around sixties banners to conceal their record of ruthless, beaver-like tunnelling to the top."

Over the years, few have had little positive to say about universities. I make this statement to elicit a dizzying list of positive comments from academics who are only triggered to action when the academy is attacked.

H.L. Mencken suggested decades ago that the solution to the failure of universities was to burn the buildings and hang the faculty. It's a little drastic, but little will change as long as the faculty runs the universities. The prisoners running the prisons and the wardens are the promoted prisoners. Mostly, they use their impressive intellectual skills to defend the increasingly indefensible.

Universities are anachronisms.

Prince Philip said that universities are our society's only truly incestuous systems. After 500 years, the inbreeding is clearly showing.

They are medieval institutions which resist most efforts to make them relevant. He's used the dreaded word, which will also trigger a violent response. They will say universities are not supposed to be appropriate; a degree is not job training; our graduates have a low unemployment rate; anyone who uses the word relevant in regard to universities is clearly uneducated; anyone who questions the role of universities is equally illiterate. Academics resist relevance because they interpret it as a code word for accountability. Notice that the phrase that something is purely academic means it is irrelevant to the real world.

The fact is they are job training. What else are faculties of education, medicine, dentistry, engineering, nursing, architecture or law?

True, some research is done, but most of it, as Paglia said, is irrelevant and produced to advance the career of the professor within the system—countless pages of arcane, useless material read only by those playing the same game. The faculties are not considered job training because they are classified as professions, a designation granted by a trusting society that believed they would monitor their own behaviour. Now, they fail to do that, and worse, cover up serious problems.

What don't the academics want you to know? My gross salary is $72,000, excellent compensation for the job. However, it places me at the bottom of the full professor in my department. Several of my colleagues make at least $20,000 a year more. Yes, in the geography department at the University of Winnipeg, people are making over $90,000 per year. Yet the U of W salary scale is less than that at the University of Manitoba. Worse, it is reported that 83 faculty are over 71 years old and draw a full salary plus their pension at that age.

My contract requires me to teach three courses a year. A regular session course has three hours of lectures each week over 24 weeks. This means a total of 216 hours a year. If you work a 36-hour week for 48 weeks, you are obliged to work 1,728 hours a year. At the U of MB, the contract requires the profs to teach only two courses a year.

I am allotted money proportional to my class enrolment to hire student markers. I do not use it for this purpose. I pay a student to file my work, answer my phone and keep my office in order. (I do my own marking.)

It is unconscionable to use students as markers. The student pays for a professor when they enroll in a course. This is like paying for a Cadillac and having a Chevrolet delivered to your door.

At the University of Manitoba, professors have graduate students (known as teaching assistants. I prefer to call them slave labour) to teach courses and do marking. This is not any more justified. Surely, assessing the student's performance is the most essential task of a teacher. But here's the rub: professors are not teachers, nor are they required to have teacher training. They are hired strictly on the basis of research degrees. Promotion and tenure are granted by colleagues also on the basis of research, despite their claims that teaching skills are rewarded. Every student can relate to horror stories from the classroom.

Of course, a lack of qualifications exists from top to bottom. Most university presidents and vice presidents are in executive positions with no executive training. Most deans and department chairs are in management positions with no management training. Professors are not required to have teacher training including those in faculties of education. The irony is that the entire system tells students they must be qualified for what they will do.

The province provides large sums of money to the universities yearly, but what do the taxpayers get for their dollar? Answer: Precious little. The combined failure and dropout rate in the first year is between 40 and 50%, while less than 50% graduate. Universities cry for more money but do little to deal with this problem. Why? Funding is no longer directly related to enrolment, but someone would ask questions if they reduced intake to lower the rates. They count numbers coming in, but no one openly discusses how many are leaving. We do not consider the cost to the individual of 'failing' in the university.

A few solutions stem from this last point. We have created an educationally elite society with too much emphasis on narrow academic intellectualism. Society inherently assumes that every child going into kindergarten will end up in university. That means anyone not attending university is a dropout or failure.

Things I would recommend:

- Reduce the number of students going to university. Separate school leaving requirements from university entrance qualifications. Have the universities prepare and supervise their own set of entrance exams.
- Educate students and society that university is just another after-high school option.
- Require all faculty to chair Boards, Committees and other agencies for government as part of their contract. They would provide the intellectual framework for the discussion and become better professors because they would also have to be involved in real-world decision-making. It would also identify incompetence.
- Close the University of Winnipeg (Formerly United College.) Reduced enrolments mean all students could be enrolled at the University of Manitoba. The university needs to identify its role. It should be the

city of Winnipeg's university, as the name implies. Still, it needs to do more to work with the city, the core area, the business world or anything else in its environs. It is a suburban university where people commute in the morning and go home at night. It exists as an order-in-council and would not require legislation to be eliminated.

- Change the law on compulsory retirement for academics. Experience has value, but making way for new ideas is essential.
- Require that all administrators are qualified for the job through executive and management training.
- Require that all faculty have teacher training.
- Recognize that four universities in a province of one million is excessive.

There is no evidence that universities will make these changes necessary for today's or tomorrow's society. They are a closed society answerable only to themselves, a situation we can't afford anymore.
—*Tim Ball*

Tim, David and Ainsley in 2010

Miscellaneous Musings

H. Sterling Burnett: You've written books on climate science, including *Slaying the Sky Dragon: Death of the Greenhouse Gas Theory*. What is the thesis of the book?

Tim Ball: The original claim made was that global warming was inevitable due to increasing levels of atmospheric carbon dioxide from human activities, especially from industry. This hypothesis was based on the assumptions that carbon dioxide is a greenhouse gas and that such an increase would result in a temperature increase.

The hypothesis ignored key facts. There are three main greenhouse gases: water vapor is 95 percent, carbon dioxide 4 percent, and methane 0.4 percent. The official position is humans produce water vapor but the amount is so small relative to the atmospheric total it is reasonable to ignore it. In every historic record, temperatures have increased prior to increases in carbon dioxide. Human production of carbon dioxide is within the error factor of estimates of carbon dioxide emissions from two natural sources: the oceans and rotting vegetation.

These facts, among others explored in my book, undermine the claim human carbon dioxide emissions are driving present climate change.

From an H. Sterling Burnett's interview with Tim, *Climate Science Was Corrupted, Says Award Winning Climate Scientist*, published February 6, 2020.

CHAPTER SIXTEEN

Letter from Joe and Mary Campbell, Winnipeg

Memories of Tim

TIM WAS QUITE a force in the lives of the Campbells. A very positive force 'ab initio.'

We first met at a Christmas party for Grace Hospital staff in 1973, where Mary and Marty Ball were nursing. Tim was teaching at the University of Winnipeg. I was starting a doctoral program in clinical psychology at the University of Manitoba. Thus began a very warm and enriching relationship.

Social and Family Life

We remember the frequent dinners hosted by Marty…what a cook. Tim was a conversationalist of many hues, from humour to gripping insights into politics, climate change and the shortcomings of university undergraduate teaching. Every dinner, and there were many, was both food for the body and the mind. Tim excelled at keeping us informed and entertained. We sorely missed these dinners when Tim and Mary moved to Victoria, BC in the mid-nineties.

Tim, ever generous, frequently shared his wisdom with our children. Eoin remembers him vividly and fondly as his mentor and motivator. Cara still talks of her trip to West Hawk Lake during which Tim kept them spellbound on the topic of the Dawson Trail.

Tim became an honorary Irishman playing golf with a bunch of us on Saturdays at Tuxedo Golf Course in Shaftesbury. He also came to Hecla Island, (roughly 150 miles north of Winnipeg), for the 'Irish Open' on several occasions. I especially remember going there by bus and receiving an education on the flora and fauna along the way. It made for a fascinating and eye-opening trip.

West Hawk Lake was special. Tim built a family cottage there on weekends. The times we spent there, all five of us, were nothing short of magical. I am only realizing now how close we were, and how hospitable Tim and Marty were to us.

One memory I've relived many times. (Let's call it an introduction to sailing, or how to ruin a beautiful friendship.) Tim put me in charge of the tiller with the simple instruction to push it right or left when I tell you. "We sailed out into West Hawk with nary a bother. It was sunny and warm with a nice breeze." At last Tim said "Ok, push it right." I did with vigour and nearly capsized the wee boat. Tim very patiently explained the need to push smoothly and gently. We docked soon after to avoid further erosion of our friendship.

JOE AND MARY CAMPBELL

Academic Life

Tim was too honest and insightful for university politics. He loved his students and was many times voted the outstanding teacher of the year. On a personal level, he took charge of having my dissertation printed and delivered to Graduate Studies. I was living and working in Ireland at the time, and had not Tim selflessly undertaken this onerous chore, my PhD would have been considerably delayed. For this and so many other kindnesses, I forever owe him. He will be quite an asset to Heaven's think tank.

—*Joe and Mary Campbell*

CHAPTER SEVENTEEN

Remediation at the Penninsula—The Leaky Condo Crisis

During the First 18 years of Living at the Peninsula Condominium Units

Marg Trombley Fellow Owner—Her Own Thoughts and Opinions (she was on the Strata Council with Tim)

IN 1996, CELINE DION dominated the airwaves, Braveheart won an Oscar for Best Picture, and Canada's Mortgage and Housing Corporation released its Survey of Building Envelope Failures in the Coastal Climate of British Columbia. It was the year VIS4023, commonly known as the Peninsula Condominiums, opened its doors. Newport Realty was on hand to show prospective buyers the model unit, a live-in caretaker assured new residents the common areas would be maintained, and a fellow from the development company, Nova Fourteen, was available to do repairs and chat up the realtors. Copies of Canada Mortgage and Housing Corporation's survey were not included in the Peninsula's brochures.

One new owner, Tony Panegos, invested early in the project. His 4,000 sq. ft. on the top floor of the first tower merged three units into a penthouse and included a separate, fully functional unit that could house live-in domestics. The penthouse initially wowed guests with homage to England's Regency period and views of Victoria's spectacular Inner Harbour. It is universally acknowledged that a single man possessing a splendid penthouse must want Strata Council chairmanship.

The Peninsula's owner-developer, Kombiz Eghdami of Nova Fourteen, turned over VIS4023 to owners in 1997 after completing the second four-story tower and a chain of ten linked townhouses. Predictably, Tony Panegos nominated himself for Strata Council chair and oversaw the immediate task of bylaw creation for owners to approve at a meeting slated for the summer. Douglas Adams, author of 'The Hitch-hiker's Guide to the Galaxy,' has a favourite, quotation:

> *It is a well-known fact that those people who most want to rule people are, ipso facto, those least suited to do it...anyone who is capable of getting themselves made President should on no account be allowed to do the job.*

As a member of that council, I can admit Adams' quotation described us. Tony did everything. In fact, a fellow councillor commented that working with Tony was a pleasure because he did all the work. Bylaws approved, the council moved on to a more contentious issue, the live-in caretaker.

A woman named Pat was a sentimental hire by the developer. She'd worked for his father managing apartments in Vancouver and needed a job. A retired banker, Tony kept his eye on the budget and was genuinely concerned that her salary and the mortgage expense of her one-bedroom unit were incommensurate with her abilities. With the completion of the second tower, her workload doubled. The Strata Council decided to hold an information meeting to discuss her future with owners, and one council member resigned out of loyalty to Pat. His resignation should have been a warning.

Tony presided at the meeting in the fall of 1997. Shortly after it began, it became apparent that owners viewed the council like Goliath beating up David seated in a wheelchair. Tony's rapid-fire Greco-Italian accented English was complicated for some to understand. Adding to that, his inner authoritarian crept out in the face of palpable hostility. Tony was more comfortable hurling admonitions than receiving them.

The council underestimated the owners' fierce loyalty to Pat, their neighbour and friend. More sympathetic to her situation than to cost-benefit analysis, the loudest group in the room cried, "she stays." Shortly afterwards Tony resigned from the council and owners polarized. As we filed out that night, one man appeared particularly outraged at the chairs' performance. It was the first time I heard Tim Ball speak.

Tim and Marty Ball, retirees from Winnipeg, also bought their Peninsula condo in 1996, later moving into a more spacious, west-facing unit in the second tower. A set decorator tasked with designing a space suited for a university professor would be inspired by Tim and Marty's home. It says come in, sit down, have a cup of coffee and an oatmeal cookie and let's chat. The couple immersed themselves in post-retirement activities and, in the words of one of Tim's favourite women: "This couple is boredom's enemy."

To claim Tim's early warning system was on high alert that night might be accurate. It was indeed prophetic. Tim and Tony, with comparable experiences and abilities, would become the Peninsula's sumo wrestlers. Ultimately, one would have to push the other out of the ring.

The consequence of that ill-timed meeting was divided ownership—pro and con live-in caretaker camps made for uneasy conversations during a slow elevator ride. When the first Strata Council limped to the finish line, a pro-live-in caretaker cohort took over. It tried to establish an owner-directed garden committee only to be thwarted by Tony's court injunction. Tony also objected to Christmas lights decorating the buildings' inner courtyard. It took two years before the live-in caretaker was finally replaced by a man, Mr Val Dmiteryk, whose competence has won the devotion of everyone who lives here.

The Peninsula is an anomaly among condominiums in the Songhees. Unlike many buildings in the area, rentals are permitted. In its early days, the majority of units were owned by investors. During the late 1990s, life at the Peninsula was tense—the threat of envelope failure dominated hallway chatter and cultivated uncertainty. With the release of the Barrett report on condominium building failure, owners needed direction from the Strata Council. The Strata Property Act of B.C. demands a 75% agreement on capital expenses and requires owners to make repairs. Because the Peninsula had a mixture of resident and investor owners, their differing priorities could not guarantee a 75% vote. Councils needed help with the project's immensity and getting agreement from owners.

In 2001, the Strata Council included members with a maelstrom of agendas. Tony and Tim volunteered that year along with two US owners, a furniture salesman, me and the smooth-as-an-oil-slick Herbert Bolz. Herbert's bank, UBS, was a mortgage for Peninsula's developer, Kombiz Eghdami. Owners can see Herb's name as a witness on their copies of the buildings' blueprints. It was curious that Herb Bolz would volunteer to serve on the council. It meant a monthly air flight from Vancouver and almost daily emails concerning issues brought up by owners and the property manager.

Tim agreed to host the first informal gathering of the new council. His unit offered the most space, and he couldn't go to Tonys because he'd been banished. A year before stopping Tim from entering, Tony had physically attacked him when he tried to attend a meeting in his penthouse. Tony, however, was welcome inside Tim and Marty's unit.

The exploitation of natural fear is central to any attempt to control people. It is no coincidence that the original fear story was "Chicken Little and the Sky is Falling." As H. L. Mencken said, "…the whole aim of practical politics is to keep the populace alarmed, and hence clamorous to be led to safety, by menacing it with an endless series of hobgoblins, all of them imaginary."

Tim sensed deception and felt the engineers promoted fear the building was falling because it profited them. It was a stumbling block to any progress we would make. Tony knew the engineers were correct. Herb Bolz knew enormous money was needed to fix the building. The rest of us just grabbed our limbs and tried not to fall. Council accomplished one thing before its inevitable disintegration: selecting another property management firm, Cornerstone Properties. In an almost unheard-of action among property management firms, Proline effectively fired us.

An hour before owners met at the Leonardo Da Vinci Centre, one night in 2001, Herb Bolz's realtor called me, concerned his client had misrepresented the extent of remediation. He had. Herb owned a townhouse he rented to students, and it was clear he wanted to sell it before any hint of envelope study was approved by owners, thus putting off a future buyer. There it was, out in the open. Council had been played by Herb, whose real job was to unload ten rental units as well as his own and perhaps delay the engineers' envelope study, the starting point for all condominiums concerned about water ingress damage. In retrospect, there was good evidence

Herbert Bolz's presence on this Strata Council violated the Strata Property Act's standard of care (Bylaw 31). Owners should not have elected him in the first place.

Before the meeting began, Tony quit, I quit, and Tim was left with whatever remained of the Strata Council. Much to his credit, he finished out his term and, at some point, realized the buildings would have to be fixed. Herb Bolz managed to unload the ten units to a Vancouver businessman, Derek Lee.

In 2004, Tony Panegos and a group of owners formed Waveland Ventures. Without the requisite 75% agreement, owners could petition the court to order an administrator as an impartial third party to oversee remediation. Tony approached Ian Stuart. Ian had been a property manager with Newport Realty and represented the Peninsula for a short time. Tony might have believed he had some influence over the young man. The group retained Nanaimo attorney Cora Wilson, an expert on leaky condos. On June 29, 2004, the Honourable Madam Justice Anne Winter MacKenzie granted the petitioner's appointment of Ian Stuart as administrator. No one represented most resident owners at this hearing except Tim Ball, who was there as a respondent, illustrated by attorney Alan Tryon.

It cannot be stated strongly enough that Tim's willingness to defend the Peninsula against Tony and their friends' ill-advised plan for partial remediation has never been fully appreciated. With Tim's name as the respondent, owners were advised of future decisions. Only some owners in the history of the Peninsula have invested in it as heavily as Tim.

Peninsula residents recognized Tim's motives as honest ones.

Ian's underperformance as an administrator soon became apparent, forcing a subsequent Strata Council to retain attorney Tino di Bella. This is where Tim's actions the previous year paid off. A recognizable body of owners was concerned enough that Tony's plan had failed. There would be adequate consensus to get on with the messy and expensive ordeal that was our inevitable future.

In 2005, owners united. The council needed a vote to oust Tony from the Strata Council. Summoned to a meeting for that purpose, we watched Tony stand before us like a rich man's tiny son, all dressed up, longing to play with the raggedy street urchins, yet wary of the stones in their hands. He refused to resign. This forced owners to vote against him while he witnessed the count. Scrubbing off his remaining shards of dignity, he begged for help from Derek Lee, whose ten rental units and ten votes would have kept him on the council. It didn't happen, and Tony marched out of the basement of the Leonardo da Vinci Centre.

Had he remained for the entire meeting, he would have heard engineer Bruce Cheadle's report. Bruce presented a different scenario for building repair. Rather than replace the windows and brick siding, he recommended removing the entire exterior. This was the more expensive option. Cheadle explained the only way to survey the extent of damage was to go all the way. Owners agreed, and Tino di Bella prepared for court.

In December 2005, Tino di Bella represented the owners in the petition against Waveland Ventures. The judge, concerned there was no one from the group in court except attorney Cora Wilson, expressed uncertainty over proceeding with the request to change administrators. Here, the best witness for the owners turned out to be Tony's lawyer herself, Ms Wilson, who advised the judge there was no new information and, "by the way, your Honour, I don't want to represent my client anymore, would you care to sign these papers releasing me?"

Remediation began.

Despite the messiness and noise, rebuilding the Peninsula's exterior also repaired social connections. Tim's humanity and decency overpowered much of the negativity we'd experienced. Along with Joanne Emerson, Graham Zuril and Bob Hawes, reasonable people got things done.

> *Never doubt that a small group of thoughtful, concerned citizens can change the world. Indeed, it is the only thing that ever has.*
> —Margaret Mead.

Rebuilding revealed sloppy construction practices. Over 127 structural deficiencies were discovered as workers chipped off stucco and brick. One section of the second tower had to be propped up because the original framework's construction proved woefully inadequate. Many issues from the Barrett report's assessment of building practices and vague codes appeared as work continued. The building boom of the 1980s attracted new and inexperienced workers unfamiliar with the construction trades in general and local rules in particular. The Peninsula condominium was a monument to this under-regulated industry.

The report further states:

> *At the end of construction, the developer or contractor would be dissolved, thereby removing any legal recourse by those wishing to make a financial claim for construction defects. While considered unethical 'shell games,' these practices were not illegal.*

Nova Fourteen dissolved too. Mr Eghdami never appeared in court.

Despite physical evidence and findings in the Barrett report, Tony clung to his original concept and said as much in a letter slid under owners' doors:

> *At the beginning of remediation, I encouraged you to go for it at a cost of less than 3 million dollars. You listened to Ball, Hawes, Trombley and company, and we spent $12.5 million (sic). The first Administrator (Stuart), who had a successful record on remediation, quit in disgust after being attacked by the usual crowd. The current Administrator has stretched remediation from an estimated 18 months to more than three years at a salary of $4000 per month—and has not yet rendered an account. The longer he stays on, the longer he gets his money. Is this a condo of fools? You bet!*

Over the years, Tim shouldered the brunt of these word storms. The criticism was undeserved. Evidence that a shifty developer shoddily built the Peninsula could not be denied. Owners had a choice: fix it or walk away. They chose to fix it properly, despite the cost and much thanks to loans from CMHC. Respondents listed on Tony's Waveland Ventures petition drifted away, leaving him with negligible support and malingering rage.

Owners thought the project was near completion, but in December 2009, lawyers Tino di Bella and Bruce Cheadle, the engineer, advised the Strata Council that the townhouses needed to be in order. I went back to CMHC for loans and almost another year of work.

At the end of remediation, with all the bills tallied, Tim, along with Bob Hawes, Graham Zuril, and Joanne Emerson, met with lawyer John Adams, who represented the Peninsula in its lawsuits against whatever contractors still existed, the City of Victoria and the Peninsula's architect. They signed the non-disclosure agreement, a common practice for settlements of this type, and owners received a portion of the millions of dollars spent. A later payment would be forthcoming, much, much later.

It must be noted that during this time, Tim underwent open heart surgery. Missing in action briefly, he bounced back and continued to serve on the council despite (perhaps) his wife's concern.

Lois Hayes of Newport Realty chaired the Strata Council for several years. She represented the interests of Derek Lee, the Vancouver businessman Herb Bolz had convinced to buy his ten units. Condominiums, where one person holds a large block of units, make passing special resolutions difficult if a 75% vote is required, even though only a 50% majority is needed. So, the council was in constant negotiations with Derek, and having Lois there made life easier. After remediation, she stepped down, and Tim became chair again. From 2006 to 2015, Tim has served, maintaining a steady helm.

Due to a conflict of interest with di Bella, who also represented our property management firm, Cornerstone Properties, the council decided to hire Vancouver attorney Alison Baker, who was not as conflicted and was familiar with the Peninsula's internal politics. She was asked to contact di Bella to return to court to dismiss the administrator and pay the owners their refunds. Tino procrastinated, and did he acknowledge Ms Baker's emails or letters?

The Peninsula is not alone in prodding Tino di Bella to get things done. This review from a Victoria website is similar to what the council experienced:

In our property purchase, he represented the Strata. He was highly unresponsive (caused significant delays and related costs in getting our permit), highly unprofessional (rude, arrogant and hiding behind a VISA machine that had to be fed before he would release the Strata approval letter when I was in his office), not knowledgeable (in light of the unnecessary steps he took us through with the Strata), expensive (considering much less could have done to address the Strata's needs), and always armed with excuses for not getting things done. The Strata is now seeking to replace him, and he has been equally unresponsive when requested to hand over the files.

During remediation, the Peninsula fought a war on two fronts. There was the day-to-day battle of noise and dust, windowless walls and hard-hatted men. The other was Tony Panegos. Living with a constant, irrational presence is tiresome. People with dissenting opinions became enemies to be publicly thrashed. In a small community of condo owners, the tension could be overwhelming.

The judge at that court hearing had never experienced the extent to which condo life can intensify disagreements. Was Tony Panegos a narcissist? Maybe. Tim might have sensed it on that evening in the fall of 1997. And early on, Tony recognized Tim would be a threat.

What the judge didn't have access to was years of outrageous behaviour. Most of the anger was directed at Tim, the man who played Tony's game of hiring a lawyer and doing battle in court. Tim won the decision to proceed with the expensive remediation owners wanted. Tony never forgave him. All he could do was lash out on paper. Fed up with Tony's behaviour, owners supported Tim and continued to elect him to council until 2015.

Tino di Bella finally summoned the energy to mail owners their refunds and sign off on remediation, releasing Bruce Cheadle from his duties. Tony's health deteriorated along with his finances. He and his partner listed their penthouse, gradually reducing the asking price over the years it was on the market, eventually selling it and moving to a smaller space overlooking the Olympic Mountains on Dallas Road. Tony died a few years ago. His obituary never appeared in the local paper. Reputedly, Tino di Bella wanted notification of his death to ensure Tony had moved on.

Tim quietly resigned from the Strata Council in 2015. His departure deprived owners of publicly acknowledging his devotion to us and paying tribute to him. An AGM, chaired by Tim, meant owners could get a fair hearing. He combined amiability with business and left the drama to the McPherson Playhouse. Council members weren't micromanaged under Tim's leadership, allowing us to proceed like mature sloths, climbing the condominium journey slowly but with more assurance.

A fourth property management company, Firm, took over, and Tim left the council in the hands of six people with Strata Council experience.

Condominium communities have a more transitory residency than single-standing house neighbourhoods. Today's council and many new residents didn't go through the Peninsula's war years. When Tony's name is mentioned, eyes glaze, saying, "Get over it," like the judge who advised us to stop behaving childishly and move on. A reasonable person would come to the same conclusion. But it wasn't like that. You can't comprehend the tumultuous environment of the Peninsula's early days if you've never experienced continuous manipulative and abusive behaviour and unjustified criticism. Tim stood up to the bully and shoved the pompous sumo wrestler out of the ring, using common human decency as leverage.

Thank you, Tim, for your time, idealism, humanity, and willingness to stand up for the Peninsula.
—*Marg Trombley* (Marg died on July 27, 2022.)

Marty writes:

Tim was in the hospital and was not aware enough to understand Marg's death. He often said she was a knowledgeable and dedicated person—also such a great support during the bad years of condo remediation.

Tim and I very much appreciated Margaret Trombley's explanation of what the owners went through in great detail. She neglected to mention the $21,000 Tim and I loaned the Strata Council to pay the lawyers upfront before they would take on our struggle for justice. We needed much more time to go to the owners and hit them with a special assessment. Being president of the Strata Council, Tim felt it was his responsibility to pay that amount and worry about getting it back from the owners later.

I adamantly objected. We were the closest we had ever come to a divorce.

After five times in court and eight years later, many owners died, moved, or forgot what Tim and I did for them. When we finished remediation, Margaret emailed the remaining owners to suggest that each contribute $500 to reimburse us. We have received $4,000 to date.

The cost for our unit's remediation was $146,000. The square footage of each unit determined this cost. After the council sued the developers and builders, Tim and I were reimbursed $25,000. The government allowed us ten years to pay our loans interest-free. A few had to move because they could not afford to pay these loans—many a tear shed. All the condos around us suffered much the same injustice.

Letter from Mr. Val Dmiteryk—Caretaker at the Penninsula Condominiums

I have been a member of the Peninsula for over 20 years and have had enough time to figure out many things here. I watched how people live, how they communicate and react to various life situations. From the very beginning I was imbued with respect for many of the residents of the Peninsula.

Tim had the habit of going for a walk every day as I worked outside or inside. I often met with him. After a few short conversations, even with my not very good English, I realized he was a very well educated and honest person. It was clear that he had excellent communication skills and knew how to keep up a conversation on any topic. Later I found out he was a professor at the University of Winnipeg.

At some point the people of the Peninsula voted Tim in as president of the Strata Council. People living here for a long time remember those days. It was just before the remediation of the complex started. As a result, Tim and his Strata Council had to go through the hardest time in the history of the Peninsula running business of the corporation. At the start, Tim spent a lot of time in consultations with engineers, builders and layers. He also tried to assure those owners who disagreed with some of the details of the remediation process. From the very beginning until its completion, Tim was always aware of the ongoing process. He often asked me about how the repair was done and if there were problems.

Working with Tim, I have always had his support. He often asked if I needed any help to carry out my duties.

Tim was always interested in how things were in my homeland (Ukraine) and also how my family were doing.

Working at the Peninsula I became convinced that Tim was a very good man, he is one of those people who are respectful to others and would give you a hand if you need it.

My wife and I and our three children came to Canada with five suitcases and a few thousand dollars in my pocket. It was a very hard time for us. Despite the fact that we could not find a job in our specialties, my wife and I found jobs and life began to change for the better. Soon our older daughter said that she was going to get married. Our financial situation was not so good and we could not pay for the wedding. I asked Tim if there were any projects such as painting or anything else coming up at the Peninsula that I could do on my vacation to make extra money. Tim found a better option. He introduced me to someone who gave me a few jobs which I could do on weekends and after regular working hours. My whole family worked on those projects and we made my daughter's wedding possible. Tim, thank you very much for that.

I have always been skeptical about the clownery that has begun in the world with the loud name 'Global Warming.' Those who are behind this will, of course, get a lot of money and more power. It reminded me of a plot from a science fiction novel, *The Air Seller*, by Russian writer Alex Belayev written almost 100 years ago in 1928 where a megalomaniac villain Bayley plans to create an oxygen deficit and then start selling fresh air, thus eventually becoming the master of the world. There was a character who realized what Bayley was doing. He did everything possible to let people know about it and ultimately saved the world from disaster. In real life we have brave people who tell the world what is really happening, and Tim is one of them.

Once I heard a radio broadcast where a familiar voice was talking about what was happening in the world. That voice belonged to Tim. Not believing what the media is trying to convince people about the climate, I started listening to weekly programs with Tim's participation on this radio.

Tim has a heightened sense of justice and being an honest person, he cannot stand aside when people are misled. In his various speeches and lectures all over the world he tries to tell people the truth and point out those who are involved in the deception. He has different life principles than those who are behind the idea of global warming.

What he is doing is a very dangerous activity and it is not for everyone. Only people with strong characters who are confident in their beliefs can do this. As Immanuel Kant once said, "Character consists in the ability to act according to principles."

In the USSR where I was born, historically and traditionally, the military personnel were treated with great respect, and when I learned that Tim served in the RCAF, my respect for him became even greater. I am so proud that I knew Tim personally.

"It is part of a good man to do great and noble deeds, though he risks everything." Plutarch
—*Mr Val Dmiteryk*

Miscellaneous Musings

"Certainly the concept that human CO_2 causes warming and climate change was based on unproven theory used by people with an ideology. They used instruments of state to dominate the science. They also attacked and abused anyone who dared to pursue proper science. The small group who controlled the IPCC were unlikely to change their tune. A pattern that was borne out by the release of IPCC Report AR5 in September 2013, which denied the fact that for 17 years global temperature declined slightly while CO_2 levels continued to increase."
—Tim Ball, from *The Deliberate Corruption of Climate Science*

CHAPTER EIGHTEEN

Tribute to Tim by Ian Jessop—Radio Talk Show host on CFAX in Victoria, BC from Jan 22, 2015 to July, 2016

DURING MY INTERVIEW to host a talk show on CFAX Radio in Victoria, British Columbia, the station manager asked what kind of a show I wanted to do. "I want to do something different," was my reply. "Okay," he said, "Just don't get us sued."

At the time, there was a lot of discussion and interviews with global warming advocates, and I was searching for someone who could legitimately argue the other side of the issue. We should hear both sides of the issue instead of ignoring (censoring) those opposing views. But, at the time, I was having trouble finding anyone since the media mainly ignored opposing views or legitimate scientists.

I mentioned this to the station manager, who said, "We used to have a guy on the air who took an opposing view, and he lives here in Victoria. His name is Tim Ball." Bingo! I contacted Tim, and he graciously agreed to come to the program.

Tim knew very little about me then, and I knew nothing about him. During the interview on our first show, the phones lit up with the critics wanting to condemn Tim for various reasons, saying he wasn't a climate scientist, his information was not accurate and a whole host of nasty pejorative comments to attempt to discredit Tim's background and research. It was a fascinating hour, and I told Tim we should do this every month, which we did for three years.

Each time Tim was on the program, the naysayers would call in droves and make nasty comments, but as the months went by, those calls became fewer and fewer. We even started to get calls and comments from people who supported Tim's position. As the weeks passed between interviews, I sometimes got calls asking when Tim would be on again because they found his views exciting and informative.

The one interview that stands out is the debate between Tim and Green Party Leader Elizabeth May, who, for months, refused to debate Tim but finally relented after I publicly stated she refused to participate.

https://www.youtu.be/k0lh2Wi8AAQ
http://https://www.youtube.com/watch?v=k0Ih2Wi8AAQ

There was no warmth between the two of them in the studio. During commercial breaks, they never spoke to each other, and when it was over, they departed without comment.

We didn't always talk about the global warming issue during our many interviews. There were shows where Tim would tell fascinating stories of the people who worked for the Hudson Bay Company in Canada several centuries ago and their hardships. Like many listeners, I was astounded by Tim's encyclopedic knowledge of detail. It truly amazed me, and I'm sure many listeners, how he could recall names, dates and stories of Canadian history. His recall was brilliant.

But then, unexpectedly, the axe came down in the summer of 2016 when Bell Media, the Toronto owners of CFAX, began firing on-air staff to cut costs, and I was part of that. When I informed Tim of what transpired, he blamed himself, which certainly wasn't the case.

Over the following months, we would still go for coffee to talk about anything and everything. Of the thousands of people I have interviewed over the years, Tim Ball was my favourite. He was knowledgeable, kind, caring and very much concerned with helping people who went to him asking for advice. Tim is a friend, and I'm proud to know such an honourable man.

—*Ian Jessop*

CHAPTER NINETEEN
Malcolm Roberts

HELLO, I'M SENATOR MALCOLM Roberts—a senator in Australia's national parliament.

Today, I want to share with honest people around the world my experience of a remarkable Canadian who has worked to protect and restore our freedom around our planet.

He has courageously devoted almost five decades to supporting us all because he loves science, especially what it has given our human species. He has campaigned voluntarily to restore scientific integrity because he knows science is vital for human progress and freedom.

Canadian climatologist Professor Tim Ball had a severe heart attack a couple of weeks ago, and Canadians asked me and others worldwide to write a bio.

I'll now read to you (see website below) what I have written because Professor Ball has helped me enormously, as you'll soon see. I've called my piece:

Celebrating Tim Ball

https://www.youtube.com/watch?v=IyOHndWpcPk&t=95s

Celebrating the world's most knowledgeable climatologist and climate scientist is easy yet difficult.

Celebrating how he helped me enormously gives an insight into Tim, the depths of his pain and his hopes for humanity, human civilization and our planet.

Until his recent illness, when I called or wrote for advice on climate or related matters, he was available. Always amicable and generous. Always ready to guide or correct me on any loose or incorrect assumption in my questions or conversation.

Yet my appreciation is deeper because his advice and counsel are always practical. It's always immediately helpful.

As with all great educators, Tim does not instruct; he assists people to discover for themselves because that maximizes connection and ownership of the learning.

When needed, though, Tim can be appropriately blunt and direct. Engagingly direct. Refreshingly courageous. Demonstrably honest.

I feel confident and reassured because I know that I will get more than direct answers to my questions since Tim always freely shares a depth and breadth of knowledge across many topics and issues, many disciplines of science and well beyond science into human behaviour and politics.

His mind knits data, information and philosophies into a holistic synthesis that captivates for its comprehensive completeness, elegance and sheer beauty.

Through Tim, I discovered, or in some cases confirmed, the reasons for the United Nations' profound corruption of science rooted in acts almost half a century ago in 1972, found in the actions of a few crooked academics and bureaucrats, as well as those many academics, innocently fooled or naively co-opted in their clutching to academic grants, or whose work was distorted to the United Nations yoke.

Tim's knowledge objectively and factually encapsulates those UN foot soldiers, conflicts of interest and, when necessary, their professional or academic history and past misbehaviour.

Tim never judges these people; he discusses their behaviours and motives, whether financial or academic or reputational—sometimes with a clever quip that summarized so clearly, cleverly and entertainingly.

I always appreciate the depth of his generosity. His love of science. His passion for science, material gifts, and understanding of human behaviour and civilization.

Tim understands science's crucial role in ensuring freedom of thought and exchange of ideas, liberating humanity from the control of nature's naked power, and on a human level, the liar's control, the bully's control, the financial baron's control, the political manipulator's control, the spin doctor's control, the bureaucrat's selfish control, the propagandist's control.

History shows that science brought objectivity, and with that came greater fairness and liberty from tyranny. It ushered in greater freedom.

Tim's depth of knowledge covers and crosses many topics. His ability to weave the pure sciences into human behaviour brings common sense, understanding with clarity, and sincerity rare in everyday interactions.

Tim can sensibly and credibly discuss any topic and make sense factually with an amazing grasp and recollection of solid data.

Although we had been exchanging ideas for a few years, as I was writing my first speech to the Senate in 2016, I called him for advice on a simple matter. During our chat, he uttered something so simple yet profound that revealed the enormity of the UN's climate lie. I immediately wrote it into the speech.

"The sun warms the earth's surface, the surface warms the air." Thus, the atmosphere cools the earth's surface. Those who understand this immediately begin to see the tip of the UN's deception.

Yet ignorant journalists went apoplectic partly because it challenged their ignorance and gullibility and partly because it profoundly challenged and laid bare the UN's climate deceit.

Tim had that ability to expose and often disarm the charlatans and the deceivers that are all too common in academia, journalism and politics today.

His knowledge and ability to connect across climate, nature and humanity in many ways is inspiring, uplifting, and encouraging. Reassuring.

The origins of the climate scam and how the UN developed into a terrorist organization falsely spreading fear are well understood and easily referenced among his many contacts, including accomplished authors, scientists and true environmentalists.

His understanding of human behaviour, politics, bureaucracy, globalist elites and internationalist entities explains in simple terms the motives and methods of UN crooks, including Maurice Strong, the mastermind who fathered the UN's climate scam now crippling economies worldwide.

It is this type of understanding that shows why it is so important to expose the UN despite it continuing to hide beneath the depths of a few powerful and well-connected plutocrats and technocrats whose deception and subtlety enabled many people, including academics, to be fooled without empirical scientific evidence. Indeed, they unwittingly contradicted or neglected empirical evidence while entrancing in groupthink and group-speak that unconsciously became a vehicle for the UN's lies.

These are the UN's unwitting foot soldiers who bristle into illogical, emotional denial when held accountable.

Tim knows of the academics corrupting the science and the early genuine climate scientists like Hubert Lamb, whom the climate mafia later used to destroy his pioneering work in Britain.

The clarity, depth and breadth of Tim's knowledge enabled him to understand academics' vulnerability to being misled and played. He spotted the corruption early in the UN's march and, for almost half a decade, called it for what it is: an anti-human corruption and deceit of science for which humanity is paying and will pay enormously—economically and in terms of the self-chosen and unelected elites, more significant control over all humans.

Tim is a practical man who is academic in the sense that he understands how academia and science work, yet not in his approach. He is of the natural world as a result of his search and rescue missions over Canada's Arctic and especially his deep love and admiration for nature and the grandness and wonder of our immense and all-powerful universe.

A true environmentalist.

Whenever I request it, he always provides references, sometimes including prominent scientists among his contacts.

Yet his humility ensures that he never seeks praise or adulation. He shares freely.

His modesty means he brushes it off instead of taking credit for identifying fellow Canadian Maurice Strong as the father and creator of the UN's false climate claims and political campaign for unelected global governance and control.

Yet, Tim has the true scientist's most remarkable trait—keen, objective observation.

For these reasons, he agonizes over the UN's relentless dishonest co-opting of pseudo-science to push criminal activities and political agenda.

Tim's Message is One of Hope in Humanity and, Thus, Hope for the Future

Yet, as an advocate for science and humanity, he tirelessly works to restore scientific integrity. He values science's true power beyond the scientific realm to liberate humankind.

That is another dimension in celebrating what I value and appreciate in Tim.

His is a love of science, not a mere understanding. His gratitude is for what true science has given humanity. We know that when scientific integrity is restored, it will give all people an amazing and abundant future.

I feel deep gratitude, enormous respect and a sense of honour for having the opportunity to work with this giant of men.

To personally experience his breadth and depth of skills, intelligence and dedication is to have been blessed with a deeper understanding of a remarkable and beautiful human and to see a glimpse of selfless devotion to humanity.

My memories are of calling him with a question about climate or science and coming away after a two-hour chat filled with awe for nature, humanity—and Tim, changing me from puzzled to smiling, indeed beaming. Excited and ready for more work to restore scientific and political integrity.

He did all this for free. He withstood attacks from climate charlatans who slapped lawsuits on him in a vain attempt to shut him down using the deep pockets of billionaires funding their climate activism—some for their own personal gain.

He stood up. Often. Always.

When Michael Mann, that serial misrepresenter of climate, science and humanity, slapped him with a lawsuit, people worldwide spontaneously donated hundreds of thousands of dollars to enable Tim to defend himself. Suddenly, the little scientist from Victoria on Vancouver Island could stand as the giant he was. In court under oath, Tim's team slayed Mann, the UN's darling climate activist-convincingly.

The UN's pin-up boy was destroyed in a court under oath, and the UN's core climate argument was smashed. And Tim did it with assistance from genuine international scientists who testified on the science.

What keeps him strong? On course? True?

Strong guiding qualities deep within, pervading every atom of his being and personality.

Tim's immediate helpfulness would have been a burden on ordinary women. Yet, until his recent sickness, his caring wife Marty always happily handed the phone to him when I called because Marty knew the value of Tim's work and knew how much he was loved, respected and needed worldwide.

Indeed, I enjoy chatting with Marty and appreciate her love for Tim.

I'm on Board with Tim and the Truth

Tim is among the last of the true Renaissance men. He accurately and confidently covers climate and climatology, hard sciences, the environment, politics and policy, human development, human behaviour, history, geography, governance, basic economics, education, the United Nations and the people driving its globalist agenda, and so many more topics.

His love of humans and humanity is inspiring. His life and leadership are a beacon for humanity, science and politics.

We all need to do more than admire his qualities and example. We must live as he does: having the courage to call out people who misrepresent science, nature and humanity, regardless of whether they are globalists like Michael Mann, Canadian Greens like Andrew Weaver, charlatans and hucksters like Al Gore, or the rat's nest of academics and collaborators in my country, Australia, that are misrepresenting humans, science, nature and climate as they feed on monetary gifts from politicians corrupting science.

Academics like Tim Flannery, Will Steffen, David Karoly, Ove Hoegh-Guldberg, John Cook, Ross Garnaut, Matthew England, Lesley Hughes, Andy Pitman, Kurt Lambeck, Stephan Lewandowsky and others who benefit financially, politically and/or, in their cloistered careers, as parasitic foot-soldiers for the corrupt UN's climate con. Tim's desire is pure—not for ego and adulation.

Instead, he is reassuring. Forgiving. Encouraging. Helpful in intent and in practice.

I am dedicated to his cause, humanity's ageless cause: protecting humans and restoring scientific and political integrity and freedom.

Finally, after years of UN propaganda hijacking the public, I need to remember that a scientist is a person who follows the scientific method and promote the objective process and system for acquiring knowledge to understand nature for the benefit of humanity and the sake and purity of knowledge.

Science consists of describing, understanding and explaining natural phenomena to define relationships between cause and effect; to then hypothesize cause and effect; to measure to obtain data to confirm, disprove or modify the hypotheses; and for others to then use data and logic to try to disprove hypotheses all to apply the proven relationships to enhance human living and minimize the costs of our actions, whether on each other or nature. While climate scientists study narrow factors affecting climate, climatologists study climate holistically to understand climates or climatic conditions. Tim is a scientist, a climatologist and a first-rate human. He is knowledgeable, practical and an honest man of courage who loves nature, humanity and truth. He does so with demonstrable courage, intellect and integrity. I thank Tim and Marty and celebrate their courage, integrity, competence, generosity and love for nature and our role in nature as humans.

"Their gifts to humanity and their love of freedom for us all."
—*Senator Malcolm Roberts*

Tim in Hawaii 2013

Miscellaneous Musings

"In climate research and modelling, we should recognize that we are dealing with a coupled non-linear chaotic system, and therefore that the long-term prediction of future climate states is not possible."
From *The Deliberate Corruption of Climate Science* by Tim Ball

CHAPTER TWENTY

Tribute to Dr. Tim Ball, by Patrick Hunt, Tim's Friend April 2020

> If you can keep your head when all about you
> Are losing theirs and blaming it on you,
> If you can trust yourself when all men doubt you,
> But make allowance for their doubting, too;
> If you can wait and not be tired by waiting,
> Or being lied about, don't deal in lies,
> Or being hated, don't give way to hating…

Read the rest of Rudyard Kipling's poem If, and you will have read the biography of Dr Tim Ball because "If" sums up the way he does life.

Tim is a brilliant man who had time to educate me when I asked. I first met him as Dr. Ball when he spoke to the Rotary Club of Victoria in 2005 about the lack of correlation between atmospheric CO_2 and the average earth temperature. His talk was an eye-opener for me because, until then, I had not thought much about the science behind the popular meme that mankind was the major cause of global warming. He also gave evidence of the correlation between temperature and the sun's variable output and the Earth's relative position to the sun.

His talk encouraged me to think, read, and research, and eventually, I agreed with him that anthropogenic CO_2 is not the cause of global warming. I met and communicated with Tim over the last 15 years. He gave freely of his time and expertise.

As I got to know him, I learned what price far lesser men had extracted from him. I refer to the SLAPP (Strategic Litigation Against Public Participation) lawsuits and the blackballing of him by the media and the global warming alarmists. They attack the man but hardly ever counter his evidence or scientific reasoning. Through that process, I saw not only that he is of strong character, always a gentleman, and always polite to his detractors, but I also saw firsthand what a rock and supporter he had in his wife, Marty. One does not put one's home on the line to fight a lawsuit backed by a global warming industry without a partner willing to risk her nest. Marty knew their risk, but she did so willingly, wholeheartedly, and feistily.

With each passing year, Dr Ball's science is confirmed by the evidence, while the global warming models have been consistently wrong, and their proponents are changing their story from 'Global Warming' to 'Climate Change.'

Canadians and the world are so lucky to have a man willing to speak truth to power in such a forceful, tireless, understandable and graceful manner. I am privileged to call Tim Ball my friend. He truly is a man whose life embodies IF. In Rudyard Kipling's words again:

IF by Rudyard Kipling

> "If you can talk with crowds and keep your virtue,
> Or walk with Kings—nor lose the common touch,
> If neither foes nor loving friends can hurt you,
> If all men count with you, but none too much;
> If you can fill the unforgiving minute
> With sixty seconds worth of distance run,
> Yours is the Earth and everything that's in it,
> And—which is more—you'll be a Man, my son!"

"If you can dream—and not make dreams your master,
If you can think—and not make thoughts your aim;
If you can meet with Triumph and Disaster
And treat those two impostors just the same;
If you can bear to hear the truth you've spoken
Twisted by knaves to make a trap for fools,
Or watch the things you gave your life to, broken,
And stoop and build them up with worn-out tools:"

"If you can make one heap of all your winnings
And risk it on one turn of pitch-and-toss,
And lose, and start again at your beginnings
And never breathe a word about your loss;
If you can force your heart and nerve and sinew
To serve your turn long after they are gone,
And so hold on when there is nothing in you
Except the Will, which says to them: "Hold on!"

"If you can talk with crowds and keep your virtue,
Or walk with Kings—nor lose the common touch,
If neither foes nor loving friends can hurt you,
If all men count with you, but none too much;
If you can fill the unforgiving minute
With sixty seconds' worth of distance run,
Yours is the Earth and everything that's in it,
And—which is more—you'll be a Man, my son!"

A Tribute: An Inspiration, Mentor and Friend by Sheila Zilinsky—Author and Podcaster

If I could define a true influence on my life and someone who had a great impact on the trajectory of my life it would undoubtedly be Dr Tim Ball.

Tim and I met in 2009 shortly after I heard him on a radio show. I was jaw dropped at his entire two-hour interview riddled with passion and knowledge. If knowledge is power, powerful it was. I never forgot the way his honesty and transparency gripped me. It stirred in me and never left. I remember trying for weeks to get a hold of this man I had heard that night on the airways who had impacted me so deeply. He had conveyed so simply all the many things I had come to know working for government for a decade, but didn't know how to express.

Tim Ball became a true friend and an incredible mentor to me. He taught me many life lessons including what it means to never stop fighting for what you believe in, no matter the cost, no matter the repercussions; how to always go forth with a spirit of courage and determination in all that you do. It's something I apply in my everyday life as well.

I remember moving to Victoria in 2012 and I was so thrilled to finally get the chance to meet Tim in person. What an incredible honour it was. It still feels surreal to have the true honour of his friendship, and his time. Dr Tim Ball is a humble and unselfish example of a true role model and true inspiration.

He is a man who believes with all of his might that the truth must be told despite consequences; knowing that standing up to powerful interests and injustice carries a price. Tim's struggles have become all our struggles; his triumphs, our triumphs. His ethics and dignity are unimpeachable.

It is hard to capture in words what Tim Ball means to the people he inspires. Given the sweep of his life, the scope of his accomplishments, the adoration that he so rightly earns, it's tempting to view Tim as an icon, smiling and serene, detached from the tawdry affairs of lesser men.

Everything Reminds Me of Tim

Tim shows us what is possible not just in the pages of history books, but in our own lives as well. He shows us the power of action; of taking risks on behalf of our ideals. Tim taught me the power of ideas, but he also taught me the power of action. He has taught me the importance of reason and common-sense arguments; the need to study not only those with whom you agree, but also those with whom you don't agree. It was like the quote from H.L. Mencken that stayed with me "The whole aim of practical politics is to keep the populace alarmed (and hence clamorous to be led to safety) by an endless series of hobgoblins, most of them imaginary." Tim always had the perfect quote to go with his incredible teachings. He has a profound ability to connect the dots and tie up with a bow.

It was always like you get the dessert with an extra helping of whipped cream, and then the cherry on top. That was how he delivered each one of his on-air or in-person messages.

I always loved when Tim was on my show when he would tell one of my favourite stories, as only he could tell it. He fully understood a joke he heard as a teenager: A man is on a soapbox at Hyde Park Corner, London. He is haranguing the crowd with a series of promises prefaced with the phrase "Come the Revolution…" After several promises he says, "Come the Revolution we will all wear shirts and ties." A voice at the back shouts out, "But I don't want to wear a shirt and tie." To which the speaker replies, "Come the Revolution, you will do what you are bloody well told."

Tim's knowledge of history was prolific. The chat rooms on our radio shows were often ablaze with comments like "Wow, Tim is a walking dictionary." Or "Wow, now it all makes sense."

Tim had an inconceivable way of making everything make sense.

Tim had the true gift of teaching. He combined history and science in a compelling and intriguing way. I've never heard anything like it—before or since!

But as Tim shows with painstaking patience, is that he is not afraid to compromise for the sake of a larger goal. True to his vision of the precious freedoms of us, here in the West, and what our founders fought to preserve and protect. As Tim says, America wasn't the last bastion of freedom, it was the first and only. I love the way Tim can make information exciting and history come alive. His narratives are unmatchable, but more than information, Tim teaches that too many of us sit on the sidelines: comfortable in complacency or cynicism when our voices must be heard.

Tim reminds us that pushing for truth and standing up for what is right is our responsibility. Tim's willingness to expose the truth reminds me of a bible scripture that I am fond of, Ephesians 5:11, "And have no fellowship with the unfruitful works of darkness, but rather expose them."

May we all search for Tim's largeness of spirit somewhere inside of ourselves. And when injustice weighs heavy on our hearts, when our best laid plans seem beyond our reach, let us think of Dr Tim Ball and his moral courage and his love and concern for all kinds of people.

Each man must respond to the call of God, and his own God-given talents in his lifetime and not in someone else's time. I have said many times, it isn't how long one lives, but how well. It's what one accomplishes for mankind that matters. I believe Dr Tim Ball has made a huge impact on mankind. In his boldness and in his bravery and in his unwillingness to compromise when it comes to the truth.

I have so many fond memories of my early days on radio with Tim as my co-host, and then as a regular guest for over a decade. I was thrilled when he wrote the forward to my book Green Gospel. It still means so much to me. Sitting under Dr. Tim's tutelage and being part of our many off-air discussions and phone conversations has come to be a true blessing in my life.

I gleaned so much knowledge from Tim that goes beyond mere learning.

I consider it such an honour and privilege to call Tim Ball my friend. Tim is truly my hero and my role model: one of the most inspiring men of our generation.

—*Sheila Zilinsky*, **April, 2020**

Tim Ball Remembered by James Corbett of the Corbett Report, Japan

In 2009, after having interviewed Dr Ball on the phone a few times, I was taking a trip to Canada and I stopped off in Victoria so that I could interview Dr Ball in person.

Now, I had no idea what to expect from that encounter. I thought that we might meet up, go to some café or some public space somewhere, record a short interview, and say, "Nice to meet you, see you around."

That was not what I got.

Instead, I got Dr Ball meeting me on foot for a little walking tour of Victoria, where he regaled me with stories about the city and various people and places and events from its history.

And then he took me back to his home. His wife, Marty, got us settled in and comfortable, and then Dr Ball opened up. We talked for hours—literally, hours and hours—about the history and philosophy of science and politics and all sorts of things.

It was a fascinating conversation, and, unfortunately, only a short bit of that conversation was recorded on camera, but I got to a sense of who Dr Ball really was that day. That sense only confirmed what I had gathered in our talks up to that point—namely, that Dr Ball was a genuine person who had a real passion for science and research and collecting information and synthesizing it, and thinking about science on a meta level as well.

He was a deep thinker on these issues.

So, when I read the types of attacks, smears and slanders that were being written about him in the mainstream corporate-controlled press, it certainly was an eye-opening experience. This was something that I talked about in an article that I wrote in November of 2009, just as "Climate-gate" was breaking:

As someone who spent his entire scientific career fighting the alarmists—first the ones who were whipping up hysteria over the coming ice age and then the ones (sometimes the same ones) who were whipping up hysteria over global warming.

Dr Tim Ball is no stranger to the Denial Machine smear. In fact, he was one of the scientists singled out in the CBC documentary on the subject. According to the twisted logic of the CBC filmmakers, he doesn't toe the global warming line, therefore he must be funded by Big Oil. It doesn't seem to bother the producers of the documentary that they offer not one shred of evidence for that assertion. The logic of the situation demands it, so it must be true.

For someone who supposedly receives secret backdoor money from the Exxon bigwigs, Dr Ball lives a remarkably low-key life. When I met him for an interview in Victoria earlier this year, he was neither lighting cigars with Big Oil-supplied $100 bills nor driving a gas-guzzling SUV. Instead, he was on foot and he took me on a walking tour of the beautiful B.C. capital, regaling me with stories about the town's history and demonstrating a genuine enthusiasm for the local tradition and culture of his adopted hometown. We passed several hours talking about the history and philosophy of science, and what strikes one about him when engaged in such a conversation is that he has read, researched, and retained a voluminous amount of material, not just on his specialty of climatology, but of scientific history generally.

I will forever be grateful for the generosity of spirit that Dr Ball displayed to me and to all the people with whom he shared his intellect, his wit and his gifts.

—James Corbett

Thoughts and Opinions by Harv Chapple

Dear Marty,

I have waited some time before sending this to you. I have wanted to form some thoughts about Tim and what he meant to me and many others.

Listening to a Victoria radio station many years ago, I heard a radio guest talking about how the media and the government twist the news and sometimes report actual lies to the public. This piqued my interest immediately.

We were in the lawn care business and although we were applying only registered products approved and considered safe, the press reported we were "killing people and destroying the environment." We felt alone and downtrodden by the media.

Upon further listening I learned that the guest was experiencing the same treatment about climate. I had to contact this guy as I knew we were miles apart in what we were trying to say, but we were strong 'kindred spirits' in our quest. I talked to, emailed, met with, and suggested he talk to our international convention in Niagara Falls and another one in Kelowna.

Of course, it was the one and only Tim Ball.

I had such a feeling of relief, knowing that others were having the same issues. He helped raise my spirits and gave me the strength to continue my journey trying to educate the public.

I appeared before Vancouver City Council, many other local town and city councils, appeared on the Bill Good Radio Show in Vancouver and was interviewed by the media several times. I don't think I could have done it without the help and support of Tim.

TIM AND HARV AT KELOWNA INTERNATIONAL CONFERENCE

He was a very special man. All I wanted to do was run my lawn care business and enjoy a good family life. Tim and I had many conversations about our similar paths on the trail of life. I cannot possibly relay to you how much I respected and admired Tim's great abilities and knowledge.

His anecdotes and examples of what he had done over his career were amazing. His memory was like an encyclopedia. His sense of humour was so entertaining.

When I hear about the atrocious things going on in our world that are put down to so-called climate change I immediately think of what Tim would say to refute it. Unfortunately we regular citizens don't have the megaphones and amplifiers that government and media have. But those of us in the know are educated enough to realize that the emperor has no clothes. Someday the pendulum will swing back in the direction of sanity and Tim will be sitting, smiling and watching the results.

My life has changed knowing Tim Ball. I am a better, stronger, more self-assured and more knowledgeable person because of him. You were so lucky to enjoy your time together.

Sincerely,

—*Harv Chapple*

Ken Rowan—A Good Friend from Victoria Golf Club

For me, ground zero for the climate debate (there really shouldn't even be one...but I digress) is Tim's extraordinary book *Human Caused Global Warming: The Biggest Deception in History*. The book boils down all the salient facts, including the pseudo-science of bogus 'Anthropogenic Global Warming' theory and the carefully orchestrated manipulation of Maurice Strong and the corrupt IPCC. It's a must read! Unlike many high profile 'climate posers' like David Suzuki, Andrew Weaver and Elizabeth May, Tim Ball has impeccable credentials in climate research and discussion. He has a PhD in climatology from the Queen Mary College, University of London. He taught climate courses through the department of geography (no climate-only department) at the University of Winnipeg for many years.

I had the pleasure of meeting Tim three years ago after he gave an enriching lecture to a casual group of interested listeners at Victoria Golf Club. I took him to lunch shortly thereafter and got to know him better through periodic get-togethers and countless conversations through email, telephone, etc. What struck me about Tim was not only his superb knowledge of climate but also his strong background in political and economic history from the Enlightenment onwards. Marrying the disciplines of politics, economics and climate today can be a volatile combination in this age of unrest we live in. What impresses me about Tim is his cool demeanour; his courage to speak firmly and truthfully to several hostile people with a militant pro AGW (Anthropogenic Global Warming) view. Tim has so many facts on his side and dismantles the climate alarmist simply yet elegantly. It's a pleasure to listen to him!

I first became aware of the environmental debate going back to the early '90s and the Rio Earth Summit. Back then I was still under the impression that climate scientists were more afraid of a new 'ice age' (Time Magazine cover 1975) than any warming. Gradually I began to hear more about the Intergovernmental Panel on Climate Change (IPCC) and AGW theory.

In the late 1990s (maybe year 2000), I worked at an investment bank in Calgary called First Energy Capital. I listened intently to a boardroom presentation by an engineer named Allan MacCrae (an old colleague of Tim's) who effectively and persuasively debunked the AGW doctrine and, in, particular Michael Mann's 'hockey stick' theory.

This presentation really had an effect on me because I couldn't understand why such shady and deceitful AGW science was being presented to us in the media. Worse, the powerful, influential leaders in the oil patch didn't seem to pay much attention. Jean Chretien was Prime Minister then. One notable Calgary energy leader said "it's easier to pay a small inconsequential carbon tax" than fight the lefty media pumping out the AGW nonsense. What a costly mistake that attitude has been to Calgary, to Canada and the entire world, given the dependance on reliable energy (cheap hydrocarbons) to support their standard of living.

This black hole of disinformation combined with apathy from the energy sector has allowed the average Joe to slowly listen to mainstream media, acknowledge and then subliminally believe AGW/global warming/climate change dogma as truth! How sad, corrupt and wrong is that?

This ate away at me for years! I did read and listen to occasional skeptics of AGW in the media but most mainstream sources (think CBC, CNN, BBC, etc.) pump out the same alarmist propaganda. Thank god for Tim Ball! His book was a huge lightbulb moment for me. Everyone should read it.

My final comment on Tim (I admit my bias. I like and respect Tim very much!) is his bravery! He has been lampooned, harassed and ridiculed by so many on the left I've lost count. (None of his opponents have credentials nearly as worthy as his.) He has fought several (SLAPP) lawsuits (Michael Mann, Andrew Weaver) over the past decade or so, virtually on his own. He has suffered enormous financial and reputational wounds while guys like Mann, Weaver and Suzuki ride the 'climate change gravy train.' Undeterred, Tim Ball sticks to his guns because he knows the facts and will not be bullied.

When the world and media finally wake up and acknowledge the enormous, corrupt deception of AGW and climate change dogma, Tim Ball will be recognized as one of the giants in repelling the lies and standing up for truth and the scientific method.
—*Ken Rowan*

Miscellaneous Musings

Tim Ball exposes the political machinations of climate scientists who are more concerned about protecting their turf and pushing their agenda than actually pursuing science. The extent of deception truly boggles the mind. From control of scientific journals to control of public discourse through hired PR agencies, to manipulation of Wikipedia and of course the infamous Climategate which was again covered up using PR agencies and sham investigations, the behaviour of these superstar climate scientists has been dubious and quite unlike real scientists.

Tim asks some very important questions: why do scientists need a PR agency to defend their science? Why do they need to crush all voices that try to disprove them, when the entire basis of progress in scientific research lies in disproving existing theories? To what extent will the world have to pay the cost of these false theories, and what is the cost we have already paid?
—*Amit Thadhani*

Everything Reminds Me of Tim

CHAPTER TWENTY-ONE

Mark Steyn's Article on his Website, September 26, 2022—'Ball's Bearing'

Ave atque vale (hail and farewell : I salute you, and goodbye)

https://www.steynonline.com/12840/ball-bearing

I AM IN a cold rage, which is never the best temper in which to write. But over the weekend came the news from his wife Marty that Tim Ball had died.

Tim was a Canadian scientist who dissented from the global warm-mongering that has deranged our politics, and put out the lights at the Eiffel Tower, and is on course this winter to freeze and starve Europe's elderly. In the course of his pushback against the madness, Tim reprised an ancient Pennsylvanian jest and applied it to the creator of the famously dodgy global-warming hockey stick, Michael E. Mann: Dr. Mann, he remarked, belongs not at Penn State but in the state pen.

Cute.

But any joke about Mann is no laughing matter. So the 'warmatollah' determined to destroy a retired University of Winnipeg professor.

Mann filed suit against Ball in British Columbia, and then just sat it out, knowing that (to reprise my old line) the process is the punishment. Three years ago, Mann lost the case for failure to prosecute. As in his suit against me in the District of Columbia, the plaintiff had refused, for years, to do the elementary things necessary to settle a legal matter, such as providing evidence of damage. In the crap-hole of American justice, at least as evidenced by my own experience, judges let him get away with that. But in Canada the court wearied of the obvious delaying strategy, and ruled against the vengeful climate mullah.

He lost; Ball won. That is a fact, even though Mann and his doting Mann-boys continue to deny it. For anyone more sentient than the average Mann groupie, you can read the BC Supreme Court judgment for yourself:

https://www.steynonline.com/documents/9740.pdf

As is customary in civilized jurisdictions (i.e. not the American courts), the prevailing party's legal bills are paid by the loser—or, as they say in Canada, 'costs follow the event.' Roger McConchie, Mann's counsel, accepted his client's liability for Dr. Ball's expenses. See page six of Mr Justice Giaschi's ruling:

MR. MCCONCHIE: Costs follow the event. I have no quarrel with that.

https://www.steynonline.com/documents/9740.pdf

By then, both Tim Ball's retirement savings and his health had been drained and depleted by a decade of Mann's frivolous, dilatory litigation. He was broke in both body and bank account.

Had Mr McConchie's client been an honourable man (I know, I know, we are dealing with unimaginable hypotheticals here), he would have paid Tim a seven-figure sum. Instead, Tim's family now requires a GoFundMe campaign to cover the costs of his modest burial. His friend Anthony Watts will be posting details of that later today.

I had not thought it possible for me to loathe and despise Michael Mann any more than I did. He chose the jurisdiction in which he sued Tim Ball, as he chose the jurisdiction in which he sued me (the District of Columbia, where justice goes to die). And, when that jurisdiction found him liable, he simply rejected the plain meaning of the judge's decision and holed up beyond the court's reach. The contemptible Mann has had three years to remit what he owes, but he has not paid Dr Ball a penny.

And no doubt this evil man and those who abet his vile schemes are laughing at the penury unto death they forced on a brave man. Michael Mann filed a frivolous suit he had no intention of bringing to trial, but he succeeded in hounding Tim Ball into the grave.

Tim bore all this with great fortitude. The last time I saw him was at a 'denialist' gala in Washington where all the Commonwealth wallahs—UK, Canuck, Oz, Kiwi—had been seated together, presumably so the Yanks didn't have to risk being exposed to some unfortunate social faux pas like an accidental Loyal Toast.

Despite being visibly ground down by Mann's frivolous litigation, Tim was on grand form that night, full of life and full of laughs. He had all the qualities of a true warrior: courage, integrity, indomitable resilience, and, in his quiet dignified bearing, a rueful acceptance of the costs they impose. The ugly husk of a human being that is Michael Mann could destroy Tim's savings and his health, but he could not destroy Tim's spirit.

There will be a reckoning for the slug Mann. In the meantime, you can gain a sense of Tim Ball and his enviable inner strength from this Heartland Institute awards night not so long ago:

Tim Ball Receives the Lifetime Achievement in Climate Science Award

https://youtu.be/XFlJVotNW-g

Tim's Thank You for the Achievement Award

https://wattsupwiththat.com/2022/09/25/tom-harris-presentation-of-the-lifetime-achievement-in-climate-science-award-to-dr-tim-ball-international-climate-change-conference-13-washington-dc-july-2019/?utm_source=rss&utm_medium=rss&utm_campaign=tom-harris-presentation-of-the-lifetime-achievement-in-climate-science-award-to-dr-tim-ball-international-climate-change-conference-13-washington-dc-july-2019

Publisher's Note by Ken Coffman—Stairway Press

As Tim's editor and publisher, he and I were business partners for over ten years. This gave me a unique perspective about his mind and work.

Tim was a polymath—a renaissance man—and as mentioned elsewhere, a walking encyclopedia. The depth and breadth of his knowledge was amazing to witness and his apparent implacability was an inspiration. He was so sure of his facts that he could not be derailed by smokescreen nonsense that worked well for progressive activists like Al Gore, Elizabeth May, Gavin Schmidt, Michael Mann and endless others involved in the climatology scam.

To say I admired Tim is a massive understatement.

My first knowledge of Tim was his contribution to *Slaying the Sky*

Dragon: Death of the Greenhouse Gas Theory—an early book in the Stairway Press portfolio.

From back in 2011, Tim's thought-provoking words were my first exposure to his thinking.

> The most fundamental assumption in the theory that human CO_2 is causing global warming and climate change is that an increase in CO_2 will cause an increase in temperature. The problem is that in every record of any duration for any period in the history of the earth exactly the opposite relationship occurs: temperature increase precedes CO_2 increase. Despite that, a massive error was developed and continues.

In all the years since this controversial book was published, I am unaware of any corrections. If you search, you'll find lots of criticism, but no dispute of the underlying math and science. As an engineer, accuracy and data are important to me.

In this, Tim and I were kindred spirits.

Tim's next book from Stairway Press was *The Deliberate Corruption of Climate Science* with a nifty cover by Cartoons by Josh.

Again, you will find a lot of criticism, but no errors of fact or science. I am constantly watching. There are many contrary opinions, but if a critic found an error, we would apologize and correct it, but it hasn't happened so far.

On his own, Tim self-published a smaller and more accessible (less technical) version of TDCoCS called *Human-Caused Global Warming*.

Stairway Press is proud to publish the reprint.

Over a decade after Slaying the Sky Dragon was published, a follow up collection was published called Slaying the Sky Dragon: Victory Lap. Again, Tim's contribution was a key part.

Here is a clip from Tim's introduction:

> I wrote a foreword for the first edition of Slaying the Sky Dragon. I did not think I would write such a foreword again because all the issues, problems, and limitations of climate science and climate change were identified, which, supposedly, means they were halfway to solution. The problem is—for the mainstream—neither the foreword nor the book changed much. It proves, once again, that a big lie has a mass and momentum that truth struggles to overcome.

As Tim notes, it's amazing that activist climatologists were so influential—and got so wealthy—with baseless, nonsensical scientific arguments. But, they did. Slowly, we see consensus science crumbling and its corruption exposed. Tim played an important role. Why it took so long is a question for the ages.

Tim was a tireless and persuasive public speaker.

A happy memory for me was his 2014 presentation at a Skagit Public Utilities District meeting in the quaint little town of Mount Vernon, Washington where I lived at the time.

As always, he was willing to answer any and all questions and was extraordinarily generous with his time.

I whole heartedly agree with Michael Coren's assessment of Tim:

> *Tim Ball is a highly qualified and experienced academic with an expertise in historical climatology who rejects most of the current hysteria around climate change and global warming. He is a modest, gentle man who, in spite of his enormous work in the field and the chairing of inquiries and commissions into environmental causes, is now libelled, slandered, abused and threatened for his opinions.*

Recently, the algorithm and data used to create Michael Mann's famous (and completely phoney) hockey stick graph was reverse engineered by Hampus Soderqvist and publicized by Steve McIntyre at his ClimateAudit website. Here's a comment by Steve:

> *Although Mann claimed statistical "skill" for each of the eleven steps, he did not archive results of the 11 individual step reconstructions. In 2003, we sought these results, ultimately filing a formal complaint with Nature. But, to its continuing discredit, Nature supported Mann's withholding of*

> *these results. Despite multiple investigations and litigations, Mann has managed to withhold these results for over 25 years.*

You read that right. Mann kept his methodology secret for over 25 years. And, when finally discovered, it was by a diligent forensic investigator, not via disclosure by Mann.

Knowing Tim as I did, he would have been completely delighted by this disclosure. There are many sadnesses about losing Tim—this is one to add to the list. In my vivid imagination, I hear him chortling as the unveiled facts validate what he told us all along. As he said long ago, Mann should have been in the state pen, not at Penn State.

Will deadbeat Mann ever pay court-ordered restitution to his estate?

Only time will tell.

Tim was a mentor and inspiration on a relentless mission to educate his fellow man. I admired him. I miss him.

Let's end with a quote:

> *It's easy to create progressive delusions to justify bureaucratic despotism. Mary McCarthy was correct when she said bureaucracy is the rule of no one—the modern form of despotism. Unfortunately, when you push back, then you experience how freedom of expression is muzzled by an unaccountable bureaucracy using and misusing the rules and the law. The price is higher—financially, emotionally, and productively—than most citizens can pay. You can fight city hall, but don't expect them to make it easy.*

—Dr. Tim Ball, Environmentalist, Public Speaker, Consultant, Author and Columnist

—*Ken Coffman*

Dr Tim Ball, a Great Teacher who Deserved the Order of Canada
by Tom Harris

We have recently said goodbye to dozens of outstanding scientists who fought long and hard in support of real science to contest the global warming scare. Drs Tim Ball, Jay Lehr, Bob Carter, Fred Singer and Patrick Michaels were the heroes I knew best.

It may come as a shock to some readers to see Tim Ball, PhD (Climatology, Queen Mary College, University of London, England), on that list.

Most people thought he was virtually indestructible and would live to 100, fighting the good fight with good humour and solid science for many more years to come. 'Ball' was certainly the right last name for Tim. After all, the harder you throw a ball against a wall, the harder it comes back. Dr Ball obviously followed the Churchill idiom that:

TOM HARRIS

> *If you have an important point to make, don't try to be subtle or clever. Use a pile driver. Hit the point once. Then come back and hit it again. Then hit it a third time—a tremendous whack.*

Dr Ball certainly gave the climate scare a tremendous whack. He was straight forward and honest, never hiding from the truth and always getting right to the point. And unlike most scientists who make many of us feel dumb by speaking in jargon only fellow experts can understand, Tim had a way of communicating that made the exceptionally complicated field of climate change understandable by everyone.

With patience, humility, and the gifts of a natural teacher, Tim built up his listeners understanding and self-confidence. This was not surprising. After all, as a climatology professor at the University of Winnipeg, he won many outstanding teaching awards. All this resulted in him attracting a far wider audience demographic and swaying public opinion far more than we could ever hope to reach with our technical conference presentations and scientific papers.

And this is precisely why Tim was so often in the crosshairs of the climate alarmist movement.

They knew he had tremendous impact on the public through radio, TV, newspapers and in presentations. Even today, the Bing search engine yields about 32 million results for "Tim Ball" and "Climate Change."

During the day after one of Tim's articles was published on the Drudge Report, he received approximately 1,000 e-mails from the public, 90% of which were supportive. And, believe it or not, he answered over 500 of these e-mails personally. The amount of work he did was incredible.

While the vicious attacks he endured were ultimately hard on Tim, who passed away last September at the age of 84, (https://generalistjournal.com/timothy-francis-ball-obituary/) and his wife Marty, in the final analysis, I hope his family realize that the animosity from enemies of our society was a compliment in a rough sort of way.

It reminds me of when World War II Lancaster bomber pilot, the late Sandy Mutch, a steadfast climate realist himself, encouraged me to not back off when the going got tough.

Sandy explained:

> *On bombing raids over Europe, we could tell we were closing in on the target when we started to get the most flak.*

That occurred because critical German assets were usually surrounded by anti-aircraft guns that filled the sky with AAA fire. And, instead of being deterred by this resistance, it told Bomber Command precisely where the next wave of aircraft should concentrate their attack.

Mutch, who held a Masters of Science degree and even prepared some of his own YouTube videos on climate change, (https://www.youtube.com/@alexandermutch6629/) continued:

> *Anyone who wants to kill the dangerous and unfounded climate scare...should focus on exposing the shaky science behind climate alarm. That is the Achilles heel of the whole movement. Shoot it down and you win the war!*

Dr Tim Ball, who spent nine years with the Royal Canadian Air Force as a radio navigator, was clearly right over the target in the climate war. We are so fortunate that he was the right man, in the right place at the right time.

And so he suffered the slings and arrows for all of us for decades.

Tim stood up to aggressive lawyers in terrible court cases. He handled overconfident and ignorant politicians with grace in government hearings. He faced uninformed, arrogant radio and TV talking heads, making sure to get his message out to a public thirsting for honesty and real science. And he gave literally thousands of presentations to audiences large and small, young and old all over the world, no matter how he was smeared.

When I think of Dr Ball, I think of one word in particular, and that is "courage." He's one of the bravest people I have ever known.

Of all the scientists I worked with since becoming Executive Director of International Climate Science Coalition in 2008, no one helped me more than Dr Ball.

One thing people didn't realize when they saw me on television or heard me on radio during the 14 years I worked closely with Tim (2006-2019) is what I did in the hours before the interview. I was almost always on the phone with Dr Ball. Always generous with his time and right up to date in current affairs and the latest climate science, he was essential to my success for all those years.

I was so happy to have had the privilege to present the Lifetime Achievement in Climate Science Award to Dr Ball at the 13th International Climate Change Conference in 2019—https://youtu.be/XFlJVotNW-g

Mutch explained:

I lost many of my best friends and colleagues in the war but we were doing it to defend our society from deadly enemies. Canada now needs leaders with the courage to stand up to today's deadly enemies, climate campaigners who are bent on destroying the energy sources we need to maintain a prosperous society.

The motto of the Order of Canada, which our country awards to people who make extraordinary contributions to the nation, is DESIDERANTES MELIOREM PATRIAM (They Desire a Better Country.)

As one of those very rare Canadians who had the courage, knowledge and skills to stand up to extremists who are destroying our nation, Dr. Tim Ball clearly should have received the Order of Canada.

(Article as published March 16, 2023. in America Out Loud, an American talk radio/website https://www.americaoutloud.com/dr-tim-ball-a-great-teacher-who-deserved-the-Order-of-Canada/)

—*Tom Harris*

Miscellaneous Musings

Science has effectively replaced God leaving society to make the decisions and take actions to resolve problems, but even this is not the real issue. Religion is about morality, a code of living, which in most cases makes the individual or group accountable for their actions.

Science is amoral, and essentially not accountable for its findings or actions. Society is left to deal with the moral and other questions that arise. Some scientists are aware of this dilemma, and a few have warned society, usually without success. For example, Einstein wrote to the President of the United States warning of the potential dangers of nuclear power and urging politicians to show leadership in controlling the threat.

At the end of the 20th century people enjoyed the advances of science and technology, but some negative side effects were becoming apparent. In most cases there were no scientific or technological solutions, the 'technological fix' was not an option. The issues required a moral answer, but these were thrust on a society morally confused.

Well, not everyone!

Those with very fundamental religious views had no problem, often aggravating the issue by taking a 'holier than thou' position. Most realized they needed a moral position but didn't want the one offered by the fundamental groups.

—Tim Ball

CHAPTER TWENTY-TWO

Letter by Susan Crockford, Assistant Prof at UVIC, Polar Bear Authority

Losing my Adjunct Status at the University of Victoria

Dr. Susan Crockford, 8 March 2023

IN JULY 2019, I lost my status as Adjunct Assistant Professor at the University of Victoria (UVic), a position I had held for 15 years. This demotion followed my removal from the roster of the university's volunteer Speakers Bureau in May 2017.

Two events appear to have precipitated these actions: a lecture about polar bear ecology and conservation status that I gave at a conference in March 2017 which was videotaped and posted online, and some highly defamatory statements about me that appeared in a widely publicized journal article in late 2017.

I suspect interference by someone with political clout.

An adjunct professorship is an unpaid position with a few responsibilities that in return allow a scholar to operate as a valid member of the academic community. Adjunct status is renewed every three years or so at the discretion of the individual department, but can be cancelled at any time with as little as two weeks' notice.

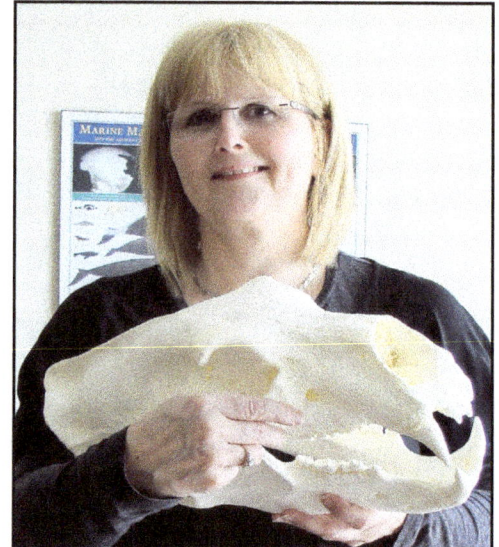

DR. SUSAN CROCKFORD, HOLDING A POLAR BEAR SKULL

I was first appointed as an adjunct in the Department of Anthropology in 2004, shortly after I had successfully defended my PhD. dissertation at UVic. As far as I am aware, there had been no complaints regarding the performance of my adjunct duties. In May 2019, my appointment was up for renewal for 2019-2021, but my application was declined. No reason was given.

In refusing to allow me to participate in the Speakers Bureau (explained in more detail below) and rejecting my adjunct status renewal application, the Anthropology Department behaved in a manner that was completely contradictory to their treatment of me regarding scholarly issues prior to April 2017.

As a consequence, their hypocritical actions took me completely by surprise.

The department was not only fully aware of my activities with regard to the polar bear status controversy, but proudly shared that information via social media. For example, twice—in June 2013 and again in January 2015—the department published announcements on their news webpage regarding opinion pieces on the status of polar bear populations I had written for the Financial Post.

In 2014 and 2017, the university paid me for several special polar bear lectures for students learning English, and in 2015, for a public lecture series on polar bears for the Continuing Education Department.

In other words, up until mid-April 2017, the University was well aware of the controversy that my work on polar bears was generating, and even paid me to talk to students about it.

The turning point was the lecture I gave at the International Climate Change Conference hosted by the Heartland Institute on 23 March 2017 that was video-taped and posted on the internet. During the question-and-answer session after my lecture, I happened to mention that over the past year I had given presentations about polar bears to elementary school classes in Victoria.

I believe that someone saw that video-taped lecture and contacted the University to complain about me talking to school children about polar bears.

About two weeks after the Heartland lecture was posted online, an email notice arrived in my in-box regarding the annual renewal of topics for the Speakers Bureau, addressed "Dear Adjunct Faculty Member." The email explained that this year there was a new requirement that adjunct professors had to have departmental approval to participate in this free community lecture service.

My department chair, Dr. Ann Stahl, refused to give her permission. She said only this:

> While I respect issues of academic freedom, your talks at schools have generated concern among parents regarding balance that have been shared with various levels of the university.

That is all: no further information about what these unspecified "concerns" were. Polar bears were never specifically mentioned and I was not presented with any avenue of appeal. No one requested a copy of my presentation or questioned me in any way about my lectures.

It was an academic hanging without a trial, conducted behind closed doors.

I did not make a public fuss about the Speakers Bureau cancellation at the time because it was already eating up too much of my valuable time during regular working hours. However, in late November 2017, a slanderous article in a science journal for high school teachers called BioScience generated international attention. It was called *Internet Blogs, Polar Bears, and Climate-Change Denial by Proxy*.

CARD FOUND IN TIM'S WALLET AFTER HE PASSED. SEEMS APPROPRIATE!

All media outlets—BC News, National Post, Victoria Times-Colonist, and eventually, even the New York Times—all repeated the authors' unfounded claims that I provided misinformation about polar bears and misrepresented myself as a person with expertise about polar bear issues, all the while suggesting I was a despicable "Climate Change Denier" (a term that deliberately equates those who question accepted authorities on the science of climate change with those who deny that the Holocaust was a real historical event).

It was an ugly few months, culminating with the New York Times piece in April 2018.

That paper and the media pile-on provided added ammunition for those who wanted to silence me. Eventually, the university bowed to the pressure. Vested interests were not only able to stop my participation in the Speakers Bureau but managed to have my adjunct status revoked.

When it really mattered, it was clear that academic freedom and freedom of speech were not concepts that the University of Victoria held in high regard.

My academic career was over.

—*Susan Crockford*

Excerpts from a Letter by Maggie Robinson, University of Winnipeg

I was the managing editor of *The Uniter*, which was the student paper at the University of Winnipeg. I was told in my interview that they had a big budget for their speaker series. They planned to have two speakers for pro-climate change, and I decided we should have another view.

I emailed Dr Tim Ball and said he would be happy to be part of our speaker series at the University of Winnipeg, where Tim taught for 25 years. Tim responded, "It would be a miracle if they allowed me within ten miles of the campus."

I contacted the different departments at the University, including Geography and History, that I was planning on asking Tim to speak. I also sent a cc to the president, Lloyd Axworthy, at this time.

The first interview I got was from the Head of Geography. He said immediately, "I will protest if Tim Ball gets within ten miles of campus." Tim was right.

All the departments and the president said there was no other side of the climate story.

Many meetings were held, and no matter how I argued and emphasized that many students highly favoured having Tim speak, they accused me of being rude, immature, complacent and intransigent. They also suggested that I resign and seek counselling or face being fired.

I was fired.

—*Maggie Robinson*

***TIM OFTEN SAID THE WEATHER WAS MORE
UNUSUAL THAN USUAL***

CHAPTER TWENTY-THREE

Tim's Article in *Country Guide Magazine*, March 2004

Picture a World Without People

WE'RE TOLD HUMANS are changing the climate, but how do we know? How much change would occur if we weren't here? It's like cloud seeding: how much rain would fall if the clouds weren't seeded? We know climate and nature change a great deal, but we don't know the full extent or all the mechanisms of change.

Environmental extremists believe we shouldn't make any changes to the world around us. Some even say humans shouldn't be here at all. Greenpeace, in its book on *Global Warming*, says carbon dioxide is added to the atmosphere 'naturally and unnaturally.' By unnaturally, they mean the human contribution, which implies humans are not natural, or at least what we do is not.

How do you get a measure of nature before humans came on the scene? Geology and biology offer some clues, but they're crude measures. You need early human measures of an essentially unsullied landscape and a vast part of Canada offers that possibility.

From the moment Hudson Bay Company (HBC) adventurers left England and set foot in North America they were mapping, measuring and recording. Their enterprise was completely weather-dependent. Weather determined food supply for the animals they trapped for fur and food.

The HBC archives were brought to Winnipeg from London in 1970 to celebrate Manitoba's 100th birthday and the company's 300th. They included 12,000 maps, more than 250,000 photographs, journals of daily weather, employment records, trade and ships' logs as well as scientific reports of all kinds.

All HBC materials and documents from Canada went to the company's governors in London and most of the scientific information and materials were passed on to the Royal Society. The 18th century was a time of extensive exploration and scientific advance. One of the focal points was Hudson Bay.

There were aboriginal people in most regions when Europeans arrived, but their numbers were small and sparse; the land was essentially uninhabited. Detailed descriptions provided by HBC personnel paint the picture of a virgin landscape. The amount and range of information they gathered is without equal.

Newton produced his theory of gravity in 1687 but it needed proof before it could become a law. In 1769 the transit of Venus across the face of the sun, a rare astronomical event, provided an opportunity to solidify the theory. Two astronomers, William Wales and Joseph Dymond, went to Churchill, the best place for observation, in 1768 and spent 13 months waiting to observe the 7-hour event. Determine how long Venus takes to cross the sun and then, knowing its speed, you can calculate the size of the sun. A simple triangulation provided the distance of the earth from the sun.

A precise measure of the size of our solar system was critical to Newton's theory that gravity was a force determined by the mass of each planet as a function of distance. Wales and Dymond weren't successful in their efforts. Their instruments were inadequate. A couple of minutes error in the timing made their observations useless. Of more significance, they brought the first thermometers to Canada and left them for HBC use. The company later arranged for more thermometers from England in 1811. Employees were given good instructions. Thomas Topping notes in 1811 at Churchill, the thermometer should be kept where the direct and reflected rays of the sun cannot affect it. Ironically, severe weather of the period, particularly from 1790 to 1820, caused a dramatic drop in the number of animals. William Cook notes on April 9, 1811, "scarcity of furs around Factory is without parallel."

The great variation of climate from year to year and decade to decade as recorded in HBC journals is noteworthy. On January 18, 1807, John McNab reports, "Winter continues uncommonly mild." This is followed by, and probably related to, a July 17 entry, "A summer of scarcity."

Just 15 years earlier, Joseph Colen records on February 5, 1792, 'they [Natives] also inform me that the winter set in so early that many swans and other waterfowl were froze in the lakes and they found many not fledged, they likewise say the snow is remarkably deep.'

This early and unique information about birds and climate and many other items are covered in the recent publication. 18th Century Naturalists of Hudson Bay, written by Stuart and Mary Houston—and me. It's available from McGill-Queens University Press. Stuart is the world expert on great horned owls, long-eared owls, great snowy owls and other Arctic species My contribution was a knowledge of Canadian climate and climate change. Together we have been able to credit men who provided material for the most remarkable archives in the world, those of the HBC, and left us data on erratic weather—from a time when mankind's footprint on the earth was negligible in comparison to what it is today.

Mackenzie King said "Canada's problem is too much geography and not enough history."

He wasn't correct; we have lots of both.

The problem is we know very little about either.

—*Tim Ball*

The Rock 98.5 Radio Station in Yorkton, Saskatchewan by Jack Dawes

(Tim was a frequent guest on Jack's program, discussing climate as it relates to farming, because Jack's primary audience were prairie farmers.)

Today, we acknowledge a great Saturday night event which inducted our long-time sports broadcaster friend Randy Atkinson (along with others) into the rejuvenated Yorkton Sports Hall of Fame—but Sunday morning was the other side of the coin!

That's when we learned of the death of Dr Timothy Ball in Victoria—he had been in poor health for several years—and died at age 84 on Saturday.

Some classified Tim Ball as a 'climate change denier' because he fought to show that so-called man-made climate change is closer to modern mythology than it is to fact. He wrote several related books, *The Deliberate Corruption of Climate Science* and *Human-Caused Global Warming: The Biggest Deception in History*.

Ball rejects the scientific consensus on climate change and has stated that he believes global warming is occurring but that human carbon dioxide is not the cause.

However, the (supposedly unbiased) Wikipedia people go to great lengths to discredit Dr. Ball's contention that climate change is cyclical in world history.

The infamous 'hockey stick' graph incident—where warming numbers were 'doctored' to point to high rates of climate warming—is just one example of Ball's point of altered data.

Over the past few years, Ball's opponents have pursued what is known as 'SLAPP' lawsuits—seen by some as spurious endeavours to discredit his climate approach.

Dr Ball and his wife Marty spent years (and we believe) hundreds of thousands of dollars of their life savings fighting off and winning at least some of those lawsuits.

Tim Ball drew heavily on the Hudson Bay Company Archives and their data on the climate of northern and western Canada. Did he know climatology? Even the critically oriented Wikipedia summary agrees reluctantly!

Rest in Peace, Climate Truth Warrior!

"Sometimes I wear this in court. It's my frivolous law suit."

—*Jack Dawes*

Thoughts and Opinions by Andy Rowlands, Birmingham, England

My Impressions of Dr Tim Ball

I first became aware of Tim when I watched *The Great Global Warming Swindle* on TV in 2007. Some years later on a social media platform, I found his son David was a member of the same climate-related group that I was.

David saw some posts I made and suggested I should submit my essay to the website Tim had helped create: Principia Scientific International, which I did, and they published it.

David suggested that if I wrote any more articles, Tim might be able to check them for accuracy. When I wrote a second essay, I emailed Tim from his website and he very kindly read it and suggested a few corrections.

To say I felt honoured is an understatement.

I submitted several other articles over the following months to PSI, and the editor of the website subsequently asked me to combine two articles I had written about the court case with Tim and the fraudster Michael Mann, which would form a chapter in a new edition of their Slayers book, for which Tim was to write the forward.

I have yet to meet Tim, but in the Swindle programme, and in his emails with me, he came across as totally honest and forthcoming, and spent much of his time refuting sensationalist claims about our climate with actual facts. Tim was also the first person I heard say if a country declares an emergency, it allows that country to bring in a whole new set of rules governing the population, such as curfews, and restrictions on things like civil liberties, the free movement of people and freedom of speech.

He was referring to the 'climate emergency', but we have seen exactly what he predicted during the pandemic.

—*Andy Rowlands*

Tim, Chris and Marty in the 1980's

Miscellaneous Musings

Establishment "science" is no longer about truthful facts, but about politics and profiteering. No one outlines that better than Dr. Tim Ball in *The Deliberate Corruption of Climate Science*.

He extensively examines the leaked "climate-gate" e-mails, showing how the warming alarmists worked to fix the "science", in an attempt to "prove" that anthropogenic global warming is real.

He names the names and quotes their exact words from the e-mail messages that were hacked and made public from a still—as of yet—unknown hacker. This is a very well-written, timely, and important exposé of the compromised climatologists—from the United Nations Framework Convention on Climate Change to the climate professors at the grant-funded universities. Their quest to twist "science" to fit their political purposes is laid bare by their actual words. This is a must read for every policymaker who might be considering a carbon tax, as well as any lay person who simply wants to know the truth.

Dr. Ball lays out the truth in plain English for everyone to easily understand.

—Darren Weeks

CHAPTER TWENTY-FOUR

Should '*Global Warming*' Fraudsters Spend Time in the Clink?

Thoughts and Opinions from Pat Boone October 30, 2019

GENTLE READER—and fellow taxpayer—let us again examine an important and unfolding story of global climate science fraud unreported by 'fake news,' or to put it more tactfully, inaccurate, biased and selective mainstream media.

The recent Mann vs Ball lawsuit verdict, dubbed the 'science trial of the century,' has profound repercussions, which spurred me to write this series of articles (this is the third if you're counting).

Please pay attention—or you'll feel ashamed in the next few months as the truth of this worldwide deception is exposed for all to see.

Penn State professor Michael E Mann's recent million-dollar libel case against fellow climate scientist Dr Tim Ball was dismissed due to Mann's 'inexcusable delay' The judge found in favour of Dr Ball, the plaintiff, and Professor Mann was ordered to pay a hefty fine and all court expenses when he refused to produce the scientific basis for his widely acclaimed and accepted claim that the world is on the verge of deadly Global Warming!

PAT BOONE

Why is this so important?

Sceptics say that Mann is part of a criminal climate conspiracy. They assert Mann's alarmist and iconic 'hockey stick' graph—the cornerstone of United Nations' global warming fears—was created from 'secret science'—intentionally secret because it is fraudulent.

In 1999, Dr Mann and his graph were the international game-changers, appearing largely unknown and un-credentialed, as if from nowhere. The hockey stick showed 'unprecedented' increases in modern global temperatures.

Mann told reporters, "I found myself at the centre of what is arguably the most suicidally contentious issue that we face today: the issue of human-caused climate change and what to do about it."

The only thing unprecedented, says Dr Ball, is how rookie Mann suddenly appeared soon after being awarded a 'rushed through' PhD and swiftly appointed Lead Scientist by the U.N.'s Intergovernmental Panel on Climate Change (IPCC).

Were you aware of any of this? Was anybody aware of this, including the 'mainstream media' that swallowed it hook, line and sinker?

Mann's tree ring temperature proxy graph was speedily and widely accepted when it suddenly appeared, despite the reality that most scientists who had studied this knew that higher temperatures than today existed during the Medieval Warm Period (MWP).

Understand: it was, and is, known that the world's overall climate was considerably warmer than now—and there was no industrial revolution upon which to blame it.

Climate campaigners and policymakers alike hysterically touted the new hockey stick graph while those promoting one world government and control were avidly and insistently sounding the 'Chicken Little, Sky is

Falling' fallacy!

Sceptics smelled a rat, and Dr Ball was sued by Professor Mann—for publicly joking that Mann was a fake and 'belongs in the state pen, not Penn State.'

This lawsuit dismissal should have been front-page news, but the media have largely ignored it. Wonder why? The leading proponent of 'Global Warming' was being called out as a fraud in public court!

But if he was truly concerned for his professional and personal reputation, all Mann had to do was show his data and workings in court. He wouldn't, evidently, he couldn't, so he refused.

And his reputation has now sunk to the point where a reputed 97% of scientists admit that Mann and his hockey stick theory seem to be a fraud.

It is made out of thin air, not globally warming air.

Despite this lawsuit taking over eight years, Mann stubbornly hid his secret numbers from the court. His case was dismissed for 'unreasonable delay'—Mann's 'secret science' was staying secret.

Like you, I'm now asking for common-sense proof.

My previous column was an appeal to reason addressed to all parties. Even non-scientists can see the dilemma. I urged Mann to 'cough up' all the data, which any honest scientist would do. If it's reality-based, let's all see it, not just blindly take your word for it, as we have to date.

You know, as well as I do, how all this looks.

If the scientific 'basis' for the 'Global Warming' scam is bogus, then real scientists should and could have known it long ago.

Who and what persuaded them to go along, unquestioningly, like proverbial lemmings? Could it be big money, elite interests, even cabals who see this as a means of assuming control over all production, industry and fuels worldwide, telling us what we can and can't do, 'for our own good.'

These 'experts' had us believing temperatures would skyrocket, flooding coasts. Properties and communities would be devastated. Remember when President Obama promised to shut down all coal mining and set about to do it?

The first prominent Chicken Little, Al Gore, revealed the Inconvenient Truth that he was continent-hopping in his gas-guzzling private jet—and the Obamas recently purchased a $15 million beachfront mansion, which the globally warmed oceans will surely wash away—right?

Do they know something we don't?

Suppose I still have your attention, and I hope I do. In that case, you may still be wondering about the actual scientific evidence showing that all this 'Global Warming' data are 'hokey,' not 'hockey,'—so let me take you briefly 'into the weeds' of actual data.

Steve McIntyre, a respected Canadian statistician, does this yeoman's work.

McIntyre checked to see if Mann had done what any diligent scientist would do—perform tests (i.e., an r-squared statistic—[coefficient of determination]) to uncover any unforeseen errors in creating his graph. The U.S. House Energy and Commerce Committee's Wegman Commission (2006) asked McIntyre to assist in its investigations.

Wegman wanted answers about the controversial graph and asked Mann whether he had calculated such a verification r-squared statistic and asked what it was.

Mann refused to provide the test numbers, even in response to a congressional inquiry.

He provided code, which revealed that Mann calculated a verification r-squared statistic check during the summer of 2005.

Likewise, the National Academy of Sciences similarly asked Mann questions on whether he performed the verification regression tests to verify whether his graph's hockey stick shape was correct.

Then Mann caught himself in a lie.

Our errant hockey stick professor flatly denied calculating that—saying that it would be a 'foolish and incorrect thing' to do—even though his own source code, produced for the House Energy and Commerce Committee, showed that he had calculated the r-squared regression statistic: he didn't report it. One would assume, therefore, it didn't validate his theory!

Do you smell what I smell? Remember Bernie Madoff—the financial 'genius' who blatantly defrauded many experienced and very wealthy famous people of a reported $50 billion, and we taxpayers of billions more?

Well. Bernie was sentenced to jail for several lifetimes—and this effort to stampede all of us into giving up our liberties to produce and create, and go about our lives freely as we have become accustomed to in modern society, is a multi-trillion dollar scam of intentionally fraudulent data and pressure.

Might there be a vacancy next to Bernie Madoff's empty cell? (he died in 2022??)

—*Pat Boone*

[My gratitude to scientist Tom Tamarkin for the spadework and verifiable references herein.]

Miscellaneous Musings

Tim Ball's Student Exercises

The ideal exercise is to establish a weather station at the school. When I helped schools do this I have had support from Parent Teachers groups and from local businesses: power utility companies are usually very willing to help. You can also get help and advice at least from the government. Environment Canada or the National Oceanographic and Atmospheric Administration (NOAA). Automatic instruments are not expensive and can be hooked directly into a computer preferably in the library were all have access. A list of providers of instruments is available at the end of this section.

The values of this project for students are:

1) They learn about quality, location and reliability of weather instruments.
2) They learn about official weather instruments and weather stations.
3) They learn about the collection of data; a fundamental part of all aspects of understanding the environment and society.
4) They can compare their results with local, national and international weather stations and with other schools who keep similar records.
5) They learn about the problems of maintaining long term records and develop an obligation to those who went before them and those who will come after.
6) They will learn about local and microclimates as their record differs from other stations in their community or in neighboring communities.
7) There are many exercises the students can do with their information, including providing the data for the local radio or TV stations.

A list of topics for students to investigate in a way the teacher can define depending on their particular location and resources available. Some of these topics will be unknown to most students but the questions will take them on a voyage of discovery.

1) Investigate paintings, drawing and photographs as evidence of previous climates.
2) Examine the changing western view of the world starting with Neptunism, through Uniformitarianism to Chaos theory.
3) Compare this view of the world with other cultures such as China and India.
4) How is sea level measured? How has it changed over time, especially since the last Ice Age? What is the difference between eustatic and isostatic changes?
5) Who was Milutin Milankovitch? How was his work a culmination of research from James Croll on? How did it explain the occurrence of Ice Ages?

CHAPTER TWENTY-FIVE

Dedication by Kim Purdy, May 2023, Calgary, AB Canada—A Dear Friend of Tim's

IT IS A SINCERE honour to accept this invitation to share with you how the amazing Dr Timothy Ball has impacted my life and how his family have become dear friends and true inspirations to me and many others.

As a freedom-fighting truth seeker with a keen awareness of the racket that global warming began to ignite, I had become increasingly concerned about the one-sided storyline pushed by Al Gore, Michael Mann and other politicians, then undisputed by so many. This was around the time I learned of Tim's work regarding the global warming narrative, where only one obvious side of the story and singular agendas were being pushed forward.

A worldwide man-made global catastrophe would be inevitable if we did not concur with those particular ideologies and did not do something immediately. Thus, Tim inspired me to align with his utter determination to expose the facts, to tell the truth, and never back down, even in the cold and often overwhelming face of adversity. Tim had found a hill to die on, and he fought for this truth to the end of his life.

With virtually no debates or contests between the cheerleaders of global warming and those who held opposing ideas and solutions, dissension from these leaders was severely shunned, attacked, and criticized; the credibility of the opposing intelligence was immediately questioned, and their reputations became deflections from the benign subject on the centre stage.

While Tim was not the only great mind questioning this official narrative, I daresay he suffered the most for demonstrating an alternative view of the global warming landscape. He pressed hard that the official hockey stick narrative was grossly overstated, even inaccurate and that the science needed to be completed. This, I believe, is a crucial cause of why he became a primary target for the catastrophic corroboration of climate change promoters, who dragged Tim's fighting spirit right into the fires of the courthouses. Tim's fighting spirit and utter conviction to deliver the true facts brought me even closer to this war. Tim became such a dedicated mentor to me after I met him at a conference in Calgary where he, Marc Morano, and I shared dinner one evening and quickly became allies to the cause.

Tim's vast knowledge of a multiplicity of subjects was impressive from the start, coupled with his incredible life's work. His perpetual education on worldly matters seemed infinite. He continued sharing this vast knowledge far and wide with all who cared to listen until he could no longer travel due to health restrictions. Unstoppable, he later turned to other formats, such as guesting on radio and other recorded interview opportunities.

What I came to understand about Tim was that even though he was faced with years of lawsuits that threatened his livelihood, his reputation and that of his family, he never once relinquished or denied an opportunity to tell the truth or expose the flaws in the storylines he encountered throughout his journey. The fact that so many of his colleagues came to bat for him during his court battles, where he never abated a challenging argument, is a testament to his spirit and the reason he garnered such great respect from so many communities of science.

I am proud to state that I had many long conversations with Tim during and around these difficult times, wherein my respect and admiration for this rock-solid individual flourished. Near the end of the court battles that ensued for years, at a significant loss of personal finance and security, he and his family began weathering the wear of its negative results. One day he told me he did not know how much more zeal he had left in his tank, how many more unimaginable hardships he could face or surmount. Somewhere and somehow, Tim always seems to find his reserve tank and push on.

A true and rare Canadian hero. A brilliant beacon for the entire world who sadly bid farewell to a most magnificent man. Tim Ball's incredible work, his legendary spirit, his tireless dedication and effort will never be extinguished in the hearts, minds and agendas of those of us who knew him, loved him and continue to carry his torch for the truth and to dispel the mythical global warming narratives.

—*Kim Purdy*

CHAPTER TWENTY-SIX

Dr Tim Ball Defeats Michael Mann's Climate Lawsuit!

Written by John O'Sullivan, Published on August 23, 2019

Supreme Court of British Columbia dismisses Dr Michael Mann's defamation lawsuit versus Canadian skeptic climatologist, Dr Tim Ball. Full legal costs are awarded to Dr Ball, the defendant in the case.

https://www.desmogblog.com/sites/beta.desmogblog.com/files/Mann-Ball%7B154653b9ea5f83bbbf00f55de12e21cba2da5b4b158a426ee0e27ae0c1b44117%7D20Libel%7B154653b9ea5f83bbbf00f55de12e21cba2da5b4b158a426ee0e27ae0c1b44117%7D20Claim.pdf

THE CANADIAN COURT issued its final ruling in favour of the dismissal motion that was filed in May 2019 by Dr Tim Ball's libel lawyers. View the judge's decision here:

https://principia-scientific.com/wp-content/uploads/2019/09/mann-judgement-canada.pdf

The plaintiff Mann's 'hockey stick' graph, first published in 1998, was featured prominently in the U.N. 2001 climate report:

https://www.nature.com/articles/33859.epdf?

The graph showed an unprecedented spike in global average temperature in the 20th Century after about 500 years of stability:

https://wattsupwiththat.com/2009/12/12/historical-video-perspective-our-current-unprecedented-global-warming-in-the-context-of-scale/

Skeptics have long claimed Mann's graph was fraudulent.
    On Friday morning (August 23, 2019) Dr Ball sent an email to WUWT revealing:

https://wattsupwiththat.com/2019/08/22/breaking-dr-tim-ball-wins-michaelemann-lawsuit-mann-has-to-pay/

"Michael Mann's Case Against Me Was Dismissed This Morning by The BC Supreme Court and They Awarded Me [Court] Costs."

A more detailed public statement from the world-renowned skeptical climatologist is expected in due course.
    Professor Mann is a climate professor at Penn State University. Mann filed his action on March 25, 2011 for Ball's allegedly libellous statement that Mann *"belongs in the state pen, not Penn State."* The final court ruling,

in effect, vindicates Ball's criticisms.

Previously, on Feb 03, 2010, a self-serving and superficial academic "investigation" by Pennsylvania State University had cleared Mann of misconduct. Mann also falsely claimed the NAS found nothing untoward with his work.

https://hockeyschtick.blogspot.com/2011/03/there-he-goes-again-mann-claims-his.html

But the burden of proof in a court of law is objectively higher.

Not only did the B.C. Supreme Court grant Ball's application for dismissal of the 8-year, multi-million dollar lawsuit, it also took the additional step of awarding full legal costs to Ball.

This extraordinary outcome will likely trigger severe legal repercussions for Dr Mann in the U.S. and may prove fatal to alarmist climate science claims that modern temperatures are "unprecedented."

https://wattsupwiththat.com/2009/12/12/historical-video-perspective-our-current-unprecedented-global-warming-in-the-context-of-scale/

According to the leftist The Guardian newspaper (Feb, 09, 2010):

https://www.theguardian.com/environment/2010/feb/09/hockey-stick-graph-ipcc-report

The wider importance of Mann's graph over the last 20 years is massive:

> *Although it was intended as an icon of global warming, the hockey stick has become something else—a symbol of the conflict between mainstream climate scientists and their critics.*

Under court rules, Mann's legal team have up to 30 days to file an appeal. [update October 09, 2019: Dr Mann did NOT seek to formally appeal the Decision]. The Judge's Decision is here:

https://principia-scientific.com/wp-content/uploads/2019/09/mann-judgement-canada.pdf

Hockey Stick—Discredited by Statisticians in 2003

In 2003 a Canadian study showed the hockey stick curve *"is primarily an artefact of poor data handling, obsolete data and incorrect calculation of principal components."* When the data was corrected it showed a warm period in the 15th Century that exceeded the warmth of the 20th Century.

So, the graph was junk science. You could put baseball scores into Mann's Climate model and it would create the hockey stick.

But the big question then became: did Mann intentionally falsify his graph from motivation to make profit and/or cause harm (i.e. commit the five elements of criminal fraud.)

No one could answer that question unless Mann surrendered his numbers. He was never going to do that voluntarily—or face severe consequences for not doing so—that is, until Dr Ball came into the picture!

Evidence in Legal Discovery and the Truth Defence

Dr Ball's legal team adroitly pursued the 'truth defence' such that the case boiled down to whether Ball's words (***belongs in the state pen, not Penn State***) after examining the key evidence (R^2 numbers) fairly and accurately portrayed Mann.

The aim was to compel the plaintiff (Dr Mann) to show his math working out to check if he knowingly and criminally misrepresented his claims by resorting to statistical fakery (see: "Mike's trick" below).

In the pre-trial 'Discovery Process' the parties are required to surrender the cited key evidence in reasonable fashion, that they believe proves or disproves the claim.

Despite Ball's best efforts over eight years, Mann would not agree to surrender to an open court his math "working out" —the R^2 regression numbers for his graph (see Mann's latest obfuscating Tweet in the 'update' at foot of this article).

But throughout 2017 and 2018 any reasonable observer could see through such endless delays from the plaintiff—all just attritional tactics.

https://principia-scientific.com/breaking-key-un-climate-fraudster-makes-concessions-tim-ball-lawsuit/

The Penn State professor had persistently refused to honour the binding "concessions" agreement he made to Ball which ultimately gave his legal team the *coup de grâce* to win the case for the defendant due to Mann's "Bad Faith" see: legal definition here:

https://legal-dictionary.thefreedictionary.com/bad+faith

Dr Ball always argued that those numbers, if examined in open court, would have conclusively prove Mann was motivated to commit a criminal fraud. It was at this point legal minds could discern Ball was closing in on victory—a triumph for "David over Goliath."

And Mann certainly is a science "Goliath." Ever since featuring so famously in the UN IPCC 2001 Third Assessment Report (TAR) Mann's graph has been an iconic image cited relentlessly by environmentalists clamouring for urgent action on man-made global warming.

Will US President initiate an investigation into the now disgraced "world-leading climate change scientist"?

For the past two decades the biased mainstream media has acclaimed Mann as "a world-leading climate scientist" and last year he was heralded as their champion to help dethrone "climate denier" President Trump.

Indeed, not just a fawning MSM, but many hundreds of subsequent climate studies have relied on Mann's findings. Mann's reputation was such, that most climate researchers merely accepted his graph, a typical example of groupthink.

Dr Ball has long warned that if the world was permitted to see behind the secrecy they would be shocked at just how corrupt and self-serving are those 'scientists' at the forefront of man-made global warming propaganda.

As anyone can tell by contrasting and comparing the graphs (Mann's version top, Ball's below) it is obvious there exists a massive discrepancy in the respective findings.

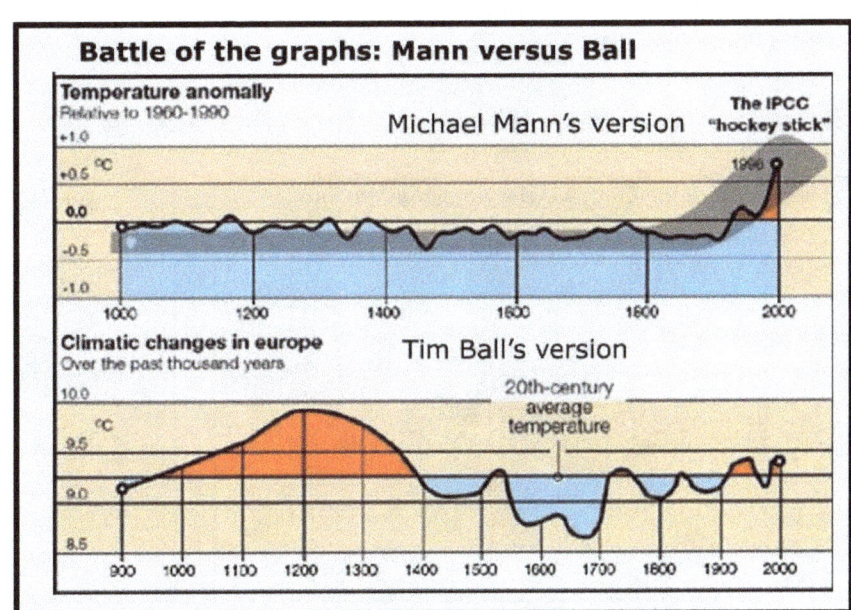

Contrast and compare Dr Mann's dodgy graph with Dr Ball's more reliable version—based on that of the renowned Hubert. H. Lamb:

https://wattsupwiththat.com/2012/06/24/hh-lamb-climate-present-past-future-vol-2-in-review-part-i/

…and see how Mann fraudulently altered the proxy climate date with a "hockey stick" shape to falsely show the dramatic uptick with modern temperatures rising "catastrophically" to fit the fake UN IPCC doomsaying narrative.

Have Skeptics Ever Proven that Mann's Graph was Deliberately Faked?

Answer: No. This is because Mann has always refused to release his R^2 regression numbers for independent examination.

He claimed his secrecy was justified because he held "proprietary rights" (article by Tim Ball for Principia Scientific, https://principia-scientific.com/the-ipcc-and-proprietary-rights-does-the-law-trump-justice/ over them (i.e. personally valuable intellectual work product, you see). So "valuable" to Mann was the secrecy of his metadata that losing a multi-million-dollar lawsuit and his reputation was the ultimate price he was prepared to pay. While steep, I guess, that's preferable to serving a long federal prison stretch, right?

Before Ball's glorious court victory, little more could be conclusively proven other than the hockey stick graph uptick stupidly (and unscientifically) relies on the proxy evidence from the tree rings of a single Yamal larch!

Mann could thus sleep safe in the knowledge that as long as statistical experts remain deprived of any conclusive proof of his intent to defraud, they could only find him guilty of incompetence.

Putting Mann's Fraudulent Graph Under the Microscope

Mann's goal was to make the Little Ice Age (LIA) disappear, as we explained in our previous article on this issue.

https://principia-scientific.com/what-michael-manns-hockey-stick-graph-gave-to-un-climate-fraud/

The LIA was an especially cold era that ended around 1840 and since then global temperatures have gradually risen. But government "experts" like Mann have sought to use statistical trickery to make such natural variation appear as "man-made" warming.

Apart from playing with statistics Mann made his proxy fit the thermometer data by adding thermometer values to the proxy values known as "Mike's trick" in the climate gate email scandal:

https://www.telegraph.co.uk/comment/columnists/christopherbooker/6679082/Climate-change-this-is-the-worst-scientific-scandal-of-our-generation.html

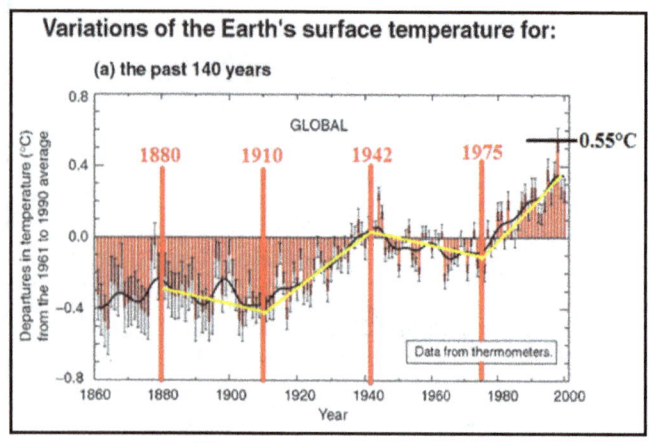
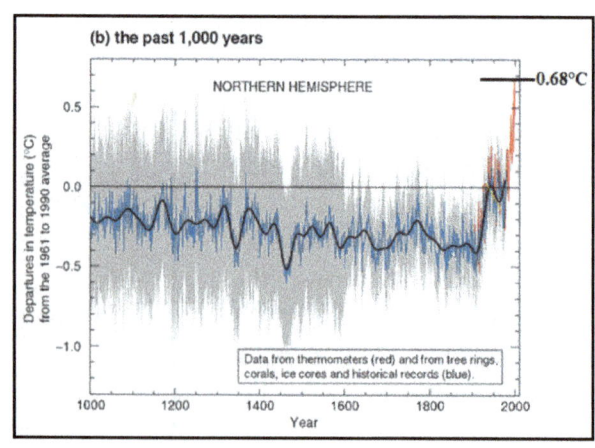

Everything Reminds Me of Tim

From the emails released during the Climate-gate scandal:

https://www.conservapedia.com/index.php?title=Climategate

Professor Phil Jones, Britain's top climate scientist at the University of East Anglia was shown to have written the following to his alarmist colleagues. There is some analysis here:

https://jhammerton.wordpress.com/2009/11/29/climategate-on-the-mikes-nature-trick-email/

The email, sent by Professor Phil Jones of the CRU in 1999, states:

Dear Ray, Mike and Malcolm,
Once Tim's got a diagram here we'll send that either later today or
first thing tomorrow.
I've just completed Mike's Nature trick of adding in the real temps
to each series for the last 20 years (ie from 1981 onwards) and from
1961 for Keith's to hide the decline. Mike's series got the annual
land and marine values while the other two got April-Sept for NH land
N of 20N. The latter two are real for 1999, while the estimate for 1999
for NH combined is +0.44C wrt 61-90. The Global estimate for 1999 with
data through Oct is +0.35C cf. 0.57 for 1998.
Thanks for the comments, Ray.
Cheers
Phil

This has the Hockey Stick Graph **showing the same cooling from 1942 to 1975** as the HadCRUT3 data as posted in the IPCC 2001 AR3.

In 1942 there was just 4.0 Gt of emissions increasing to 17.1 Gt by 1975 but since this 425% increase in CO_2 emissions didn't cause any global warming during this 33 year period; the conjecture of CO_2 emissions induced (catastrophic) global warming was proven false.

Readers interested in gaining a deeper understanding of what is likely to eventually be exposed as a criminal conspiracy between Mann and other "elite" researchers should see "The Hockey Stick Illusion" by Andrew Montford:

https://www.amazon.com/Hockey-Stick-Illusion-Andrew-Montford-ebook/dp/B0182I73BA

Victory that Comes at Great Personal Cost

Behind the scenes, gathering the resources, mental, scientific and financial, there is an untold burden of defending these cynical SLAPP suits.

Lest readers forget, it is mostly in the service of misguided public policy, with massive funding and connivance from political operators in play, that fake scientists like Michael Mann and Andrew Weaver acquired such esteemed public positions.

They are not only despicable human beings they are a disgrace to all decent scientists.

Readers will be aware that this author has been a staunch friend and ally to Tim throughout the hardships of this protracted 8-year legal battle.

Our reputations were routinely trashed by our enemies, so it is sweet justice that the court has now given legal credence to Tim's famous words that Michael Mann **"belongs in the state pen, not Penn State,"** a comical reference to the fraudulent "hockey stick" graph that knowledgeable scientists knew to be fakery.

[Author Note: Being very much a party to these legal proceedings (having provided Dr Ball with the financial security of a legally-binding indemnity in the event Tim lost) it is a monumental vindication of my faith in Tim's cause. In effect, I "bet the farm" on Tim winning, as graciously reported by Jo Nova (below)]

Knowingly Fraudulent and Corrupt

During 2018, while Tim Ball's hard work was winning "concessions" from Mann's legal team in Canada:

https://principia-scientific.com/breaking-key-un-climate-fraudster-makes-concessions-tim-ball-lawsuit/

South of the border, (on April 20) a shameless Mann wrote in Scientific American this utter nonsense:

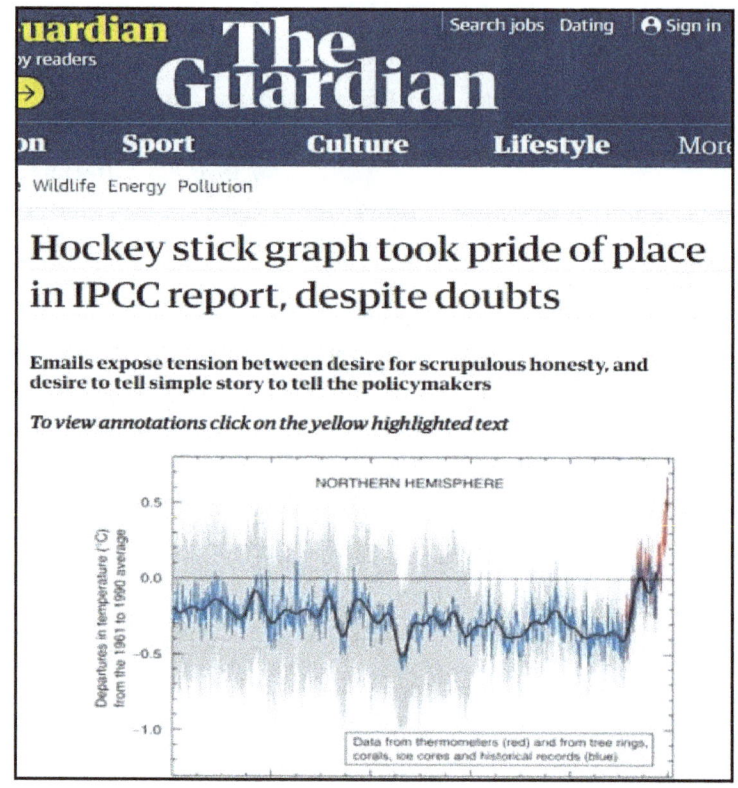

Yet, in the 20 years since the original hockey stick publication, independent studies, again and again, have overwhelmingly reaffirmed our findings, including the key conclusion: recent warming is unprecedented over at least the past millennium.

Gullible and brainwashed greens and the many self-serving politicians swallowed up this garbage.

Dr Ball Expresses Gratitude to Principia Scientific International

Speaking in this 2018 video…transcription of first three minutes of video here:

https://principia-scientific.com/video-dr-tim-ball-on-importance-of-michael-mann-lawsuit/

…on the gravity of what some scientists have called "the science trial of the century," Dr Ball revealed his gratitude to his colleagues at Principia Scientific:

Dr Tim Ball:

I know John O'Sullivan who set up the Principia site and I know I wrote a foreword and a chapter in one of the books they produced called *Slaying the Sky Dragon*.

https://www.amazon.com/Slaying-Sky-Dragon-Greenhouse-Theory/dp/0982773412

John O'Sullivan comes from his anti-government [stance], very legitimately and unfortunately, it's not until you've actually directly personally experienced it, that is, challenging the government—that you realize how nasty they can get. So John knows very well how nasty these things can get—that anyone that dares to challenge the authorities.

And so, Principia was set up for that reason, and John was the one that helped me set up the PayPal so people could help me financially so, that's my disclaimer with that.

As Jo Nova Reported on the joannenova.com.au Blog:

https://joannenova.com.au/2012/01/john-osullivan-puts-his-house-on-the-line-more-than-any-skeptic-ought-to-be-asked-to-do/

John O'Sullivan is putting in above and beyond what any single skeptical soul ought to.

He's already been a key figure helping Tim Ball in the legal fight with the UVA establishment, which has spent over a million dollars helping Michael Mann to hide emails. The case was launched by Michael Mann, but could turn out to do a huge favour to skeptics—the discovery process is a powerful tool, and we all know who has been hiding their methods, their data, and their work-related correspondence.

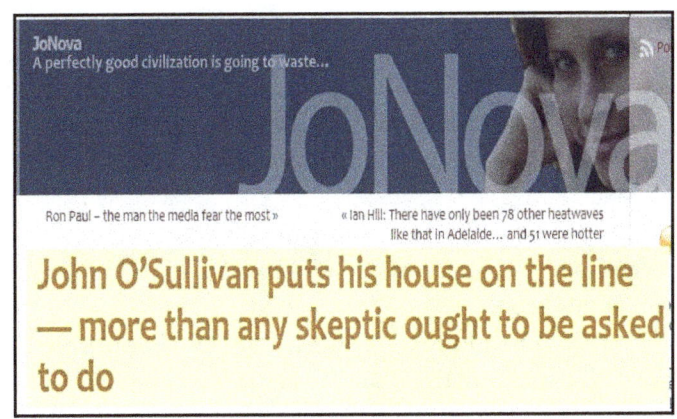

Tim Ball and John O'Sullivan are helping all the free citizens of the West. The burden should not be theirs alone. There are many claims for help at the moment, but that is a sign that the grand scam is coming to a head. Jo

Two out of Two Major Court Wins by Ball Versus Junk IPCC Scientists

Dr Ball, now affirmed as a courageous champion of honest science, has assured his place in the annals of real climate science. His gift to the world was sacrificing eight of his senior years, when he could have been enjoying his retirement, to exposing key players in the biggest science fraud of all time.

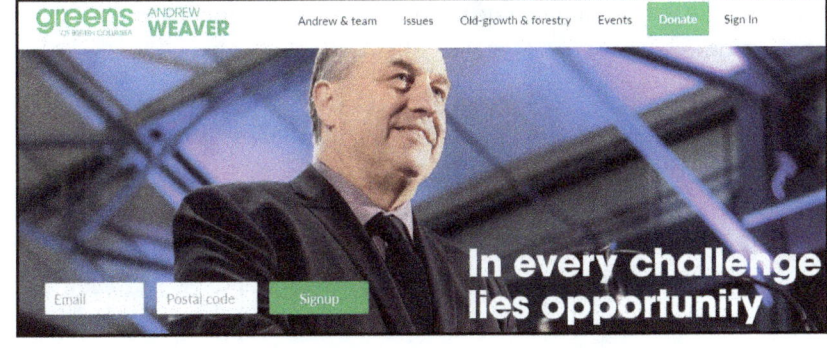

People too easily forget Dr Ball has defeated in expensive legal battles not just one top UN IPCC climate scientists, but two!

This latest victory is the second this champion of climate skepticism has enjoyed in the last 18 months in this same jurisdiction—both for "defamation," both multi-million dollar climate science claims.

We reported (February 15, 2018) on Dr Ball's first crucial courtroom win against Dr Andrew Weaver (photo, right), another elite junk scientist (a UN IPCC lead author in climate modelling) and British Columbia Green Party Leader.

https://principia-scientific.com/update-tim-balls-huge-courtroom-win-now-targets-michael-mann/

Pointedly, at the time, Dr Ball wanted to emphasize an extremely salient fact:

> While I savour the victory, people need to know that it was the second of three lawsuits all from the same lawyer, Roger McConchie, (photo, right) in Vancouver on behalf of members of the Intergovernmental Panel on Climate Change (IPCC).

In effect, there is more than mere coincidence that Dr Ball, a world-leading skeptical climatologist, was systematically targeted for legal retribution time and again by political groups such as the unscrupulous Climate Science Legal Defence Fund.

As a retired scientist in his 80's, Tim was a "soft target" and the stress of these lawsuits put an enormous toll on his health.

Not to be outdone, Tim has used his time wisely to write a damning book of the 30-year back story of the great climate fraud titled *The Deliberate Corruption of Climate Science* and I heartily recommend that interested readers buy it.

https://www.amazon.com/Deliberate-Corruption-Climate-Science-ebook/dp/B00HXO9XGS/ref=sr_1_1?

It is also not often reported that the funding in Canada for these extravagant **SLAPP lawsuits** is believed to be from the David Suzuki Foundation, a hot house for extreme environmental advocacy and Big Green policy promotion.

What is a 'Strategic Lawsuit Against Public Participation' (SLAPP Suit?)

Wikipedia offers a fair definition:

> "A ***strategic lawsuit against public participation*** (***SLAPP***) is a lawsuit that is intended to censor, intimidate, and silence critics by burdening them with the cost of a legal defence until they abandon their criticism or opposition.[1] Such lawsuits have been made illegal in many jurisdictions on the grounds that they impede freedom of speech.

In the typical SLAPP, the plaintiff does not normally expect to win the lawsuit. The plaintiff's goals are accomplished if the defendant succumbs to fear, intimidation, mounting legal costs, or simple exhaustion and abandons the criticism. In some cases, repeated frivolous litigation against a defendant may raise the cost of directors' and officers' liability insurance for that party, interfering with an organization's ability to operate.[2] A SLAPP may also intimidate others from participating in the debate."

Update (August 24, 2019):

Dr Mann Posted on Twitter In Reply to this Article:

Mann's statement is here:

https://twitter.com/MichaelEMann/status/1164910044414189568

In short, Mann's ugly responsive legal statement is (a) stark admission he lost fair and square, and (b) a disingenuous argument that the dismissal was granted merely on the basis of Mann's "delay" in not submitting his R^2 numbers in timely fashion.

Well, Mikey, You are the Plaintiff and Tim Gave You Over 8 YEARS 'To Get Your Case Together!'

On that point, this is where readers may wish to refer to the article "Fatal Courtroom Act Ruins Michael 'Hockey Stick' Mann" (July 4, 2017).

https://principia-scientific.com/breaking-fatal-courtroom-act-ruins-michael-hockey-stick-mann/

In it we offered analysis as to Mann's fatal legal error. As Dr Ball explained at that time:

> *Michael Mann moved for an adjournment of the trial scheduled for February 20, 2017. We had little choice because Canadian courts always grant adjournments before a trial in their belief that an out of court settlement is preferable. We agreed to an adjournment with conditions. The major one was that he [Mann] produce all documents including computer codes by February 20th, 2017. He failed to meet the deadline.*

As I explained in the article, Mann (and his crooked lawyer) had shown bad faith, thereby rendering his case liable for dismissal. I urged Tim to pursue that winning tactic and thankfully he did.

Assisting Dr Ball has been a huge honour for me and probably one of the greatest achievements of my life. But Tim only won this famous courtroom battle thanks to massive worldwide grassroots support.

We can only continue to fight these protracted lawsuits with your kind support.

Marty's comments:

> *The judge (Skolrood) stated at the first trial that he would not speak to the Science of Climate as he was not knowledgeable enough and would not give his opinion. In his synopsis after the first trial, he said, "the article was poorly written and lacked credibility." So, he did have an opinion about the subject and wanted Andrew Weaver to know it.*

JOHN O'SULLIVAN OF PRINCIPIA-SCIENTIFICA

Weaver stated that he would appeal and did so. The courts granted him that privilege even though his lawyer applied late. (They would not have given Tim the same freedom had he been late in filing.) The three judges on the Appeals Court decided that Tim's comment was defamatory even though no one presented new evidence.

Tim would also like me to mention Andrew Weaver's "Wall of Hate" in his office at the University of Victoria. (He holds this position, and is also MLA for the Green Party of BC. He resigned in 2020 from that position.) This "Wall of Hate" contains all the photos and articles by people who disagreed with him, and Tim's picture and the piece that Tim wrote for The National Post were in the centre.

(By the way, Andrew Weaver's lawyer could not find anyone who had read this NP article besides Andrew Weaver.)

The National Post also won its first trial and lost on appeal.

Miscellaneous Musings

Tim Ball at the Heartland International Conference on Climate Change, 2014

CHAPTER TWENTY-SEVEN
Canada Free Press

TIM WROTE MANY, many articles for Canada Free Press and proved very popular. Once the lawsuits came in, Judy Macleod, editor of CFP was forced to discharge Tim from her website by writing the article noted below. We don't know who forced her to write this—or did they write it for her?

Judy McLeod's Apology for Tim on her Website

Since posting the apology last week, Canada Free Press has stripped it from their website along with Ball's biography and virtually everything he ever wrote for the site. The full text of the retraction is as follows:

> On January 10, 2011, Canada Free Press began publishing on this website an article by Dr. Tim Ball entitled "Corruption of Climate Change Has Created 30 Lost Years" which contained untrue and disparaging statements about Dr. Andrew Weaver, who is a professor in the School of Earth and Ocean Sciences at the University of Victoria, British Columbia.
>
> Contrary to what was stated in Dr. Ball's article, Dr. Weaver: (1) never announced he will not participate in the next IPCC; (2) never said that the IPCC chairman should resign; (3) never called for the IPCC's approach to science to be overhauled; and (4) did not begin withdrawing from the IPCC in January 2010.
>
> As a result of a nomination process that began in January, 2010, Dr. Weaver became a Lead Author for Chapter 12: "Long-term Climate Change: Projections, Commitments and Irreversibility" of the Working Group I contribution to the Fifth Assessment Report of the IPCC. That work began in May, 2010. Dr. Ball's article failed to mention these facts although they are publicly-available."
>
> Dr. Tim Ball also wrongly suggested that Dr. Weaver tried to interfere with his presentation at the University of Victoria by having his students deter people from attending and heckling him during the talk.

[We have the audio proving that Tim was heckled by Weaver's students. Tim also took a taxi to and from the university in case he was harassed. I remind you again of Weaver's wall of hate in his office.]

> CFP accepts, without reservation there is no basis for such allegations.
>
> CFP also wishes to dissociate itself from any suggestion that Dr. Weaver "knows very little about climate science." We entirely accept that he has a well-deserved international reputation as a climate scientist and that Dr Ball s attack on his credentials is unjustified.

[Weaver is an oceanographic and atmospheric scientist using computer models to determine climate patterns and an associate of Michael Mann's. They met regularly at the Stonehouse Pub at Swartz Bay]

> CFP sincerely apologizes to Dr. Weaver and expresses regret for the embarrassment and distress caused by the unfounded allegations in the article by Dr. Ball.

—Judi McLeod, Canada Free Press

CHAPTER TWENTY-EIGHT

Newspaper Articles

Tim's Letter of the Day—Times Colonist, July 13, 2005

Climate Studies have Basic Flaws

THE WORLD HAS gone mad.

African dictators and Swiss bankers rub their hands in glee as Bono and other rock stars convince our bonehead leaders to send an extra $25 billion per year their way.

Next they plan to "stop global warming", a ridiculous concept if there ever was one. Yet the world will now spend literally trillions of dollars on the non-existent problem based on the scientific knowledge of untrained environmental lobbyists while ignoring the increasingly vocal cautionaries from world climate experts that the science is fatally flawed.

All one need know about that crusade is that global warming fears are based on the predictions of computer models that do not even include the effects of clouds and have failed in every prediction to date. They also assume an increase in carbon dioxide due to human activity will result in a temperature increase when the science shows that temperature increases before carbon dioxide.

In other words, the fundamental basis of the models is also wrong.

Heaven help us, because our leaders won't.

Rock On!   Tim Ball, Victoria

ARTICLE AS IT APPEARED IN THE TIMES COLONIST

Opinion Pieces

An article in *The Globe and Mail* on August 12, 2006 by Charles Montgomery followed by a rebuttal in the *National Post* on August 23, 2006 by Terrence Corcoran.

Nurturing Doubt about Climate Change is Big Business.

On a cloudless morning in June, Tim Ball has joined a hundred-odd members of the Comox Valley Probus Club for a buffet of coffee, cinnamon buns and pink lemonade. As this group of retired business people wraps up its monthly meeting, Dr. Ball surveys the crowd and runs a hand over his suntanned dome.

He does not appear the least bit fatigued, which is remarkable considering that the 67-year-old former University of Winnipeg professor has spent much of the past couple of months crisscrossing the country, addressing community forums, business groups, newspaper editorial boards and politicians about climate change.

He has been nearly as dogged as Al Gore, whose own globe-hopping slide show is the subject of the hit documentary film An Inconvenient Truth.

But that is where their similarity ends.

Dr. Ball clutches a cordless microphone and smiles out at the sea of white hair. He teases the audience about their age, throws in a hockey joke, then tells the crowd that, unlike Mr. Gore, he is a climatologist, and he is not at all panicking about climate change.

"The temperature hasn't gone up," he asserts. "But the mood of the world has changed: it has heated up to this belief in global warming."

Over the next hour, Dr Ball stitches together folksy anecdotes with a succession of charts, graphs and pictures to form a collage of doubt about the emerging consensus on climate change. There's a map of Canada covered in ice 20,000 years ago—proof, he says, that wild swings in the Earth's temperature are perfectly normal. There's a graph suggesting that atmospheric carbon dioxide is at its lowest level in 600 million years.

Gaining momentum, he declares that Environment Canada and other agencies fabricated the climate-change scare in order to attract funding for propaganda and expensive attempts to model climate change using supercomputers.

"Environment Canada can't even predict the weather!" he bellows.

"How can you tell me that they have any idea what it's going to be like 100 years from now if they can't tell me what the weather is going to be like in four months, or even next week?"

As proof of the climate-change conspiracy, Dr. Ball shows the crowd a graph with a kinked line jigging across it. This is the famous "hockey-stick graph" published by Pennsylvania State University scientist Michael Mann and his team in 1999, which shows temperatures to be fairly stable for hundreds of years, then rising rapidly in the past few decades. Mr. Gore, among many others, uses it to illustrate the case for global warming.

Dr. Ball claims that the Mann team "cooked the books," and that its blunders were confirmed just a few days previously, in a report to the Congress by the U.S. Academies of Science. "He threw out all the data that didn't fit his hypothesis," Dr Ball says, without offering evidence to support the charge. His outrage is now as searing as the baking sun outside. "I personally think [Mann] should be in jail!"

In fact, Dr Ball says, the real danger for Canada is not warming, but cooling: "It's like Y2K," he concludes. "We all just need to calm down."

He is met with raucous applause. It is as though a weight has been lifted from the audience's collective shoulders: what a relief to learn that this global crisis, one they keep hearing will bring extreme weather, submerge small island nations and devastate economies, may be nothing to worry about.

Few in the audience have any idea that Dr Ball hasn't published on climate science in any peer-reviewed scientific journal in more than 14 years. They do not know that he has been paid to speak to federal MPs by a public-relations company that works for energy firms. Nor are they aware that his travel expenses are covered by a group supported by donors from the Alberta oil patch.

Most Canadians recognize, of course, that fossil-fuel businesses could lose large sums if the federal government moves to curtail green-house-gas emissions.

But they may not realize that by quietly backing the movement behind maverick figures such as Dr Ball, the fuel industry—with its close ties to the party that brought Prime Minister Stephen Harper to power—is succeeding, bit by bit, in influencing both public opinion and Canadian policy on global warming, including the international Kyoto Accord.

An Ipsos-Reid poll released in May found that, despite increasing scientific evidence to the contrary, four of every 10 Canadians surveyed still agreed with Dr Ball's assertion that climate change is due to natural warming and cooling patterns.

"He is a very entertaining performer, very slick," says Neil Brown, the Conservative MP for Calgary-Nose Hill, who attended a presentation Dr Ball made to a caucus of Calgary Tories. "When someone shows up and tells me that the Earth is actually cooling, then it gets my attention."

The scientific mainstream is unequivocal that global warming is real, happening at a rate unprecedented in human history, and most likely caused mainly by man-made greenhouse gases. Last year, the national academies of science of all the Group of Eight industrial nations, representing most scientists in the developed world, sent a joint message to their leaders urging prompt action.

In February, the United Nations and the World Meteorological Society's Intergovernmental Panel on Climate Change (IPCC), which brings together more than 2,000 scientists to review tens of thousands of peer-reviewed papers on climate science, will release its fourth report. The authors say it will contain a warning that human-caused global warming could drive the Earth's temperature to levels far higher than previously predicted.

Andrew Weaver, the Canada Research Chair in Climate Modelling and Analysis at the University of Victoria, and a lead author of a chapter in the upcoming IPCC re-port, gives a frustrated sigh at the mention of Tim Ball's cross-country tour.

"He says stuff that is just plain wrong. But when you are talking to crowds, when you are talking on TV, there is no challenge, there is no peer review," Prof. Weaver says.

Like other senior scientists, he charges that Dr Ball's arguments are a grab bag of irrelevancies and falsehoods: "Ball says that our climate models do not [account for the warming effects of] water vapour. That's absurd. They all do."

Likewise, he says, Dr Ball's claims that climate change could be explained by variations in the Earth's orbit or by sunspots are discounted by widely available data.

Many of Dr Ball's other points are easily refuted. Consider the hockey-stick graph: he was right that the U.S. Academies of Science had delivered a review of climate science to Congress.

But their report concluded that temperatures in the past 25 years really have been the highest in 400 years. Moreover, the panelists assured reporters that there was no evidence at all that the Mann team cherry-picked its data—completely contradicting what Dr Ball told his audience in Comox.

"What Ball is doing is not about science," Prof. Weaver says. "It is about politics."

Leaders throughout Europe have accepted the IPCC position on climate change, and have been looking for ways to take collective action, primarily via the Kyoto Accord.

Yet North Americans have lagged behind, hamstrung by a lingering debate in the media and among politicians about climate science.

How did this doubt take hold?

In a now-infamous 2003 memo, U.S. pollster and consultant Frank Luntz advised Republican politicians to cultivate uncertainty when talking about climate change: "Voters believe that there is no consensus about global warming within the scientific community. Should the public come to believe the scientific issues are settled, their views about global warming will change accordingly. Therefore, you need to continue to make the lack of scientific certainty a primary issue in the debate," wrote Mr. Luntz (the italics are his own).

Nurturing doubt about climate change science has become big business for public-relations companies and lobbyists south of the border.

From 2000 to 2003, Exxon Mobil Corp. alone gave more than $8.6 million (U.S.) to think tanks, consumer groups and policy organizations engaged in anti-Kyoto messaging, according to the company's own records. Those groups promote the minority of scientists who still dispute the IPCC consensus on climate change, creating the appearance of widespread scientific disagreement.

Mr. Luntz met with Mr. Harper in May, but the Conservatives already had adopted his advice. The Prime Minister was emphasizing that climate change was but an "emerging science" long before he cancelled an array of programs designed to promote energy conservation.

For example, Environment Minister Rona Ambrose, the MP for Edmonton-Spruce Grove, has talked up the flaws of the Kyoto accord, while steadfastly rejecting its modest emission-reduction targets. On June 30, the government simply got rid of its main climate-change website (*www.climatechange.gc.ca*), which once contained educational materials for teachers.

However, given the resonance of the climate-change issue with most Canadians, political leaders cannot afford to denounce mainstream science too loudly. That task has instead been taken up by activists in the Conservative Party's Alberta heartland.

Over the past four years, a coalition of oil-patch geologists, Tory insiders, anonymous donors and oil-industry PR professionals has come together to manufacture public consent for Canada's withdrawal from Kyoto. Through a Calgary based society ironically dubbed the Friends of Science, they have leveraged Tim Ball and a handful of other "climate sceptics" onto podiums and editorial pages across the country.

While the federal government stalls, the skeptics preach doubt, softening the public for a diluted "made in Canada" climate policy. Dr Ball acknowledges that when he meets with business leaders and politicians, he advises them to weigh the high price of action against more cost-effective "lip service".

These efforts may help delay emissions caps for years. Not bad for a campaign that began with bitch sessions among a clutch of oil patch retirees.

"We started out without a nickel, mostly retired geologists, geophysicists and retired businessmen, all old fogeys," says Albert Jacobs, a geologist and retired oil-explorations manager, proudly remembering the first meeting of the Friends of Science Society in the curling lounge of Calgary's Glencoe Club back in 2002.

"We all had experience dealing with Kyoto, and we decided that a lot of it was based on science that was biased, incomplete and politicized."

Mr. Jacobs says he suspects that the Kyoto accord was devised as a tool by United Nations bureaucrats to push the world toward a global socialist government under the United Nations. "You know," he says, to this day, there is no scientific proof that human-caused CO_2 is the main cause of global warming."

He managed to insert that last message into the Canadian Society of Petroleum Geologists official statement on climate change in 2003.

But he and his fellow Friends of Science decided that if they wanted to have broad influence on climate policy, they needed money to stage events, create publicity materials, commercials and a website, and reach the media and politicians. Dr Ball spoke at the group's first fund-raiser.

But the event didn't raise enough for the group's plans. There was plenty of money for the anti-Kyoto cause in the oil patch, but the Friends dared not take money directly from energy companies. The optics, Mr. Jacobs acknowledges, would have been terrible.

This conundrum, he says, was solved by University of Calgary political scientist Barry Cooper, a well-known associate of Mr. Harper.

As is his privilege as a faculty member, Prof. Cooper set up a fund at the university dubbed the Science Education Fund. Donors were encouraged to give to the fund through the Calgary Foundation, which administers charitable giving in the Calgary area and has a policy of guarding donors' identities. The Science Education Fund, in turn, provides money for the Friends of Science, as well as Dr Ball's travel expenses, according to Mr Jacobs.

And who are the donors? No one will say.

The money is "not exclusively from the oil and gas industry," Prof. Cooper says. "It's also from foundations and individuals. I can't tell you the names of those companies, or the foundations for that matter, or the individuals."

When pushed in another interview, however, Prof. Cooper admits, "there were some oil companies."

The brilliance of the plan is that by going through the foundation and the university fund, donors get anonymity, and their donations get charitable status. In the past two years, the Science Education Fund has received more than $200,000 in charitable donations through the Calgary Foundation. Yet its marketing director, Kerry Longpré, said in June that she had never heard of the "Friends of Science." The foundation, she said, deals only with the university, which is left to administer donations as it sees fit.

Prof. Cooper and Mr. Jacobs both affirm that the Science Education Fund paid the bills for the Friends" anti-Kyoto video, *Climate Catastrophe Cancelled*. It features Canada's most vocal climate skeptics, including Dr Ball, University of Ottawa hydrologist and paleo-climatologist Ian Clark, Carleton University paleo-climatologist Tim Patterson, University of Ottawa lecturer Tad Murty and retired meteorologist Madhav Khandekar, who has done communications for the oil industry funded Cooler Heads Coalition.

It also includes Sallie Baliunas, a senior scientist with the George C.Marshall Institute in Washington, a fiercely anti-Kyoto think tank that has received hundreds of thousands of dollars from Exxon Mobil.

Roman Cooney, the University of Calgary's vice-president of external relations, insists that the "Friends of Science" is neither affiliated with nor endorsed by the school. And when he saw the university's coat of arms on early copies of the anti-Kyoto video, Mr. Cooney ordered Prof. Cooper to remove it.

There is a letter-sized piece of paper bearing the words "Friends of Science" taped to the wall in Kevin Grandia's Vancouver office. From that single sheet, he has strung a web of string, leading to the names of individuals, free-market think tanks, private companies and charitable foundations. And from them more strings lead, invariably, to the names of energy corporations.

Mr. Grandia is being paid full-time by James Hoggan and Associates, a public-relations firm, to examine the connections between fossil-fuel companies, the climate skeptics and the Public Relations industry itself.

"Follow the money trail," says Mr.Grandia, ball of string in hand. "Why the hell do all of these lead back to oil and gas?"

Take Fred Singer, a former professor of environmental sciences at the University of Virginia, who supplied one of the charts for Dr Ball's slide show. A string leads from Mr. Singer's name straight to Exxon Mobil, which has given $20,000 (U.S.) to his Science and Environment Policy Project, according to the oil company's 1998 and 2000 grant records.

Other strings loop from Mr Singer to Shell, Arco, Unocal, Sun Energy and the American Gas Association. In a Massachusetts Superior Court deposition, he acknowledged that he had consulted for all those companies, as well as the Global Climate Coalition, whose members in industry spent tens of millions of dollars to fight the Kyoto accord in the 1990s.

Mr. Grandia's boss, James Hoggan, chuckles when he sees the wall of paper and string. Mr. Hoggan, whose clients include Alcan, CP Rail, Norske Canada and the David Suzuki Foundation, has assigned two of his 19 staffers to this bit of intra-industry tail-chasing. (It is supported by a donation of $300,000 from former Internet entrepreneur John Lefebvre, now an environmentalist and philanthropist.)

Mr. Hoggan says he got involved simply because he was angry that his peers in PR were muddying public understanding of climate science. "For years, there have been these kind of campaigns that are manipulating opinion, and not necessarily manipulating it in the direction of good public policy, but trying to fight government regulations that will cost industry money."

"It happened with the tobacco industry. It happened with the chemical industry. It happened with the asbestos industry. And now it's happening with Climate Change," he says.

"It makes me extremely angry. I don't think that the people who are involved in this should be able to get away with it. My goal is to find out as much as we can about these people and make it public. Who are they? Who is paying them? What motivates them? How is it they can sleep at night?"

Several of Mr. Hoggan's peers show up on Mr. Grandia's Friends of Science spider web. First is Morten Paulsen of the PR giant, Fleishman-Hillard, who wears three hats. In one, he's a long-time Tory/Reform/Canadian Alliance activist—the co-chair of the Alberta Conservatives 2006 convention, and onetime director of communications for Preston Manning. In another, Mr. Paulsen is the registered lobbyist for ConocoPhillips Canada, the country's third-largest oil and natural gas production and exploration company.

Mr. Paulsen also happens to be the registered lobbyist for the "Friends of Science." Indeed, he used to be listed as the main public-relations contact on the Friends" website. Then, in June, his Tory connections were revealed on Mr. Grandia's blog (desmogblog.org). Mr. Paulsen's name no longer appears on the site.

Then there is Tom Harris, Ottawa director of the High Park Group, which is a registered lobbyist for the Electricity Association and the Canadian Gas Association.

Mr. Harris has written several essays attacking Kyoto and the science behind climate change for the newspaper chain. In his articles, he quotes several members of the "Friends of Science" advisory board including Drs Ball, Khandekar, Patterson and Murty—but he never mentions his own connections to the Calgary organization.

In 2002, for example, Mr. Harris organized the Friends' first Ottawa press conference in 2002, and helped to make their video, according to Mr Jacobs. And as recently as May, he organized a trip to Ottawa for Dr Ball, paying him $2,000 to give a presentation to federal Members of Parliament.

The election of a Conservative government to Ottawa, after all, presented a golden opportunity for the "Friends of Science" to try to reopen the debate on Kyoto. This spring, they circulated thousands of *Climate Catastrophe Cancelled* DVDs among politicians and news outlets, ran a radio ad on stations in Alberta, put up a website, and jetted Dr Ball across the country for face time with media, business and politicians.

The climax of the spring campaign was an open letter to Mr. Harper, printed in the Financial Post and other CanWest newspapers on April 6. The letter, signed by "60 experts in climate and related scientific disciplines," exhorted the Prime Minister to hold public consultations on the government's climate-change plan.

Members of the climate and meteorological science establishment quickly noted that only a third of the names on the petition were Canadian. Many of them were economists and geologists, not climate experts. One of them, Gordon Swaters, a professor of applied mathematics at the University of Alberta, later said it had been unclear what he was signing and he disagreed with the letter completely.

Several of the other signatories had received money from the oil, gas and coal industries in the United States—Patrick Michaels of the University of Virginia, for example, was handed more than $100,000 for climate skeptic work by the coal-based Intermountain Rural Electric Association this July, according to the Associated Press.

"These people are ignorant. Well-meaning, but just plain ignorant," fumed Ian Rutherford, executive director of the Canadian Meteorological and Oceanographic Society, which represents 800 Canadian atmospheric and oceanic scientists and professionals.

"The Friends of Science" are driven by ideology and some kind of a misplaced understanding of how the world works. Many are what you would call paleo-geologists. Looking at the geological record, they see evidence of wild swings in climate. Of course, these swings are there: if you go back hundreds of millions of years, 40 million years, even 400,000 years, you will find wild swings in temperature over long periods of time. But that's irrelevant.

There was hardly any life on Earth, let alone human life, at that time. So their time scale is all out of whack.

"None of them ever come to our scientific conferences. They know they would be laughed out of the building. The stuff they say, some of it is so nonsensical it's hardly worth discussing."

In its own letter to the Prime Minister, the Meteorological and Oceanographic Society objected to the "Friends of Science" complaints about a lack of debate, pointing out that Canadian climate scientists from universities, government and the private sector participate actively in the IPCC's international reviews. The government, it argued, should be relying on IPCC reports for good scientific information.

But various levels of government have gone on to give Dr Ball an audience. This spring, he addressed the Alberta Tories in Calgary, as well as the province's committee on energy and sustainable development. On his trip to Ottawa in May, he met with the Ottawa Citizen editorial board, and gave his slide show to a half-dozen federal Conservative MPs and a clutch of Tory staffers. (Dr Ball is not listed in the federal government's Lobbyists Registry.)

He made a particular impression on Brad Trost, MP for Saskatoon:Humboldt: "It really broadened the perspective. You know, maybe there is more uncertainty on [climate change]. Maybe we need to put more research into this to get a better idea," Mr. Trost says. "Just like the Y2K problem, we were a little oversold on that one. You sort of wonder. Just because something is repeated often, it doesn't make it true."

"In public relations," Mr Hoggan says, "we call this the echo-chamber technique. You have Tim Ball saying the polar bears are fine. Then you get Tim Ball's PR guy writing the same thing, and then Tim Ball takes to the road, talks to reporters and does press briefings, making sure the message is repeated over and over."

The effect is to delay public judgment on climate change, and thereby delay policy.

In his speeches and interviews, Tim Ball consistently denies any knowledge that he is receiving funds from oil companies.

"I wish I was being paid by them," he deadpanned at his Comox show. "Maybe then I could afford their products."

Like Mr. Jacobs, Dr Ball says he doesn't know, and doesn't want to know, who forks out the money for expenses and activism. He simply wants to talk about the science and will do so to whomever will listen.

Certainly, climate skepticism isn't exactly making Dr Ball rich. He says that although he has earned as much as $5,000 for speeches to industry groups such as lime producers, he more frequently gives talks for free.

He is a warm, likeable character, and there is no reason to believe he is not sincere in his concern for science and public policy. He clearly relishes the spotlight, and seems to grow taller, sharper and brighter on stage. He punches the air with his microphone and breaks out into a broad grin at the crowd's response to his jabs at Environment Canada.

Still, it must take something more than conviction to propel him through the more than 100 barn-burning speeches he gave across the country in the past year. He angrily claims that his stance has led to being denied research funding from Environment Canada, although he admits that he has not personally applied for federal climate-research funding in more than a decade.

One old colleague at the University of Winnipeg puts Dr Ball's passion down to sheer anti-authoritarianism. "He is a contrarian. He lives to challenge authority,"

According to a professor of geography, who would speak only anonymously, "If the IPCC scientists suddenly recanted," he jokes, "Tim would be the first one out there saying, "Wait a minute, global warming really is happening!"

Dr Ball's adversaries acknowledge that skeptical inquiry serves to make the science better. They just wish he would conduct new research and practice his skepticism on the pages of the peer-reviewed journals.

For his part, Dr Ball insists that the reason he lobbies so tirelessly on the issue is his frustration that the skeptics' arguments aren't reflected in the pronouncements of scientific institutions such as the IPCC. Perhaps so, but his hard work is helping weaken the power of such internationally respected institutions.

The proof, for Friends of Science founder Albert Jacobs, is in the policy. "Our success is very recent, and our success is tied to the Conservative government," Mr Jacobs says. "Rona Ambrose, she has been tearing down that

Kyoto building."

The next big challenge, he says, is to reach children. The Friends of Science is now lobbying to have its message included in the grade-school curriculum.

Charles Montgomery is the Vancouver-based author of *The Shark God*. Its Canadian edition, *The Last Heathen*, won the 2005 Charles Taylor Prize for non-fiction.

The National Post Article, Refuting *The Globe and Mail* article, August 23, 2006 by Terence Corcoran

Inside the Globe's 4,200-word Hatchet Job on Climate Skeptics

It's tough dealing with facts as a journalist, but not that much of a problem if you can also lard your work with smears, innuendo, fabrications, distortions, errors, untruths and omissions gross and minor. Armed with the above, a writer named Charles Montgomery managed to get The Globe and Mail to run a piece that attempted to demolish the ideas and reputations of Canada's climate-change skeptics.

It was a masterful effort.

The Background

Titled *Meet Mr. Cool: Nurturing Doubt about Climate Change is Big Business*, the article—published August 12—focused on Tim Ball, a retired University of Winnipeg climatologist. Mr. Ball has spent much of the last decade delivering talks to whoever will listen on what he sees as the questionable science behind global-warming theory.

The real purpose of Meet Mr Cool, however, was to turn all climate skeptics into incompetent, misguided and ignorant fools who are nothing more than paid fronts for a corporate-industrial conspiracy to debunk climate change science. As Mr Montgomery put it, "Over the past four years, a coalition of oil patch geologists, Tory insiders, anonymous donors and oil-industry PR professionals has come together to manufacture public consent for Canada's withdrawal from Kyoto."

If that sounds a little Noam Chomskyish, that's because Mr. Montgomery comes from the same ideological school as the famous author of *Manufacturing Consent*. A visit to Mr Montgomery's Web site reveals a man obsessed with primitivism and dedicated to the usual leftist world views.

Touring for his latest book, *The Shark God*, about life on islands in the South Pacific, Mr. Montgomery asks the big science questions: "Can a man convince a shark to eat his enemies?" He says he found himself believing in the strangest things: rainmaking stones, magic walking sticks.

On geopolitical issues, he joins David Suzuki in idealizing Cuba as one of the world's "havens of happiness," compared with the United States and Britain. Americans, he says, are the world's least happy people "because of their consumer-driven economies." Mr. Montgomery is from the school of economics that believes the war on poverty will only be won when everybody is poor.

So we know where Mr Montgomery is coming from. Where he leads his readers in "Meet Mr. Cool" is therefore somewhat predictable. Still, he needed 4,200 words in his attempt to demolish the integrity and credibility of scientists who criticize climate-change theory. An unusually high proportion of those words convey information and ideas that are false, distortionary and misleading, that are smears and unfounded claims, that omit the truth.

Through it all, Mr. Montgomery fails to deal with the core scientific issues.

Before we get to that, the glaring irony is hard to avoid. Here is Mr Montgomery, writing in a mass media outlet, claiming that a tiny group of scientists nobody has ever heard of—the "Friends of Science"—is out to "manufacture consent" against global-warming theory, itself beyond doubt the greatest mass-manufactured consent product in history. His article even sells itself as a function of "consensus" among scientists. If any subject deserved to be dragged through the manufactured-consent filter, the vast global consent over climate change would be at the top of the list. Mr. Montgomery's piece offers good guidance on how the system of manufactured consent works to destroy those who would question that consent.

Hockey-Stick Science

The biggest little item in this effort is the blanket dismissal of Mr. Ball's claim—made during a talk to a group of citizens in Comox Valley, B.C.—regarding the famous icon of manufactured climate consent, the hockey stick. Bold-faced text is from Mr. Montgomery's Globe article.

> *As proof of the climate-change conspiracy, Dr Ball shows the crowd a graph with a kinked line jigging across it. This is the famous "hockey-stick graph" published by Pennsylvania State University scientist Michael Mann and his team in 1999, which shows temperatures to be fairly stable for hundreds of years, then rising rapidly in the past few decades. Dr Ball claims that the Mann team "cooked the books," and that its blunders were confirmed just a few days previously, in a report to the Congress by the U.S. Academies of Science. "He threw out all the data that didn't fit his hypothesis," Dr Ball says, without offering evidence to support the charge. His outrage is now as searing as the baking sun outside. "I personally think [Mann] should be in jail!"*

One could certainly fault Dr Ball for over-the-top rhetoric, something scientists of all stripes seem to enjoy. But Mr. Montgomery then goes on to present the idea that the Michael Mann hockey-stick controversy is a big fat zero, a myth promoted by climate skeptics. He does that by misrepresenting the issue.

The original hockey-stick graphic actually claimed to represent temperatures going back 1,000 years, not just "hundreds of years," as Mr. Montgomery described it. It's an important distinction. Two major reviews of the hockey stick have found it to be wrong in its 1,000-year claim. Mr Montgomery skips over that issue and makes it look as if Dr Ball had misrepresented the facts.

> *Many of Dr Ball's points are easily refuted. Consider the hockey-stick graph: He was right that the U.S. Academies of Science had delivered a review of climate science to Congress.*
>
> *But their report concluded that temperatures in the past 25 years really have been the highest in 400 years. Moreover, the panelists assured reporters that there was no evidence at all that the Mann team cherry-picked its data—completely contradicting what Dr Ball told his audience in Comox.*

Here Mr. Montgomery deliberately gets the hockey-stick issue wrong.

The 400-year confirmation is beside the point, since nobody disputes temperatures are the highest in 400 years.

The contention is over the claim that current temperatures are at their highest point in 1,000 years, which the U.S. National Academy of Science in the end concluded the hockey-stick graph failed to prove. In other words, it downgraded the major 1,000-year claim and upheld only the minor 400-year part.

Another more devastating statistical review of the hockey stick was conducted by Edward Wegman, chairman of the U.S. National Academy of Sciences committee on theoretical and applied statistics. His study found, among other things, that part of the original statistical analysis was based on "incorrect mathematics."

It dismissed the 1,000-year claim. "Overall, our committee believes that Mann's assessments that the decade of the 1990s was the hottest decade of the millennium…cannot be supported by his analysis."

For a glimpse at the Wegman report's conclusions, see the article on the opposite page by Stephen McIntyre and Ross McKitrick. Wegman also questioned the objectivity of the review process for the hockey-stick research.

The Experts

The facts behind the hockey stick would have been known to Mr. Montgomery when he went after Mr. Ball. But perhaps Mr. Montgomery can be forgiven his lapse on the facts, since he appears to have taken many of his cues from a man named Andrew Weaver.

> *Andrew Weaver, the Canada Research Chair in Climate Modelling and Analysis at the University of Victoria, and a lead author of a chapter in the upcoming IPC report, gives a frustrated sigh at the mention of Tim Ball's cross-country tour. "He says stuff that is just plain wrong...Ball says that our climate models do not [account for the warming effects of] water vapour. That's absurd. They all do." Likewise, he says, Dr Ball's claims that climate change could be explained by variations in the Earth's orbit or by sunspots are discounted by widely available data.*
> *"What Ball is doing is not about science," Prof. Weaver says. "It is about politics."*

When it comes to politics and climate science, few beat Andrew Weaver as a player. His agency, a division of Environment Canada, builds climate models and has more riding on the business of climate change than perhaps any other science group in Canada.

Among Mr. Weaver's notorious political statements is the following: "God help Canada if the Conservatives get in," he said in 2004 during one of his lobbying pleas for more funding. If that's not politics, what is? These days, apparently, federal civil servants—which is what Dr Weaver is—apparently have absolute freedom to wage partisan politics.

Also in 2004, Dr Weaver dismissed the original hockey-stick research debunking the 1,000-year claim as 'simply pure and unadulterated rubbish.' We now know that Mr. Weaver's dismissal was pure and unadulterated rubbish.

Dr Weaver reportedly claimed it is "absurd" for Dr Ball to charge that climate models "do not account for water vapour." But Dr Ball says he never said that water vapour is not accounted for in models, nor did he ever say—as claimed by Mr Montgomery—that temperatures have not risen in recent years.

Another expert brought in to discredit Dr Ball and other skeptics is Dr Ian Rutherford, a former federal civil servant from the Environment Canada fold.

> *These people are ignorant. Well-meaning, but just plain ignorant," fumed Dr Ian Rutherford, executive director of the Canadian Meteorological and Oceanographic Society... 'the Friends of Science' are driven by ideology and some kind of a misplaced understanding of how the world works. Many are what you would call paleo geologists. Looking at the geological record, they see evidence of wild swings in climate.*

I called Dr Rutherford, a retired federal environment bureaucrat. He turned out to be a motor-mouth of putdowns of scientists who don't agree with his views. He dismissed Dr Ball as a retired professor who had not produced any recent research. He said other scientists criticized in Mr. Montgomery's article are specialists in areas that are unrelated to climate and climate modelling. "they are ignorant," he said.

The fact that Dr Rutherford himself is retired, has produced no recent research and is not a climatologist—which Dr Ball is—didn't deter Dr Rutherford from labelling others as ignorant. As for his own views on climate, Dr Rutherford is locked to the idea that the great government-backed computer climate models used by the United Nations are good science and offer solid evidence that "the entire increase in globally averaged temperatures since the start of the Industrial Revolution is due entirely to man's interference with the climate."

This is simply not true. The UN's 2001 Intergovernmental Panel on Climate Change (IPCC) report says: "the

Earth's climate system had demonstrably changed on both global and regional scales since the pre-industrial era, with some of these changes attributable to human activities." [Emphasis added.]

Dr Rutherford also claims the hockey stick is a trivial issue since it plays no role in the science argument. This is also untrue. The hockey-stick chart appears dozens of times in UN and Canadian government climate reports, generally at pivotal points and as the core "iconic proof of unprecedented climate change change." It is also crucial to NGO activists: It appears, for example, as the lead graphic on the David Suzuki Foundation's climate page.

The Corporate Smear

As noted, Dr Ball is not really the target of "Meet Mr. Cool"; he's the straw man for a smear of scientists who stand apart from the so-called climate-change consensus. To better the smear, skeptics are dismissed as pawns of the energy industry.

> *Then there is Tom Harris, Ottawa director of the High Park Group, which is a registered lobbyist for the Canadian Electricity Association and the Canadian Gas Association. Mr. Harris has written several essays attacking Kyoto and the science behind climate change for the National Post and the Can West newspaper chain. In his articles, he quotes several members of the Friends of Science advisory board—including Dr Ball and Profs. [Mad-hav] Khandekar, [Tim] Patterson and [Tad] Murty—but he never mentions his own connections to the Calgary organization.*
>
> *In 2002, for example, Mr. Harris organized the 'Friends of Science' first Ottawa press conference in 2002 (sic), and helped to make their video, according to Mr. Jacobs. And as recently as May, he organized a trip to Ottawa for Dr Ball, paying him $2,000 to give a presentation to federal MPs.*

Thus begins Mr Montgomery's great steamroller through the idea that scientists who oppose the climate consensus are in the pay of corporations. It's a classic leftist trick, as if receiving money from corporations is in itself a sign of corruption.

There isn't enough space here to itemize the scores of false links and little errors that make up Mr Montgomery's fantastic tale of corporate and Tory conspiracy.

From the above sample, we have the line that links Mr Harris to the electricity and gas industries, as if he were an 'oil industry PR professional.' As Mr Montgomery was told by Mr Harris in an interview, Mr Harris has no connection with those industries. They may be clients of High Park, the company he works for, but he has no business with them. Mr Harris says he told Mr Montgomery that his funding for his climate activity came from Gerald G. Hatch, a distinguished metallurgist, former director of the Canadian Institute for Advanced Research and funder of the Gerald G. Hatch Isotope Laboratory at the University of Ottawa.

Mr Montgomery nevertheless chose to create a fictional corporate connection. Moreover, Mr Harris also says that Dr Ball was never paid to appear before federal MPs in 2002, and that the scientists who came to Ottawa recently had no connection with the Calgary-based 'Friends of Science' or the petroleum industry.

Chilling Debate

The debate over corporate backing should, in any case, be a non-issue. In the end, though, it is the most important issue to anti-corporate activists. Nobody gives two hoots about the 'Friends of Science' and the bit of funding they might have received, at most $200,000, provided by a University of Calgary fund, organized by Prof. Barry Cooper. It was used to produce a DVD about climate science that nobody has seen. It has yet to appear on any network. Compared with the Al Gore film An Inconvenient Truth and the billions spent by Ottawa on climate, skeptics are working with pennies.

The real impact of Mr Montgomery's Globe and Mail article would be to warn corporations, especially energy firms, against taking on climate-change theory. If they challenge the established climate fundamentalism, they run the risk of bringing down the wrath of activists and thereby alienating the public.

When corporations do choose to publicly oppose climate-change theory,—and few do,—they run up against people like James Hoggan, head of James Hoggan and Associates, a Vancouver public relations firm and a self-appointed iman of anti-corporate fundamentalism. Mr Hoggan compares the oil industry's largely invisible and non-existent involvement with climate skeptics with the tobacco industry's attempt to deny the risks of tobacco. 'It happened with the tobacco industry. It happened with the chemical industry. It happened with the asbestos industry. And now it's happening with climate change,' Mr Hoggan told Mr Montgomery.

According to Mr Montgomery, Mr Hoggan is a public relations man who doesn't believe people have any right to engage in public relations on behalf of views Mr Hoggan disapproves. "It makes me extremely angry. I don't think that the people who are involved in this should be able to get away with it. My goal is to find out as much as we can about these people and make it public. Who are they? Who is paying them? What motivates them? How is it they can sleep at night?"

The only role for corporations, apparently, is to join the manufactured consent and become part of the fundamentalist crusade. Otherwise, they face the wrath of Mr Hoggan and others who accept no opposition.

The Pembina Institute, an Alberta-based think-tank and major proponent of climate-change action, receives large dollops of corporate cash. Nobody sees that as a moral issue or a conflict. There is also massive corporate backing for climate action from Canada's electricity, nuclear, gas and other industries that stand to benefit from Kyoto-type accords. No complaints there either.

The Suzuki Axis

Mr Montgomery didn't have to go too far to find Mr Hoggan. The latter is on the board of the David Suzuki Foundation. Mr Montgomery works for a Vancouver graphics outfit called Emerald City Communications, which has the Suzuki Foundation as a client. Mr Hoggan, who also does work for the Suzuki Foundation, despite his role on its board, assigned two of his staff to research corporate involvement in climate issues. One of them, David Grandia, operates a hilariously warped Web site—a sort of al-Jazeera of climate theory dedicated to exposing climate skeptics as corporate/Tory thugs. It was Mr Grandia who came up with the news that Prime Minister Stephen Harper is a fishing buddy of Barry Cooper's, the professor who helped fund the 'Friends of Science' DVD. If Stephen Harper has ever fished, he has never fished with Barry Cooper.

The whole Montgomery attack on climate skeptics is, in fact, a product of a little collection of people within the Suzuki axis of climate fear, based in Vancouver.

Last Friday, I twice called Mr Montgomery at his Emerald City office in Vancouver. A guy named Chris said Charles would be in soon. Within about an hour of the second call, however, the following e-mail arrived:

> *Dear Terence,*
> *I got a message at the office suggesting you wanted to talk about climate change. Unfortunately I'll be out of the office on holiday for 10 days, then only around occasionally until Sept. 6.*
>
> *I suspect you wanted to talk about my piece in the Globe. I try to let my stories speak for themselves, and let the continued discussion about the science take place between the folks who are actually engaged in the science. If you would like to speak directly with scientists working in the field of climate, let me know and I'll forward contacts to you. I believe you are already in touch with members of 'Friends of Science,' as [their head] Albert Jacobs told me that you were their biggest supporter in the media.*
> *Cheers,*
> *Charles Montgomery*

Even in his notes Mr Montgomery gets it wrong. I have never previously talked to Albert Jacobs, never mentioned him or 'Friends of Science' in a column, never published any of their work, have in fact never been in touch with the group. Now we know how Mr. Montgomery came to believe in rainmaking stones.
—**Terrence Corcoran,** Financial Post

CHAPTER TWENTY-NINE

Radio Interview, One of Hundreds

Thank you to Ken Coffman of Stairway Press, for this transcription.

Dr Tim Ball Interviewed on the Mike Rosen Radio Show on October 4, 2011

Mike Rosen is a morning show with AM 850 KOA Radio Station in Denver, Colorado.

The 850 KOA website is www.850koa.com

Tim Ball is a co-author of *Slaying the Sky Dragon: Death of the Greenhouse Gas Theory* published by Stairway Press (www.StairwayPress.com).

Mike Rosen: On many occasions, we have brought forth for your edification and to support your position if you're one of those who are skeptical about the impact of human activity on climate change…we've brought forth any number of qualified experts in this area. Contrary to what you're told by the liberal media—there are people who are qualified scientists who haven't jumped on the AGW—that's Anthropogenic Global Warming—theory. It's just that the liberal media doesn't give voice to very many of those and deny the existence of more, much more, than a handful …and a growing number I should note, of scientists who have not entered that bandwagon…or left the bandwagon.

We'll be talking to Doctor Tim Ball this hour, and he along with a number of other qualified scientists and experts in various fields have combined to produce a book called *Slaying the Sky Dragon: Death of the Greenhouse Gas Theory*. I'll have Dr. Ball tell you about some of his colleagues who contributed to this book.

Dr. Ball himself is a renowned environmental consultant who retired as a professor of climatology from the University of Winnipeg. He served on many local boards and national committees and has chaired provincial boards on water management, environmental issues and sustainable development. He's given over six-hundred public talks over the last decade on science and the environment. He also participated in a British Channel 4 documentary…*The Great Global Warming Swindle*. That has been on my web page. Dave Lauer, my producer, would you check and see if that *Great Global Warming Swindle* link is still on my web page? We put it up there some time ago and on one or two occasions it disappeared as the link moved. It's a definitive response to the purveyors of Al Gore's kind of global warming alarmism.

This book, again, is *Slaying the Sky Dragon*…Dr. Tim Ball is with us right now. Tim, thanks for joining us this morning.

Tim Ball: Thanks for the opportunity, Mike.

MR: Tell us about the other people who collaborated with you in putting this book together.

TB: They are a group of specialists, physicists in various aspects of the atmosphere. I was very proud to be invited to join with them because I, as a climatologist, am actually a generalist. Climatology is a general discipline—it has to incorporate every aspect of the world and its atmosphere and try to put it all together in the enormous, complex puzzle that is global climate. One of the things I realized very, very early was that everybody is a specialist now a'days and of course each person is looking at one piece of the puzzle, but we really haven't got the box top and we don't understand the box top. One of my concerns all along was that CO_2 just didn't appear to be a greenhouse gas and so I was delighted when the fellow authors advised me that they had looked at the physics of it and it just simply didn't add up. So, of course, that was what enticed me. Just to illustrate the point, Mike, one of the great breakthroughs that you'd know about, and your listeners know about, was the hockey stick. This famous graph in the 2001 IPCC[1] report...

MR: This was the work of Michael Mann, if I recall.

TB: Yes, Michael Mann. Exactly. It introduced him to the world. Well, Steve McIntyre[2] was at a conference. He's a statistician...one of those specialists. And he saw this graph up on the screen—didn't know what it was, but realized from his experience of looking at mining claims, which are some of the most fraudulent things you can get. He realized what was wrong with this graph statistically. He started digging into it—discovered it was a climate graph and that's how the hockey stick got broken.

The Slayers, my fellow authors, the Slayers are doing exactly the same thing with the argument about CO_2. One of the things I want the listeners to think about is that they have managed to get the whole world focused on CO_2, which is less than 4%[3] of the total greenhouse gases and they've turned that into controlling global energy policy in a way that's completely unnecessary. The thing that bothered me all along...I knew this back in 1991, they were claiming that an increase in CO_2 would cause an increase in temperature and that was going to occur because of human addition of CO_2. They claim that would result in global warming and runaway global warming. I knew from the records, the ice core record in particular...the person that brought this out, Jean-Robert Petit[4] ...the French researcher said don't rush to judgment on this. What they were pointing at was the fact that in that record, the temperature increased before the CO_2.

Since that time, I have been challenging anybody to show me a record where CO_2 increase precedes temperature increase. Not to create hyperbole with this, Mike—hypotheses are based on assumptions. You don't attack the hypothesis; you attack the assumptions on which it's based. You saw this the other day when that group in Europe came out and said that they found something going faster than the speed of light. Einstein's theory assumes that nothing can go faster than the speed of light. If you can show that's wrong, then the whole theory collapses. Particularly, the formula, $e = mc^2$ and c is the speed of light in that formula, evolves from that. This is why I was so excited to be able to work with the [Sky] Dragon Slayers because they were able to show what was wrong with the physics of the CO_2 part of the greenhouse gas idea.

MR: Let me go back to something you said a few moments ago, since this is fundamental. You acknowledge or you recognize that the key assumption in this AGW—Anthropogenic Global Warming theory—is that climate change is caused by an increase in CO_2, but what you counter with is, that CO_2 [increase] is one of the consequences of temperature increases. That it's the result and not the cause. The cause is from other sources.

TB: Exactly. One of the things that everybody noticed...by the way, one of the keys to watch in all of this stuff is when they keep moving the goalposts...one of the classic moves of the goalposts that gave the Slayers even more credibility is they were talking initially about global warming. That was the big issue. Some are still using that phrase, but the majority moved on to climate change. The reason they did that was, beginning about 2000, the global temperatures started to go down, albeit slightly, but that's accelerating and CO_2 continued to increase. This goes to what Thomas Huxley referred to a hundred years ago as the great tragedy of science...the great bane of

---

[1] The iconic hockey stick graph was based on a 1999 Mann, Bradley and Hughes paper (*Northern Hemisphere Temperatures during the Past Millennium: Inferences, Uncertainties, and Limitations*) that appeared in the journal Geophysical Research Letters and appeared in the 2001 IPCC Third Assessment Report and the Synthesis Report Summary for Policy Makers. IPCC stands for Intergovernmental Panel on Climate Change.
[2] Steve McIntyre is the host of the popular website ClimateAudit.org
[3] Four percent includes water vapour which is by far the most dominant "greenhouse" gas. Right now, CO_2 comprises less than 390PPM (0.039%) of the atmosphere.
[4] Jean-Robert Petit, director of research at the National Centre for Scientific Research in Grenoble, France

science…a lovely hypothesis destroyed by an ugly fact.

Nature wasn't complying with their theory and their predictions. So, they switched from talking about global warming to global climate change.

This is ludicrous because the climate changes all the time. What was even more amusing to me, though not particularly pleasant, was that I was called a climate change denier on the front page of The London Times in England…with all the holocaust implications of that term. My whole career was spent trying to educate people about the extent that climate changes in relatively short time periods. They had to make the move [to climate change] because nature was not complying with their hypothesis. Focus on CO_2, that's the key, critical assumption in the whole AGW theory.

MR: Let's take a break here. When we come back, let me run by you something I crafted from a variety of corroborating sources about the relatively meager influence of CO_2 given all the other variables and you can tell me if there is anything wrong with this little calculation I've put together. Dr. Tim Ball is our guest, one of the collaborators of a book called *Slaying the Sky Dragon: Death of the Greenhouse Gas Theory*.

[Break]

MR: Dr. Tim Ball, our guest. The book: *Slaying the Sky Dragon: Death of the Greenhouse Gas Theory*. You referred to CO_2 as a trace gas. Here's a series of multiplications that gets us to the impact of cap and trade legislation as it was proposed on the percentage of CO_2 output. Number 1, all greenhouse gases account for only two percent of the total atmosphere. Is that correct?

TB: Yes.

MR: Okay. 3.62 percent…I think you rounded it up to four…only 3.62 percent of greenhouse gases are CO_2?

TB: Yeah. What I said was less than four.

MR: Okay. 3.4 percent of CO_2 is caused by human activity.

TB: That's the claim, and unfortunately the source for that is the IPCC which is the source for all the other bad science.

MR: For argument's sake, let's give them the benefit of the doubt on that one.

TB: Yeah, exactly.

MR: Twenty-two percent of the world's CO_2 emissions come from the U.S.

TB: Yes. I believe that's changed recently with the numbers out of China, but yes, for the sake of argument. As they say…close enough for government work.

MR: Cap and trade was supposed to reduce U.S. CO_2 output by fifteen percent. That's what they said. So, here's the math. If you multiply two-percent by 3.62 percent by 3.4 percent by 15 percent…you get about eight one-hundred-thousandths of one-percent. That would be the ultimate effect of cap-and-trade legislation when you qualify all of the other limitations on man's influence on the production of CO_2 gases in the atmosphere. Eight one-hundred-thousandths of one-percent. How can that be a significant factor?

TB: It isn't a significant factor. Just to put that in an even greater perspective, the way I presented it to the public, because that's the issue and it's been a problem for the Slayers, is explaining the science in a way the average public can understand. We have to hand [Al] Gore the credit for that because his piece of propaganda did a good job. The way I've explained it, if you took everybody off the planet...got rid of the industry and everything else, and left one scientist behind, to have her measure the amount of CO_2 reduction because humans are no longer here, she would not be able to measure the difference.

It's a similar kind of analogy to what you're making. The other side of it...you have to realize the evidence is showing that CO_2 is not a greenhouse gas at all. In fact, the Slayers are arguing that it [CO_2] is actually a cooling agent.

MR: Explain how that works.

TB: Because it takes in heat energy and radiates it to space.[5] The atmosphere is actually a cooling agent, not a heating agent. That's one of the fundamental problems in the assumptions they make in their greenhouse theory explanation of why the world is warmer than it should be. Think about how much the temperature drops when you get a solar eclipse...a total eclipse going by. Or how much the temperature drops at nighttime. Simply remove the source of heat energy...the sun...the Earth gets rid of that heat quickly. The Earth is basically cooled and its only heat energy is from the sun. The fundamental ideas built into their greenhouse gas theory simply don't work. Even worse than that, the Earth's atmosphere doesn't work like a greenhouse anyway. I've been arguing that for a long time.

There are certain terminologies, like holes in the ozone...there's another one, there are no holes in the ozone, there's an area of thinning, but even at its thinnest, it's one-third the average...but these things get into our lexicon and you can't get rid of them. People say it's already established because it's a word in our dictionary, therefore it can't be wrong. That's all part of the struggle. It's a struggle of terminology, of exploitation of ideas, and so on.

By the way, Mike, I gave a presentation at the recent Heartland's Conference in Washington [DC]. Behind the scenes, there is increasing discussion about whether CO_2 is a greenhouse gas or not. That's considered heresy by a lot of the skeptics. What we've had is the Warmists and the Skeptics. If you're a proper 'Skeptic'...all scientists should be skeptics, you don't accept at face-value what the skeptic is saying, though you generally agree with their approach. Saying CO_2 is not a greenhouse gas is unacceptable to the majority on both sides of the argument. That's one of the difficulties the Slayers are confronting. They're arguing it with the numbers as you're doing. Showing the numbers that show this can't possibly be a factor.

MR: I'm not even sure this conversation is taking place. The reason I say that is...I am told that you don't exist. You're a qualified scientist, a climatologist, a generalist, as a matter of fact, with a broad overview. I'm told by Al Gore and company that there are no qualified people who disagree with their theory.

TB: That was one of the first telltale signs of how political the climate change issue...the global warming issue...had become. It was Gore and others that started what is called the "consensus" argument where the majority of scientists agree and therefore, if you're in the minority, you must be wrong. What's interesting about that, Mike, is that's a political argument. Consensus has nothing to do with science. Consensus is not a scientific fact. Einstein said I can have a hundred facts to prove me right, but I only need one fact to prove me wrong...and I'm wrong. The consensus argument was started when they were promoting...the ones who agreed were all in the IPCC and

---

[5] Dr. Ball misstates the Sky Dragon Slayer a little bit here. The most powerful conveyors of heat energy are conduction followed by convection. When you add a molecule to the atmosphere that wasn't there before, this naturally increases conduction and convection which couple heat from the Earth's surface to space. This factor is not part of the accounting of any 'Warmists' analysis of the Earth's average temperature. —KLC

yet, the majority of them are bureaucrats. They're not even climate scientists at all. The numbers game underlines how political this issue has become.

MR: Let's see…there's you, there's Richard Lindzen, the meteorology professor at MIT, there's Edward Krug and Fred Singer, the climatologist, Roy Spencer, the University of Alabama climatologist, Sally Baliunas, Harvard Center of Astrophysics, Hugh Alcazar at the Lawrence Livermore National Lab, I've got a list here of about a hundred and that's only the tip of the iceberg. Doctor Arthur Robinson has signatures of thousands of qualified scientists on a petition taking issue with this global warming orthodoxy.

TB: One of the things that's gone on, and you're seeing it in your election politics…is really nasty, really dirty and really personal. What's happened…for a scientist to stand up and say they disagreed with the official science, was almost suicide. I know a lot of scientists that would say to me that they agree with you, but we're not prepared to speak out. Your funding got threatened. Richard Lindzen had that problem. The interesting side, showing how political it was, if you, as a scientist came out and said you didn't agree with the hypothesis, you were immediately branded as right-wing, conservative in Canada and so on, and that was an insult. A lot of scientists said we agree with you, but we are of a socialist persuasion or a left-wing persuasion. If we speak out, we're immediately branded as conservatives, and we don't want that.

MR: Is this some kind of global warming McCarthyism that we're talking about here?

TB: Absolutely. It's all designed to isolate and silence. Name your fellow conspirators and so on.

MR: Tim, hold that thought.

[Break]

MR: Doctor Tim Ball is our guest. Co-author, along with a number of collaborators, all qualified scientists of *Slaying the Sky Dragon: Death of the Greenhouse Gas Theory*. Finish that point you were going to make, Tim, then I'll open it up to phone calls. You were in the midst of driving home a good point when I had to break for the news. Do you recall where you were?

TB: Not really. We were talking about the McCarthyism approach…that was another sign of how political this issue had become. What they did was completely thwart the scientific method. Science works by creating a hypothesis based on assumptions…then other scientists working as skeptics try to disprove it. What they did with the greenhouse-AGW hypothesis was put it out, and, as Richard Lindzen said years ago, the consensus was reached before the research had even begun. Then they isolated and attacked anybody that dared to question it. It took the form, initially, of a few scientific arguments, but when those failed, [the arguments] became ad hominem, personal attacks. That's what happened to any of us who dared to stick our heads up. What's happened since then, and the reason you and I are talking today, is because a few courageous people, like the Sky Dragon Slayers, and others, Richard Lindzen and so on, continued to push and get evidence. As the evidence emerges, it shows that the hypothesis is wrong. It's now become so entrenched politically and scientifically with all the funding that's going to it, it's a real uphill battle.

MR: Let's take some phone calls. In Denver, Tom, you're on Denver 850 KOA.

Tom: Good morning. How are you guys doing?

MR: Great.

Tom: I heard both you guys refer to the percentage of CO_2 in the atmosphere as four-percent...

MR: No, no. You heard wrong. I went carefully through the numbers. I think I understand your...misunderstanding. To start with I said that all greenhouse gases account for only two-percent of the atmosphere. And, of that two-percent of the atmosphere, four-percent is CO_2.

Tom: Okay, yeah. That's a big difference.

MR: It's four-percent of two-percent.

Tom: If you had at the Pepsi Center ten-thousand people, and you had people who hold a card up who represented CO_2, it would be four. A total of four. It's really a small number.

MR: Four-percent of two-percent, just to clarify.

Tom: Four-percent of two-percent. Okay. Thanks.

TB: And to put that into even a better perspective, in that Center, when those people were holding their cards up, by the end of the meeting the level of CO_2 in that room would probably be close to two-thousand parts-per-million, yet nobody is suffering from it, and, of course, CO_2 levels in the past, Al Gore says 392 parts-per-million, which it currently is, is the highest ever, when it's in fact, the lowest ever. In the last three-hundred-million years, the average has been between a thousand and twelve-hundred parts-per-million and scientific proof of the importance of that is the CO_2 level plants operate best at. That's being proven in commercial greenhouses where they're pumping CO_2 in to get that level. There's a whole lot of points the gentleman brings attention to.

MR: Here's another analogy that really drives home the point and it's more graphic than percentages. A two-hundred pound man is made up of about 130 pounds or 15.6 gallons of water. Those 15.6 gallons of water, let's say, represent the entire atmosphere. Of those 15.6 gallons of atmosphere, two-percent, or three-tenths of a gallon, represents the greenhouse gas portion of the atmosphere. Of that one-third gallon of greenhouse gases. 3.6 percent or 2.9 tablespoons represents the CO_2 portion of the greenhouse gases worldwide. Of those 2.9 tablespoons of CO_2, 3.4 percent or three-tenths of a teaspoon represents the portion of the CO_2 attributable to worldwide human activity. Of that one-third teaspoon of worldwide CO_2 contribution, twenty-two percent or three-tenths of a gram is attributable to American activity. Of that one-third gram of American CO_2 contribution, fifteen percent or five-one-hundredths of a gram might be eliminated by the cap and trade and other governmental mandates. This is approximately equal to a single drop of water from an eyedropper. That's the relative nature of this.

Let's take another phone call. In Berthoud, John, you're on 850 KOA, Doctor Tim Ball, our guest. Yes, John.

John: I keep hearing its going to raise the sea level, so we took a glass of water and marked it and put an ice cube in it. When the weight of the ice lifted, the water level? When it melted out, it was the same.

MR: That's called displacement.

John: I put this to you...every time a polar bear jumps on the ice cap, it actually raises the sea level.

TB: Al Gore gets a photograph of it and claims it's dying and drowning. John, to your point, if you had a very precise measurement of the water level in that glass, it should go down because water expands when it freezes. The ice cube is actually displacing a larger amount than the water content that it's made of. The Arctic ice which is already in the ocean…when it melts, it doesn't change sea level at all. In fact, it decreases it a bit. What they are talking about is sea level rise due to melting of the big ice caps…Greenland and Antarctica. Most of them are under water, they are already displacing and raising sea level. If they melt, the difference is about seven-percent in volume between water and ice. There was an article in Scientific American about twenty years ago that said you couldn't show there'd be any change in sea level whatsoever.

John: One more question. Who melted the ice age? Was it us?

[Laughs]

TB: No, it was Barney Rubble with his cars. You know that.

MR: Didn't the Time World Atlas recently have to correct its false assertion that the Greenland ice cap was drastically retreating?

TB: Yes. What they did was, they brought out a new atlas that showed a large green area on the east side of Greenland and claimed this was dramatic evidence of the melting Greenland ice cap. The mass of the Greenland ice caps and the Antarctic ice caps have increased. One of the things about ice caps and glaciers is they are as much, if not more, a function of snowfall as they are of temperature and that fact keeps getting ignored.

MR: Let's go to Brighton. Ernie, you're on 850 KOA. Hello Ernie.

Ernie: I was happy to call into you guys this morning. I had a little thing. My son came home from Seventh grade the other day with a science project…a kind of homework assignment that struck me as very strange. I wanted to make sure I had my math correct. It was really driving home the point that as Americans using one gallon of gasoline, we produce twenty-two pounds of Carbon Dioxide—by burning that one gallon. The mathematics of that didn't make any sense to me…how you can have an eight-pound liquid convert to twenty-two pounds of a gas.[6]

TB: That's a very, very good point, Ernie. To elaborate on your point, and by the way, I urge all parents to look at what their children are being taught in school. It's frightening the degree to which one side of the argument is presented in school. I talked earlier about moving the goal posts…one of the things that they did was…as the evidence about CO_2…a gas…started to be shown to be wrong, they started talking about carbon. Of course, carbon is a solid. It had the political advantage. Carbon, that's black and dirty…that's soot. It increased the connotation of another deception they were presenting, that is that CO_2 is a pollutant. It isn't. This is all part of the political game that is being played with the science. You're very astute to observe what you did with your child's homework, Ernie.

MR: Gotta take a break…you're on 850 KOA.

[Break]

---

[6] The homework assignment is actually correct in this instance. The carbon in the gasoline, during combustion, combines with heavier Oxygen molecules to form CO_2. We're not creating matter from nothing, but it's true that burning a gallon of gas (about 6.3 pounds total—about 5.5 pounds of Carbon) will use Oxygen from the atmosphere to create about 22 pounds of CO_2. See: http://www.fueleconomy.gov/feg/co2.shtml —KLC

MR: Doctor Tim Ball, our guest. His book, along with a bevy of qualified scientific coauthors is *Slaying the Sky Dragon: Death of the Greenhouse Gas Theory*. In Denver, Matt, you're on 850 KOA. Hello, Matt.

Matt: Hey guys. What's the longer-term forecast for this whole debate? Meaning, is it ten or twenty years where we see little to no temperature rise or a temperature decrease, I guess, and it's a 'we created or saved the planet' argument? If we hadn't done what we did, we would have had catastrophe. What does it look like in ten or twenty years? How long does it take for this thing to be either squashed or realized?

TB: A very good question, Matt. A couple of interesting things. When you used the word 'forecast', one of the signs that the AGW hypothesis group were wrong, the IPCC were wrong, they stopped doing forecasts and started doing 'scenarios' because their predictions were so wrong.

That was the first giveaway.

Nature's not cooperating, and that's making the public realize there is something seriously wrong with the science. The general consensus…I shouldn't use that term, because it's political, my sense is the majority of the public understand there is something wrong. They don't fully understand. What's giving it gravity now is the grasping of it as a political…tax…vehicle. We're seeing that battle going on in Australia right now, and in other places. Also, the opportunities created by all the government funding going to alternate energies and other things. That's giving the thing momentum.

Another problem I mentioned that we Slayers struggle with…the two things they exploited, fear, the sky is falling idea, and the other is the lack of knowledge or understanding, not only of climate science, but science in general. In a university, you can divide [the students] into 80% who are art students and 20% that are science students and that's true of the general population. Nature is doing a very good job. Just a couple of cold winters really put the chill on the global warming theory and made people start to ask questions. Once we can get the politicians to listen to all sides of the debate…and that's part of the issue…then I think maybe another three or four years at the most.

MR: How dare they say the science is settled?

TB: Al Gore made that comment when he appeared before the U. S. Congress. In that appearance, he broke all the rules. For example, when I went there, I had to submit everything I was going to say. I had to be done by a certain time. Al Gore didn't submit anything. He walked in at the last minute and gave a presentation and that's was where that statement [was made], 'the science is settled'. Interestingly enough, those sorts of comments catch.

It's amazing. I was stunned when I saw it. I thought, okay, that's rubbish. But the majority, even the mainstream media, said 'hang on a minute. Science is never settled. These kind of extremist statements serve to make people stop and say 'hang on a minute. What are you really saying here?' In a way, the more silly the statements are, the better it is to show what's wrong with the science.

MR: Matt, thanks for your call. Time for one more quick call, then we're done this hour. Dick Armey coming up the next hour. In Denver, John, you're on 850 KAO, about a minute left, John.

John: Mike, thank you for taking my call. I'm sure everybody will find this interesting. I am not a doubter as far as the dispute…as far as global warming. I understand…I think this is a flawed theory. But I do know it's documented that the water level of the Earth was substantially higher. So, if it didn't go into ice, what happened that we have a much larger land mass now than we had at different periods of time in our history.

TB: There are two things about that, John. One is that changes in the sea level are called eustatic[7] changes and they're occurring all the time. The biggest change occurred most recently during the last ice age when the sea level dropped about 150 meters or 450 feet as the water was taken out to form the great ice sheets on the land. The increase in sea level over the last ten-thousand years was very dramatic as that water came back into the sea.[8]

MR: You'll have to read the book: *Slaying the Sky Dragon* for the rest. Tim, thanks for being with us.

Miscellaneous Musings

TRANSCRIPTS OFFICE
STEWART HOUSE
32 RUSSELL SQUARE
LONDON WC1B 5DN

• Fax 020 7862 8300• e-mail transcripts@lon.ac.uk

Direct Line: 020 7862 8380

Ref: EISA/Int/LC/JCT/SDY   28 June 2006

TO WHOM IT MAY CONCERN

This is to certify that

Timothy Francis BALL

of

Queen Mary College

was awarded the degree of **Doctor of Philosophy** in the Faculty of Science on 26 October 1983 as an Internal Student. The Field of Study was **Climatology** and the thesis was entitled **"Climatic Change in Central Canada: A Preliminary Analysis of Weather Information from the Hudson's Bay Company Forte at York Factory and Churchill Factory. 1714 - 1852 ."**

[signature]

G F ROBERTS (Mrs)
Academic Registrar

As a PhD is awarded following a course of research, it is not possible to supply a transcript or marks and grades.

This document is not official unless it contains the stamped signature of the Academic Registrar and her embossed seal

---

[7] From Dictionary.com:
Eustatic: Any uniformly global change of sea level that may reflect a change in the quantity of water in the ocean, or a change in the shape and capacity of the ocean basins.

[8] Tim's time ran out before he was able complete his answer to this question. Here are his additional comments: "I wanted to say to the last question that there were eustatic changes of sea level but there were also isostatic changes of land level and often it is difficult to sort out what is happening along coastline. Isostatic change along the U.S. Gulf Coast has been presented incorrectly as eustatic change. You also have the problem that sea level isn't level but varies with changing gravity within the earth's crust and also with atmospheric pressure. The idea of human-caused seal level change is another example of a very complex situation being simplistically used to support a political argument."

CHAPTER THIRTY
Published Articles by Tim

Climate Change—Consensus vs. Science—Tim's article in Dialogue Magazine

Global Warming is not due to human contribution of Carbon Dioxide

—*Global Warming: The Cold, Hard Facts?* Dr. Timothy Ball, Victoria BC, February, 2007

GLOBAL WARMING, AS we think we know it, doesn't exist. And I am not the only one trying to make people open up their eyes and see the truth. But few listen, despite the fact that I was the first Canadian Ph.D. in Climatology and I have an extensive background in climatology, especially the reconstruction of past climates and the impact of climate change on human history and the human condition. Few listen, even though I have a Ph.D. (Doctor of Science) from the University of London, England, and was a climatology professor at the University of Winnipeg. For some reason (actually for many), the world is not listening.

Here is why.

What would happen if tomorrow we were told that, after all, the Earth is flat? It would probably be the most important piece of news in the media and would generate a lot of debate. So why is it that when scientists who have studied the Global Warming phenomenon for years say that humans are not the cause nobody listens? Why does no one acknowledge that the Emperor has no clothes?

Believe it or not, Global Warming is not due to human contribution of Carbon Dioxide (CO_2).

This, in fact, is the greatest deception in the history of science. We are wasting time, energy and trillions of dollars while creating unnecessary fear and consternation over an issue with no scientific justification. For example, Environment Canada brags about spending $3.7 billion in the last five years dealing with climate change, almost all on propaganda trying to defend an indefensible scientific position, while at the same time closing weather stations and failing to meet legislated pollution targets.

No sensible person seeks conflict, especially with governments, but if we don't pursue the truth, we are lost as individuals and as a society.

That is why I insist on saying that there is no evidence that we are, or could ever cause, global climate change. And, recently, Yuri A. Izrael, Vice President of the United Nations sponsored Intergovernmental Panel on Climate Change (IPCC) confirmed this statement. So how has the world come to believe that something is wrong?

Maybe for the same reason we believed 30 years ago, that global cooling was the biggest threat: a matter of faith. "It is a cold fact: the Global Cooling presents humankind with the most important social, political, and adaptive challenge we have had to deal with for ten thousand years. Your stake in the decisions we make concerning it is of ultimate importance; the survival of ourselves, our children, our species." wrote Lowell Ponte in 1976.

I was as opposed to the threats of impending doom (that) "Global Cooling" engendered as I am to the threats made about Global Warming. Let me stress I am not denying the phenomenon has occurred. The world has warmed since 1680, the nadir of a cool period called the Little Ice Age (LIA), that has generally continued to the present. These climate changes are well within natural variability and explained quite easily by changes in the sun.

But there is nothing unusual going on.

Since I obtained my doctorate in climatology from the University of London, Queen Mary College, England, my career has spanned two climate cycles. Temperatures declined from 1940 to 1980 and in the early 1970's global cooling became the consensus. This proves that consensus is not a scientific fact. By the 1990's temperatures appeared to have reversed and Global Warming became the consensus. It appears I'll witness another cycle before retiring, as the major mechanisms and the global temperature trends now indicate a cooling.

No doubt passive acceptance yields less stress, fewer personal attacks and makes career progress easier. What I have experienced in my personal life during the last years makes me understand why most people choose not to speak out; job security and fear of reprisals. Even in university, where free speech and challenge to prevailing wisdoms are supposedly encouraged, academics remain silent.

I once received a three-page letter that my lawyer defined as libellous, from an academic colleague, saying I had no right to say what I was saying, especially in public lectures. Sadly, my experience is that universities are the most dogmatic and oppressive places in our society. This becomes progressively worse as they receive more and more funding from governments that demand a particular viewpoint.

In another instance, I was accused by Canadian environmentalist David Suzuki of being paid by oil companies. That is a lie. Apparently he thinks if the fossil fuel companies pay, you have an agenda. So if Greenpeace, Sierra Club or governments pay there is no agenda and only truth and enlightenment?

Personal attacks are difficult and shouldn't occur in a debate in a civilized society. I can only consider them from (the perspective of) what they imply. They usually indicate a person or group is losing the debate. In this case, they also indicate how political the entire Global Warming debate has become. Both underline the lack of or even contradictory nature of the evidence.

I am not alone in this journey against the prevalent myth. Several well-known names have also raised their voices. Michael Crichton, the scientist, writer and filmmaker is one of them. In his latest book, *State of Fear*, he takes time to explain, often in surprising detail, the flawed science behind Global Warming and other imagined environmental crises.

Another cry in the wilderness is Dr Richard Lindzen's. He is an atmospheric physicist and a professor of meteorology at MIT, renowned for his research in dynamic meteorology—especially atmospheric waves. He is also a member of the National Academy of Sciences and has held positions at the University of Chicago, Harvard University and MIT.

Lindzen frequently speaks out against the notion that significant global warming is caused by humans. Yet nobody seems to listen.

I think it may be because most people don't understand the scientific method which Thomas Kuhn so skillfully and briefly set out in his book, *The Structure of Scientific Revolutions*. A scientist makes certain assumptions and then produces a theory, which is only as valid as the assumptions. The theory of Global Warming assumes that CO_2 is an atmospheric greenhouse gas and, as it increases, temperatures rise. It was then theorized that since humans were producing more CO_2 than before, the temperature would inevitably rise. The theory was accepted before testing had started, and effectively became a law.

As Dr Lindzen said many years ago: "the consensus was reached before the research had even begun." Now, any scientist who dares to question the prevailing wisdom is marginalized and called a sceptic, when in fact they are simply being good scientists. This has reached frightening levels with these scientists now being called climate change denier with all the holocaust connotations of that word. The normal scientific method is effectively being thwarted.

Meanwhile, politicians are being listened to, even though most of them have no knowledge or understanding of science, especially the science of climate and climate change. Hence, they are in no position to question a policy on climate change when it threatens the entire planet. Moreover, using fear and creating hysteria makes it very difficult to make calm rational decisions about issues needing attention.

Until you have challenged the prevailing wisdom, you have no idea how nasty people can be. Until you have re-examined any issue, in an attempt to find out all the information, you cannot know how much misinformation exists in the supposed age of information.

I was greatly influenced several years ago by Aaron Wildavsky's book *But is it True?* The author taught political science at a New York University and realized how science was being influenced by and apparently misused by politics. He gave his graduate students an assignment to pursue the science behind a policy generated by a highly publicized environmental concern. To his and their surprise they found there was little scientific evidence, consensus and justification for the policy. You only realize the extent to which Wildavsky's findings occur when you ask the question he posed. Wildavsky's students did it in the safety of academia and with the excuse that it was an assignment. I have learned it is a difficult question to ask in the real world, however I firmly believe it is the most important question to ask if we are to advance in the right direction.

Dr. Timothy Ball is a Victoria-based environmental consultant and former climatology professor at the University of Winnipeg. He is science advisor to Friends of Science [www. friendsofscience.org/] and also to the International Climate Science Coalition [www.climatescienceinternational.org/]
—*Timothy F. Ball*, PhD, Victoria BC

Methods and Tricks Used to Create and Perpetuate the Human-Caused Global Warming Deception, as published on the *Watts Up with That* website

Guest Opinion: Dr. Tim Ball—2018

These opening comments will trigger knee-jerk responses from proponents of the human-caused global warming deception. Just saying President Trump is sufficient to trigger them. However, when I add that he handled the Lesley Stahl CBS interview well, the comments will appear without them reading any further. Poke them, and they blindly respond triggered by the tunnel-vision of political ideology and the source of their funding.

This article is a response to an interesting experience involving an article I wrote for WUWT. As most readers know, I rarely reply to comments and almost never go back to read my earlier articles. While preparing to produce another article I needed to confirm something from one of these articles. I was astonished to read that in response to a complaint from two researchers Anthony added a foreword to the article.

It is Anthony's website, and he is entitled to control it however he chooses. Over the years there were several cases when he questioned, challenged, ask for a revision, or simply would not publish a comment. However, we always worked these out to our mutual satisfaction. One of the things I did to offset many of Anthony's concerns was to place the qualifier 'Guest Opinion' after each headline. Again, I am not challenging Anthony's right to add the qualifier to the article in question. My concern is what triggered his action. I immediately recognized the technique used by the perpetrators and believe that everyone should understand what was done. Problems are only problems if you are unaware of them. That is also true about biases.

I am more than qualified to speak about this topic after 40 years of dealing with all types of media and people on all sides of an issue in a variety of formats from all over the world. Besides this university of the real world, I took courses in communication and media as part of officer training in the military and continued as a student and practitioner ever since. Clear patterns emerge, a few of which I discuss here, however, the overall pattern is that the mainstream media was unchanged for at least 236 years.

It was and remains a vehicle for the power elite, as William Cowper's 1782 poem The Progress of Error reveals.

How shall I speak of thee or thy power address,
The God of our idolatry, the press?
By thee, religion, liberty and laws

Everything Reminds Me of Tim

Exert their influence and advance their cause;
By thee worse plagues than Pharaoh's land befell,
Diffused, make Earth the vestibule of Hell:
Thou fountain, at which drink the good and wise;
Thou ever-bubbling spring of endless lies;
Like Eden's dead probationary tree,
Knowledge of good and evil is from thee!

What changed was the advent of the Internet that bypassed the mainstream media and gave ordinary citizens access to more information than many governments had in the past. It meant that people using the Internet developed the methods and tricks of the mainstream media. Change the word 'press' in Cowper's poem to the Internet, and you see what I mean.

I was part of a group gathered in Washington in November 2015 to talk about policy for climate and the Environmental Protection Agency (EPA) during a campaign of Trump for the presidency. The consensus was that he should avoid making decisions based on bad science. It is bad science, but at least 80% of the public don't understand any science; therefore, they cannot identify bad science. In addition, no matter how much you prepare, somebody will ask a question you can't answer, and it only needs one. Instead, he should exit the Paris Climate Agreement because it is a bad deal and fits his main theme of improving or expunging them.

As the media loses its power and control over the information the people access most, they chose to become aggressive, uncivil, devious, and biased. I experienced it as they changed. It is telling that the Fox News slogan is 'Fair and Balanced. They did it because the competition was no longer fair and balanced. Of course, Fox News only pays lip service to the idea by having a few token liberals in what are, from my observations, contrived and stupid.

The technique of mainstream media interviews was on full display in the Stahl interview. The interviewer begins by establishing a false premise, with a false fact, or a quote from a person who doesn't know the subject. Stahl did it with the information about Greenland ice chunks breaking off and raising sea level. It is a technique used throughout the environmental and the human-caused global warming hysteria.

For example, Paul Ehrlich already established the false premise of overpopulation in his 1968 book *The Population Bomb*. In 1977 he followed it up in a book, *Ecoscience*, co-authored with John Holdren, Obama's Science Advisor with proposals for mitigating the false problem. One proposal said:

> *Indeed, it has been concluded that compulsory population-control laws, even including laws requiring compulsory abortion, could be sustained under the existing Constitution if the population crisis became sufficiently severe to endanger the society.*

That sounds reasonable on the face of it. However, you understand the deception when you ask questions that expose the technique.

- Who concluded that such laws were sustainable?
- Who decides there is a population crisis?
- Who decides when it endangers society.

In each case, the answer is, they do.

Maurice Strong and the creators of Agenda 21 introduced a similar technique when listing the Principles for that Global Policy Document. It incorporated the most popular justification for action by environmentalists, namely the precautionary principle. If the facts are not available, then argue that we should act 'just in case.'

Here it is as Principle 15:

> *In order to protect the environment, the precautionary approach shall be widely applied by States according to their capabilities. Where there are threats of serious or irreversible damage, lack of full scientific certainty shall not be used as a reason for postponing cost-effective measures to prevent environmental degradation.*

Again, it sounds reasonable, especially to the casual reader. The questions are:

- Who decides the environment needs 'protecting?'
- Who decides how to protect the environment?
- Who decides which States are capable?
- Who decides the level of capability?
- Who decides what are 'serious threats?'
- Who decides when the damage is approaching an ability to reverse it?
- Who decides what is an appropriate level of 'scientific certainty?'
- Who decides what 'cost-effective' measures are?

Again, the answer is they do.

I quickly learned that the first thing you must do is question the false premise. This brings me to the issue that triggered this article. I went back to an article on the need to address the motive behind the AGW deception. I argued that once you get the public accepting that the idea that science was corrupted to produce a predetermined outcome. This involved narrowing the science through definitions and limitations of variables to a focus on CO_2. After they accept these ideas, the next logical question is to ask about the motive? I pointed out in the article that in many recent media interviews this was one of the first questions.

Anybody who reads the comments about articles on Watts Up with That knows the pattern of responses and the core of people and their positions. I know the comments that topics will elicit. The most predictable responses are whenever the question of motive is raised. The perpetrators and ongoing supporters of the AGW deception used it to push a socialist agenda.

The complaint from the two people appeared as an article titled 'A big goose-step backward' and was referenced by Anthony Watts at the beginning of my original article.

https://wattsupwiththat.com/2014/11/23/......people-starting-to-ask-about-motive-for-massive-IPCC deception/

I will not repeat their names, suffice to comment on the obvious bias because of their positions and funding, identified by several people in their comments. As Upton Sinclair said:

> *It is difficult to get a man to understand something when his salary depends upon his not understanding it.*

I know the Upton quote is sexist as stated, but its still applicable to all with salaries.

Their complaint was about the use of the word denier to describe those who questioned the IPCC science. It was in the context of the change from Global Warming skeptics to climate change deniers. I added, the phrase, with all the holocaust connotations of the word, hence the reference to goose-stepping. They began their complaint with establishing a false and emotional premise designed to marginalize any who might question their charge. They introduced the word 'Nazi' followed by the claim I was debasing the entire debate. I never used the word 'Nazi.' I referred to the use of the term because I lived through the evolution of the word denier in the climate debate. The term was deliberately and carefully chosen for precisely the connotation I gave it.

To understand the tenor and tone of what went on, consider Michael Mann's comment in a 2004 email about the RealClimate website,

> ...the important thing is to make sure they're loosing (sic) the PR battle. That's what the site is about.

On that website, a question on 16 December 2004 asks:

> Is there really 'consensus' in the scientific community on the reality of anthropogenic climate change?

They provided their answer on 22 December 2004:

> We've used the term 'consensus' here a bit recently without ever really defining what we mean by it. In normal practice, there is no great need to define it—no science depends on it. But it's useful to record the core that most scientists agree on, for public presentation. The consensus that exists is that of the IPCC reports, in particular the working group I report (there are three WG's. By 'IPCC', people tend to mean WG I).

The second sentence is the key to their deceptive practices. They acknowledge that consensus does not apply to science, but then use it because it will deceive the public. And what is the consensus, on which they agree? The scientists at the IPCC agree, therefore there is a consensus.

In the same year, 2004, emails between Nick at the Minns/Tyndall Centre, the group involved in handling PR for the people at the Climatic Research Unit (CRU), identified their dilemma.

He wrote:

> In my experience, global warming freezing is already a bit of a public relations problem with the media.

Swedish alarmist and climate expert on the IPCC, Bo Kjellen replied:

> I agree with Nick that climate change might be a better labelling than global warming.

In that year, across the media, the term global warming was replaced by the term climate change, when talking about the work of the IPCC and the threat to the world. However, they didn't leave it there. Global Warming Skeptics became Climate Change Deniers.

Why make that change?

The switch from Global Warming was necessary to hide the fact that their theory no longer matched the evidence. It would have been reasonable to simply call those who continued to question the science, Climate Change Skeptics, but they decided not to do that.

The answer to that question involves the nature of another debate on the front page at the time, namely the battles with David Irving, renowned Holocaust Denier. He went to trial in 2001 and was sentenced and jailed in 2006. If you are interested, the recreation of the events and entire trial were portrayed in a movie called *Denial*.

The motive behind the entire misuse of climate for a political agenda was to create a world government. Maurice Strong made that clear to Elaine Dewar who concluded after five days with him at the UN and hearing him explain his goals that:

> *Strong was using the U.N. as a platform to sell a global environment crisis and the Global Governance Agenda.*

If you are not convinced that the people at the CRU would connive and manipulate both the science and the people, go and read the leaked emails.

On the back of their book, Crutapes, Mosher and Fuller summarized them for you:

- Actively worked to evade (Steve) McIntyre's Freedom of Information requests, deleting emails, documents, and even climate data
- Tried to corrupt the peer-review principles that are the mainstay of modern science, reviewing each other's work, sabotaging efforts of opponents trying to publish their own work, and threatening editors of journals who didn't bow to their demands
- Changed the shape of their own data in materials shown to politicians charged with changing the shape of our world, "hiding the decline" that showed their data could not be trusted.

If you don't think the fight is political with all the accompanying nastiness, lies and deceits, then ask yourself why, if you accept the theory of AGW you are liberal and informed. However, if you question at all, you are conservative and uninformed, regardless of your actual political views. It is the nature of the left to attack the individual in the vilest ways possible and without any evidence. It is their nature to isolate those who dare to question their orthodoxy.

No, I will not be bullied by those with a political agenda and vested interests. I stand by my comment about the connotations of the use of the phrase holocaust deniers. Besides, I lived through the war in England and know what the Germans did.

CHAPTER THIRTY-ONE
2007 to 2022

Marty and Tim 2019

IN JUNE 2007, Tim's shortness of breath became a problem. Our family doctor Dr. Ewa Jusak-Kiellerman, sent Tim to a cardiac surgeon, Dr Lynn Fedoruk. She did a quintuple cardiac bypass. Dr Fedoruk said the primary obstruction was his first heart attack in 1986. The circulation had already formed collaborative routes.

Recovery took a while, but Tim eventually returned to the lecture circuit until March 2017, when the symptoms started again.

For almost three years, I looked after him as best I could. I told him it wasn't easy to curl up your toes and die just like that. It is challenging to look after someone without the will to live. I wanted him to walk or go outside, eat properly, call friends or email them. The answer was always, not right now, maybe later.

Later never came.

He often lamented that he never made any difference to the world. He also regretted every day that he had ruined my and our children's lives. He felt abandoned by everyone, and I mean everyone.

We assured him that was absolutely not true. All the effort he spent in teaching, writing and answering media questions repeatedly was incredibly valuable, even though he felt it was meaningless. The family always looked forward to seeing him on TV, in the newspapers, or hearing him on the radio. We were always proud of his determination to speak the truth as he learned it. Tim regularly reminded me that he never even told me half of what he knew was happening in the world to protect me. He said I could not handle this if I knew what he knew. He always tried to protect me, and I appreciated it more than he knew.

He gradually slipped into more and more despair, dying inch by inch. The family and I felt helpless. He never answered the phone and eventually stopped answering emails. He used his iPad to watch documentaries and listen to music mainly. He even stopped watching sports on TV.

Beginning in March 2017 Tim could not lie flat without coughing. He slept in his easy-boy chair for four months. Tim saw seven doctors eleven times without a diagnosis. (This includes three emergency room visits, long wait times, blood tests, and X-rays.)

Even a respirologist missed the two litres of fluid on his lungs. I still find that very difficult to understand.

Everything Reminds Me of Tim

On the Saturday of the May long weekend in 2017, we made our last journey through Emergency at the RJH (Royal Jubilee Hospital). I said to Tim, this is our last hope. Nowhere to go from here today if they don't help you.

What will we do?

We were in luck. The doctor on call, Dr Bruce Sanders ordered that Tim be admitted to the Cardiology unit and have an immediate CAT scan of his chest. (We could have kissed his feet with gratitude. He believed us!!) Dr Sanders drained the two litres of fluid from his lungs the next day. They inserted four cardiac stents in Tim's heart via his radial artery two days after that.

Tim was again well enough to be sent home to recover. He continued to get short of breath on exertion. Our usual small activities, like our walks to downtown Victoria and our Cactus Club lunches on Saturdays restarted. Tim held court at the Cactus Club for over a dozen years. He loved going there with whoever could join us. Vic Dove and Elizabeth Edelbrock were our friends and regular joiners.

From October 2019, Tim could no longer make it downtown—a big disappointment. We took short walks around the Delta Ocean Pointe Resort beside our condo. We would sit on the benches in front of the hotel and look at the most beautiful harbour in the world. I relish these memories.

Tim did not care if his blood sugars were normal or whether he was eating properly. He gained weight and didn't care. He didn't shave every day, as was his lifetime habit. (When he was in RCAF survival training, he got extra marks for shaving every morning.)

On top of COVID-19, the 'Climate Change' hoax and the Great Reset, there wasn't a shred of hope left for the world now, according to Tim. On September 23, 2019, Greta Thunberg had an audience at the United Nations. At that very moment, Tim said, "It's over. We (meaning the world) are finished, and I am finished. If the world wants to be duped, let it be duped." At this point Tim totally gave up his fight for the truth.

During his last three years, his taste buds changed from savoury to sweet, which did his diabetes no good. I tried to keep his blood sugar around 10. This count is unusually high, but he would go into insulin shock if it got down to 6 or 7. None of his doctors seemed to understand that. I worried about the neuropathy in his lower legs and feet. He kept socks on day and night in case he bumped his toes. I hired a nurse who did pedicures and manicures in our home, a real treat for both of us.

Tim eventually had to use a walker. We have a fully carpeted condo and that made for softer falls, most of which were injury free until that fateful night in July of 2022 when he fell at three in the morning while heading to the bathroom on his own. He injured his left elbow, causing excruciating pain. I could not get him into his bed or a chair so I put his head on a pillow, gave him a blanket and called 911.

Marty, Tim Jr and Tim 2021

CHAPTER THIRTY-TWO

Comments by our Oldest Son, David

"There He Was…Gone!"

I FEARED SITTING down to try to describe my father. He often said we should always face our fears. We are at a junction in the complexity of this man. Dad had phobias that were almost impossible to meet. We all wanted to be open and honest, as father desired. We included the letters that lauded him while also voicing their disdain. He would have enjoyed transparency, honesty, and honour, just a few of the things he stood for.

Growing up, we presume everyone's home life was like yours. Every day we learn that this is far from true, both good and bad.

I am blessed to say that my childhood was unbelievably good. I regret not appreciating it more until I had my own family. "Too soon old, too late smart", the old men at the bar used to say. Very true.

My parents went out of their way to let us 'figure it out.' No indoctrination and looking back now, always supported whatever we chose to do.

It is surprising how much I retained of what my parents taught us, even though, at the time, I found it exceedingly dull. I was so wrong. The things we talked about and the places we visited were all exciting. They encompassed every field of study. Art, science, history, music, architecture, military events and their historical significance, geography, geology, archaeology, etc., were just a glimpse of our discussions at home and travelling. Your eyes open when you understand how things connect in myriad ways.

The first time I was able to connect historic dots triggered in me a thirst for knowledge. I love driving down roads on which I've never travelled. Finding a knowledge nugget must release endorphins in me. How else can I describe it?

Father came to respect my choice to use my hands to make a living. I was not the academic type.

Dad had trouble telling us he loved us, but his actions made it abundantly clear.

His last smile to me on the day he died said more than any words could, and it let me know I remain on the right track now.

The man stood for truth and honesty in everything. He was greatly distressed by the direction the world had taken. I made sure I let him know that he had done more than any other human being. He especially loved the average person, as he was aware that he too, was the same. He was known to have coffee with the caretakers of the university.

One thing that astounded me, and I still think he has an untapped wealth of knowledge and experience, was Dad's Contemporary World Issues class for senior citizens. I was fortunate to have been able to sit in on what was a phenomenal study in civil knowledge and open discourse. Amazing!

I met countless people who had my father as a professor and told me how much they appreciated his lectures. There are a few of these testimonial letters in this book to corroborate.

I am grateful my parents got to see that I utilized so much of what they taught me in working for my clients and became reasonably successful in my field, renovating, and most importantly, a husband and father myself. My parents remain a 'go-to' for information on any subject—my father posthumously, through his website. Mother's experience in nursing has been indispensable. One of my earliest memories was my mother taping my hamster's cheek closed after I had inadvertently given him too much food. Best mom ever.

I can only marvel at my parent's strength when my brother was dying of brain cancer.

I thought I knew how much my parents loved me until I held my children in my arms for the first time. I became love, or it became me, I'm not sure. It fundamentally changed me and still does.

I have learned to love things that are NOT perfect. I present myself as exhibit A.

The title of this segment references one of Father's litany of poignant yet silly sense phrases he used when appropriate: "there he was, gone."

He had a very sharp wit and could use this to establish a relaxed feeling in his lectures.

He was always willing to answer anyone's questions after his speaking engagements, which speaks to his confidence in his research.

His incredible memory was bested only by his mother Marjorie, from whom he inherited the ability to discuss any topic in depth, never mind being incredibly well-versed in information related to climate.

My father's disdain for bullies terrified me when I was younger, especially those who took it upon themselves to get physical. He was fearless in those situations. As I grew older, I noticed that he had only to stand up to the bully to stop them. Even though he could have physically overpowered most (you could see the glint in his eye), he never took advantage.

My father was also willing to take on the climate alarmist nonsense. His research left him no choice. Scientific credibility gave him no choice.

My hope is my father's voice is heard again through his writings. We supported him and continue to bring attention to them.

Thank you to both my parents for providing me with an idyllic childhood, the ability to understand as much of the universe as humanly possible and the desire to learn even more.

—*David C. Ball*

Comments from David's wife, Crystal

Most of what is available to the public about Tim speaks to his professional life where he can be read about as both hero or villain depending on the source and their intention. I stopped reading much of what was put into the world about Tim with its glaring gaps, misrepresentations, and downright lies long ago. It was all so nauseatingly far from whom I knew, the day-to-day Tim.

Whether you were a fan or otherwise of Tim's work makes little difference here because I will only speak to the facts about the person he was in my life.

Tim was the person who said, "How are you?" and meant it. He did not ask just to be polite; he asked because it was important. He would sit and listen. You would feel noticed. Without expectation, he freely gave away more of his time, knowledge, and resources in support of others than can ever be counted.

Tim was an educator through and through, which affected every area of his life. His capacity for knowledge was astounding. He collected knowledge like bits of treasure, absorbing the world around him, and like any educator of value, he stayed a keen and curious student. Every walk with him through Victoria was a history lesson as he shared the bits of treasure. He gladly and eagerly shared his beautiful collection of knowledge with anyone.

I turned to Tim often for insight, and with that always came support and encouragement. It was a packaged deal. And this is where I first began to feel anticipatory grief. We had nearly twenty years of emails and phone calls between us, so as he declined and could no longer participate, the absence of our conversations dug deep for me. However, until our last conversation at his hospital bedside, the support, encouragement, and

CRYSTAL AND DAVE BALL, SON DEVON, AND DAUGHTER, AINSLEY

love never stopped.

I could tell you about the day he became my father-in-law and danced and laughed with my mom, or about how he drove over 1,000 km to make sure we had a reliable vehicle, or when he took that trek again at the age of 76 to come and care for our young children while I was in the hospital.

I could tell 100 stories about Tim and how he cared for the people he loved and anyone who needed it. There are many significant memories that I and others can share about Tim, but it is the tiny stitches between important memories that tell the entire story in the fabric of his life. The words of encouragement, the acts of service, the intention, and the love tell the story of who he was, is, and will always be. Between the stories from all the people in the different spaces and eras of his life, you will see him as a whole, splendid, complicated, generous, flawed, loved, and as the villain, subject to whose story it is.

Ultimately, just a man. A good man, but just a man, nonetheless.

Steadfast at his side for more than 60 years has been Marty. From a young and beautiful couple with the world before them, she was at his side through all the trials and joys of their shared life until his last moments. Tim and Marty came a long way together, worked hard, built a beautiful life for themselves, and never stopped returning to help others.

They are people I have greatly admired and loved, with whom I have been proud to call my family.

Losing Tim was a slow process. It was in the small ways that you can see only in retrospect. His bright, active mind slowly began to become imprisoned in dementia. The daily walks to the shops to chat with all the shopkeepers while he looked for gifts, fuelled by his perpetual habit of generosity, slowly began to reduce and then stop. There are several markers of his decline that I can see clearly through my memory.

My children and I attended the final day of Appeal Court with Tim. It was like the weight of the years of fighting, all he had lost, and the ugliness of people he had been subject to while it all had sunk deep into his bones, pulling his shoulders down, his face drawn. He was not joyous as one might think with the end of the long drawn out, and, in my opinion, absurd, indulgent, temper tantrum, waste of time, energy and resources that the suit had been; he was exhausted.

We took him to a nearby restaurant, thinking that, as a person with diabetes, he possibly needed a bite to eat before we walked home. For the first time in all the years I had spent with Tim in Victoria, we called a cab to get home as he could not make it back on foot. That was one of the last times he walked through the city he loved with his grandchildren.

But this is not how I will remember him. It will be in the things he left behind. The curiosity and sparkling mind he passed down to his grandchildren. It is in the way my husband's voice softens with a lilt of laughter when he talks about his dad while growing up. In message after message of gratitude, we heard from people, telling us how he impacted their lives. It's in the love he shared with Marty. The world will remember him in its way, but I will remember him as the man who held us up repeatedly through the years. The man who kindly listened to me cry when I lost my parents and was scared and let me return the favour and hold his hand at the end when he was afraid.

Thank you, Tim, for being more than an in-law. You were a friend and a champion. I am proud to call you Dad.

—*Crystal Ball* (This is my real name.)

Comments from Youngest Son, Tim Jr

Get on with it

When Mum asked me to write a piece for her book on Dad, I considered many possible angles on how I would list his life and career accomplishments and speak to them from my perspective. After much consideration, I realized this is not what mattered to me most and did not best describe how he influenced me as a father.

The very act of procrastinating writing this piece brought back the most apparent and essential lesson that this incredible man taught me. "Get on with it." That's what he would say whenever we were putting off whatever it was, we should be doing.

It was never mean but always communicated with a grin and an 'Eric Idle' style nudge.

This phrase is more complex than it reads. It is like an onion with many layers. As I thought more and more about what he was relating to us and how it explained the man, this fatherly direction had depth beyond anything I first recognized. It would take me five decades of living to realize all that this had to offer me as a path forward.

The first layer is the obvious "Get off your backside and stop procrastinating." My father was not a religious man in terms of organized world faiths, but he understood all the adages and maxims of the world that made sense for daily life and how we should treat others and ourselves.

Dad believed Sloth was a deadly sin and could not abide laziness. He held himself to this standard and was always productive. He steadfastly worked towards security for his family, advancing his knowledge and understanding of the world, achieving advanced degrees for his career, and fighting the good fight against corruption or bullying worldwide.

The second layer is the notion of personal responsibility. No one is going to do it for you. "Get on with it" because it is your moral obligation. Again, it was not the moral duty of organized religion and the fear of eternal damnation in hell but the human element of making a better world by being productive, giving, not taking, and being responsible for the gift of life. Not wasting that precious gift.

TIM JR AND LEANN

My Pops would always say, "I am my brother's keeper, but not my stupid or lazy brother's keeper." And by 'stupid,' he meant those who consistently make poor life choices when they have every advantage.

The third and most important layer is the philosophy embodied by this statement. It is an outlook on life, our purpose as living creatures, and all others on this earth. It means that you must keep going. Sometimes survival is the goal or end game, a theme that pops up again and again in philosophical writings throughout history. What is truly remarkable is that it does not make life meaningless. It is quite the opposite. Surviving is a triumph in and of itself. You see it in the ant colony, and you see the human story.

He often told us stories of his Royal Canadian Air Force time. The one that always stood out to me is related to this third layer of meaning. They would have to go on wilderness survival exercises in Canada, during which soldiers were scored on survival skills. Dad said he received very high marks, and one reason was that he shaved every morning. The survival experts knew this was one of the most important indicators of whether a person had given up.

My father did not give up or compromise his outlook or work ethic. Sometimes that is all we've got.

My father survived all the slings and arrows and bullying

LEANN'S DAUGHTER CARLY, HUSBAND AARON, SONS LIAM, NASH AND OWEN HALLOWEEN 2023

from the corruptors of climate science as he stood firm in his belief in the scientific method, real-world evidence and freedom of speech. They did not kill him or his words and ideas. He survived because he just got on with it.

I would be remiss if I did not say how much I love and admire my father. He did so much so that we could have fun, positive childhoods.

He and my Mum were the strength and love we needed to be good adults.

—*Timothy Peter Ball Jr*

A thought from Tim Jr's wife, Leann…

The sweetest most supportive man ever…thank you for making me feel so loved.
—Love, Lee

Moon, Our Dog

We never planned on getting a dog.

Our friends heard this little dog, freezing and hungry, on their front step in January in Winnipeg. No ID tags. They advertised in the paper for someone to claim him. Nothing. They phoned us and said, "Marty and Tim, you need a dog." We replied, "No, we don't need a dog."

These friends already had a dog so there was no way they wanted him. They insisted on us just seeing him, nothing more. Ha! We fell in love with him at first sight. Our sons insisted on naming him Moon, in memory of Keith Moon of The Who musical group who died of an overdose of drugs.

Initially, Moon was ready to run away at any opportunity. He was totally white and was very difficult to see in the snow. We had the vet check him over from head to foot. He was approximately eight months old and in good health. We had him neutered so he wasn't as apt to run away. That seemed to help a little, but we never took him out without a leash.

Imagine trying to find a white dog in winter?

Fourteen years later he got cancer and had to be euthanized. He was such a part of our family that we kept expecting to see him for another two weeks.

Tim Sr missed him most but would not admit it.

CHAPTER THIRTY-THREE

My Week in Oz with Tim Ball by Dr Tony Heller

U.S. ELECTION WEEK 2016 was a very hopeful time. BREXIT won in Britain a few months earlier and there was a belief people were wresting control of their governments back from vested interests.

Tim Ball and I were invited by Australian Senator Malcolm Roberts to speak at Parliament House in Canberra.

I had never met Tim and was immediately impressed by his good nature and seriousness about communicating factual information about climate. The three of us took on most of the leading alarmists in the Australian Press Corps and left them dizzy and speechless. They really didn't know what hit them.

Tim and I then traveled to Sydney and presented to a group of skeptics, which was also great fun and very well received. Tim gave another outstanding presentation before flying off to Melbourne to speak to a group there.

The week ended perfectly with Donald Trump winning the election and for a while we all believed climate alarmism was on its last legs.

A few weeks later we met in Washington DC and gave presentations at the U.S. Congress, which were also very well received. Tim impressed his audience everywhere he spoke.

I only had the pleasure of Tim's company for a few hours, but thoroughly enjoyed them and was very impressed by his knowledge about climate and climate history.

Later I helped with his defence against the world's number one climate fraudster, Michael Mann, which Tim won because Mann never had any case. Tim was correct in his assertions about Mann and Mann was unwilling to provide documents which would have exposed him as a fraud.

—*Dr Tony Heller*

TIM AND TONY IN SYDNEY

TONY, SENATOR ROBERTS AND TIM

CHAPTER THIRTY-FOUR

THIS CHAPTER INCLUDES many things that are in a category of their own—things that tweaked Tim's brain, intrigued or amused him. Simple things.

Some originated from Tim. He often included these in his talks and lectures to keep his audience laughing and attentive. He made it very apparent that his topic was important and serious at the same time.

Once I started this chapter, I couldn't stop.

Forgive me.

"Common sense isn't very common." Voltaire.

Tim said, "If they taught common sense in the universities, they would have to bring someone from outside to teach it."

"A man's loyalty doesn't depend on what you've done for him in the past but on what you have the power to do for him (or to him) in the future. When your ability to help (or hurt) others disappears, they too, tend to disappear." Richard J Needham

"Politicians campaign on representing you in Parliament. Once you elect them, they represent Parliament to you. Their peer group changes, and, as you know, it is the strongest force." Tim

"THINK PARTNER" BY HANS-JÖRG LIMBACH, 1980, IN FRONT OF THE UNIVERSITY OF STUTTGART

"It is dangerous to be right in matters which the established authorities are wrong." Voltaire

Tim and his friend Larry Sarbit's favourite movie title, *Hurt Me, My Love*. They would laugh about the title uncontrollably. Neither one of them ever saw the movie.

"Marty is so organized, I get up in the morning to go to the bathroom. When I come back to bed, it's been made." Tim

The morning of one of our Christmases spent alone, I asked Tim, "When do you want your stuffed turkey breast?" Answer: "Tomorrow."

"My wife only serves two dishes, cold shoulder and hot tongue." Thomas McGuane

"There were seven sins in the world. Wealth without work, pleasure without conscience, knowledge without character, commerce without morality, science without humanity, worship without sacrifice, and politics without Principle." Mahatma Gandhi.

"Columbus discovered America? Did the Natives not know it was there?" Tim

"He sets himself a low standard and fails to maintain it." Winston Churchill

"The complacency of superabundance." Marshall McLuhan

Everything Reminds Me of Tim

"For in much wisdom is much grief: and he that increaseth knowledge, increaseth sorrow." Ecclesiastes 1:18

"The world is too much with us." William Wordsworth

"There is no opposite to ignorance is bliss." Tim

"Alcohol increases desire but decreases performance." Shakespeare

"I told the Queen the other day how I hate name droppers." Tim

Loquacious is a nice way of saying you talk too much.

"You cannot do a good deed for anyone without it benefiting you directly or indirectly." Many authors.

"Instant gratification isn't fast enough for me." Tim had this saying pinned on his office wall at the University of Winnipeg. Many authors said this in one way or another.

"Self-praise is no recommendation." Many authors

"If you can fake sincerity, you've got it made." E.G. Marshall

Tim worked for Peter C. Newman on the first two volumes of his trilogy on the Hudson Bay Company. (*Company of Adventurers* and *Caesars of the Wilderness*). Why Tim was willing to contribute to these volumes is no mystery. All the other professors in the history and geography departments refused because there was no money offered.
    Before proceeding, Newman sent his second wife to interview Tim at his office at the University.
    Tim said, "It's very nice to meet you, Camilla."
    Christina said "Oh, I am Christina, Peter's second wife."
    Tim said, "Oh, you didn't even have to change the initials on the towels."
    Christina laughed.
    Tim said, "I appreciate you having a sense of humour."
    She said, "When you're number two, you need a sense of humour."

"The more outrageous the lie, the more people believe it." Joseph Goebbels

"If God gave you a talent and you didn't use it, you are useless." Tim

"The majority of men live lives in quiet desperation." Henry David Thoreau.

Plausible Deniability denies involvement in illegal or unethical activities because there is no clear evidence to prove involvement—a term used in law and politics.

"The urge to save humanity is almost always a false front for the urge to rule." H.L. Mencken

"They knew the cost of everything and the value of nothing." Unknown

"A farmer is the only person in our economy who buys everything at retail, sells at wholesale and pays the freight both ways." John F. Kennedy

Marty Ball, et al

"I may not agree with everything you say, but I would fight your right to say it to the death." Voltaire

"One of life's greatest pleasures is getting into a cosy bed after a hard day's work, knowing you don't have to get up early the next morning." Unknown

"I live with fear every day; sometimes, she lets me go golfing." Unknown.

"As cool as the underside of the pillow." Unknown

"It's not that the wind blows; it's what the wind blows."

"Cell phones are the new instrument of torture." Unknown. Tim agreed.

"If you predict that the weather tomorrow will be the same as today, you have a 60% chance of being correct." Tim

"I lack credibility being a Climatologist who preferred to live in Winnipeg." Tim

"If you want anything done, ask a busy person." Tim

Over 3 million big birds are killed by windmills each year worldwide, but all you see on national television is one lone duck covered with oil.

Everything Reminds Me of Tim

Gradualism: a policy of gradual reform rather than sudden change or revolution. A word Tim often used in his talks. (The frog in the pot of increasingly warmer and warmer water.)

Tim was going to form a 'Down with Spandex Club' He said many times, "Many should never wear Spandex."

Whenever Tim had to fill out a form that asked for religion, he would put Druid. No one ever questioned him about it.

"Government Committees of Inquiry always preset the Terms of Reference. That way, the outcome is predetermined by them." Tim

One in Tim's senior citizens class said he always read the newspaper a week late. His reasoning was it takes all the urgency out of the news. Clever.

Tim often said of the Conservative Party of Canada. "They circle the wagons and shoot inwards."

China. "Let the sleeping giant lie; if he awakes, the whole world will hear him roar." Napoleon

On my return home after a fortnight away, Tim said, "Celibacy isn't funny, you know."

"It is difficult to get a person to understand something when their salary depends on not understanding." Upton Sinclair

"We now live in a nation where doctors destroy health, lawyers destroy justice, universities destroy knowledge, governments destroy freedom, the Press destroys information, and our banks destroy the economy." Chris Hedges

"Marriage is the only punishment where you get more time for good behaviour." Tim

"Good guys finish last." Leo Durocher and many others.

"It's a nice day somewhere." Tim

"We all know the type of person who carries a zip-lock bag full of kale." Senator John Kennedy, Louisiana, USA

"Something is fascinating about Science. One gets such wholesale returns of conjecture out of such trifling investment in facts." Mark Twain

"I still need data. It is a capital mistake to theorize before one has data. Insensibly, one begins to twist facts to suit theories, instead of theories to suit facts." Sherlock Holmes, Esq. *A Scandal in Bohemia.*

"The mediocre teacher tells, the good teacher explains, and the superior teacher demonstrates. The great teacher inspires." William Ward.

"Success means something other than that we earn money and live in the most prominent house in town. It means we are daily striving toward a goal that we have independently chosen and is worthy of us as persons. A goal, whatever it may be, gives meaning to our existence. The carrot on the stick keeps us striving and interested and gives us a reason for getting out of bed in the morning." Earl Nightingale

"Extinction is the norm. Survival is the exception." Carl Sagan

"What are you wearing to the costume party, Tim?"
"I am going as an afterthought," Tim said.

Tim got a hole-in-one on the second at the Victoria Golf Club. There was no excitement from him. Tad Anzai, a golfing mate and friend, called to tell me, or I may never have known.

Tim always referred to himself as a grizzly old bear or a curmudgeon.

"Money isn't everything but keeps the children in touch." J. Paul Getty

Tim has given thousands of interviews over the years. He always started and ended with, "thank you for the opportunity." Not, "thank you for having me (on)."

I never saw Tim chew gum. He was taught in boarding school that it was cheap. He wouldn't let me chew it either.

"It is no longer the tail wagging the dog; it's the flea on the hair on the tail wagging the dog." Tim

Tim commented about the drought in the 30s; "you saw the neighbour's land coming at you vertically. The dust was unbelievable, but the pioneer's family still managed to get dressed in white clothing to go to church on Sundays." Tim often wondered how they managed to do that when they lived in sod huts.

Tim's birthday was on November 5. That is Guy Fawkes Day in Britain. Tim always said, "G.F. was the only guy that went to Parliament with good intentions." (G.F. attempted to blow up Parliament.)

Marty asked Tim at about 4 PM daily, "Would you like a cup of tea, Tim?"
Tim, "I would **love** a cup of tea. Will you join me?"
Marty: "Of course I will."
Tim: "Do you have a cookie to go with that?"
Marty: "Of course I do."

"A principle is when you won't listen to another opinion." Dr David Starky

Probity. A word that very well describes our Tim. Integrity, honesty and decency.

Everything Reminds Me of Tim

"What do you say when you receive a $50 gift card for a restaurant with a $350 minimum charge?" Jimmy Failla of Fox News

Psychology: "The odd studying the id." Tim

A Presbyterian is afraid that someone, somewhere is having a good time.

"The USA will pay a very high price for freedom." Author unknown.

The inscription on a hypochondriac's gravestone. "I told you I was sick."

"Power tends to corrupt, and absolute power corrupts absolutely. Great men are almost always bad men" Lord Acton, 1887

"Walking shoes. Isn't that a minimum requirement for all shoes?" Unknown.

"When you come to a fork in the road, take it." Tim

"A sense of humour is necessary for a successful marriage." Tim

Jane Goodall spoke in Winnipeg at the Odeon Theatre. Tim was engaged to give a short talk before Jane. He came on stage, and the first thing he said was, "I never thought I would ever be a warm-up act for the chimpanzees." An audience of 2,000 gave an uproar of laughter and applause.

"Students graduating from high school these days are functionally illiterate. Being bilingual makes them functionally illiterate in two languages." Tim

Our friend Larry Anderson had a few girlfriends after he and his wife divorced. One lady friend came from out of town and stayed with Larry on the weekends. She wanted to move in permanently, but Larry said no. He claimed she would start 'nest-building' as soon as she moved in with him. On her way out the door for the last time, she said to Larry, "I thought you were better than nothing, but you're not."

Tim called the mosquito Manitoba's Bird of Prey.

"We spend so much money trying to save money." Tim

A country and western song called, "I've got tears in my ears from lying on my back and crying over you." Check it out!

"If we learned from the past, we wouldn't repeat the mistakes." Many quoted this.

"If a man knows more than others, he becomes lonely." Carl Jung

"Marriage ruins a perfectly good relationship."—many authors.

When the Canadian athletes went to the Olympics in Japan in 2018, they were each given forty condoms by our Government. Tim said he sure wishes he was an Olympic athlete.

Tim had a nun-teacher at the convent in Chippenham, Wiltshire, UK. He called her Sister Hell on Wheels.

True story: Graffiti in the ladies' washroom at the University of Winnipeg. They had a list on the wall of the ten best-dressed women at the U of W. Tim was number nine. Ha! Tim was the only prof who wore a jacket, shirt and tie daily. His colleagues considered him a stuffed shirt. The only way you could tell the difference between the professors and the students was the students carried books.

When we first moved into our condo in Victoria in 1996, our superintendent was a large woman named Pat. On arriving home from one of his walks, I asked Tim, "did you see Pat? Tim answered "Yes, but I outran her."

"He was a very humble man. He had a lot to be humble about." Winston Churchill

"When a mother is happy, the whole family is happy." Tim

Did you know you can live forever on potatoes and butter? Did Tim read that somewhere? I don't know.

A mature senior student, Gordon McIlroy, once asked Tim, "What is your goal in the classroom?" Tim said, without hesitation, "To provide an environment and encouragement for every student to use their abilities to the maximum. The decision was then theirs."

I did a lot of knitting. I often sent Tim to buy my wool. He said, "If anyone is looking for me, I'm the guy in downtown Victoria carrying a backpack full of wool."

Our friend Larry Anderson often said, "The Jehovah's Witnesses should deliver the mail and the deaf should live near the airport."

Tim said of Opera. "I keep thinking they will break into a nice melody."

Tim was continually accused of being a shill for the oil companies. He never got a nickel from them. They wanted nothing to do with him either. "As if I don't care about the environment? Why would anyone dirty their own nest? Everyone can clean up the rivers and oceans. Where are all these environmentalists who care for Mother Earth? Why don't they spend their protesting time cleaning up the planet?" Tim

"Rather fail with honour than succeed by fraud." Sophocles

When Tim started teaching at the University of Winnipeg, it was "publish or perish." When he left, it was "get funding or perish."

"Most of the world is unoccupied, with most people concentrated in flood plains, such as in China along the Yangtze (Chang Jiang) River and deltas, like the Nile in Egypt. Canada is the second largest country in the world, with approximately 33.6 million residents. (2009). California had a 2008 population of 36.8 million people. Statistically, the entire population fits certain islands, such as the Isle of Wight off the south coast of England or regions, like half of Alberta. For example, Texas at 7,438,152,268,800 square feet divided by the 2015 world population of 6,774,436,692 gives 1098 square feet per person. Fitting them in is different from the ability to live there. Population geographers distinguish between ecumene, the inhabited area, and non-ecumene, the uninhabited areas. Habitable areas change all the time. The area of the habitable Earth has changed because of technology, communications and food production capacity. Tim from his book, *The Deliberate Corruption of Climate Science*."

Tim read about a study done on 1,000 CEOs in the USA. One question read, "were you spanked as a child?" All answered yes. Next question: "did you deserve the spanking?" All answered yes.

Tim gave thousands of lectures but never gave **the** speech. He would write a few words on a little piece of paper. That was all. It was difficult for Tim when the organizations wanted a written copy of his speech. He often told me his brain came to life when he was in front of an audience. He loved teaching, and it showed.

"Do you pick your friends, or do they pick you?" Tim and I asked that question many times over the years.

Tim says he has never seen Dolly Parton's face.

There was a counterfeiter that printed $20 bills. It cost him $25 to print each one.

If a man thinks he is more intelligent than his wife, he has a brilliant wife. Unknown

Tim often asked someone, "How is your soul?" These people were always someone special in his life.

A song sung by Peggy Lee moved Tim. "Is That All There Is?" The lyrics are incredible.

Question: "What does your daddy do?"
Answer: "I don't know."
Question: "Does he shower before he goes to work or after he comes home from work?"

Question: "Are you comfortable?"
Answer: "I make a living."

Clean water is the resource of the 21st century. Canada has the most significant amount of the world's clean water supply. The government is already selling it.

Tim always walked on the left or right side of hallways or staircases so the carpets wore out evenly.

Tim often said his brain was full of useless trivia.

"I have been rich and poor. Rich is better." Many said this.

"Polygamy is two or more wives too many; monogamy is one wife too many." Tim

"I have forgotten many things over the years, but I have never forgotten to eat." Tim

Tim stood very proud when he heard the Kings College Cambridge Choir sing 'Jerusalem.' The only time he looked back. Occasionally over the years, I asked Tim, "Do you ever get homesick or want to return to Britain?" Answer, "Occasionally, but I am a Canadian now and try never to look back."

"If you are a jerk before you get your doctorate, you are still a jerk when you graduate." Many authors.

"The problem for the world is the industrialized countries, and it is our job to do away with them?" Maurice Strong of the United Nations was born in Oak Lake, Manitoba, Canada. He said this in 1992 at the Rio de Janeiro Climate Conference. This started the cabal on Anthropogenic Global Warming.

Our good friend Dr. Howard Guest wore the same tuxedo on his 50th anniversary as he wore on his wedding day. He jogged six or seven miles each morning before work, summer and winter in Winnipeg. Can you imagine? Tim told me many times that Howard was a prince of a man. Both Howard and Sheena were very good friends.

They called Tim a 'Climate Change Denier.' "I am anything but. Climate changes all the time, always has, always will. Denier has all the connotations of the Holocaust, which is an insult."

DR HOWARD GUEST AT HIS 50TH, AND WITH HIS WIFE, DR SHEENA GUEST, 2008

"Who polices the police? Power without authority." Many said these words.

Tim was asked to run for all three political parties while teaching at the University of Winnipeg, the NDP, Liberals and Conservatives. He often wondered what that said about him, or them.

Tim never owned or wore a pair of jeans.

Tim was told he was the first PhD in climatology in Canada. His colleagues said that wasn't true but could never name the one who was first.

"The definition of success is doing what you love to do and making a living at it."

"Two words you cannot say too often, please and thank you."

"You have to know and like yourself before you can like anyone else." Tim

"First, they ignore you, then they ridicule you, then attack you, and then you win." Author unknown

Everything Reminds Me of Tim

Tim took out the last two words and entered, "they sue you and ruin you, and then you die."

Tim didn't know who coined the phrase, but he agreed that "politics was a blood sport." The media could make or break you in a minute.

A famous Canadian comedian, Norm MacDonald, said, "Comedians chase the applause rather than the laughs."

Tim said many times that I was bossy but not the boss.

Tim said he saw Bill Clinton hug Monica Lewinsky over 1,300 times on television. (He never really counted.)

Our friend Jane Murphy told Tim one day, "You are the nicest climatologist I know. "
Tim, "How many climatologists do you know?"
Jane, "You are the only climatologist I know."

A senior in Tim's class once told him, "I still look through 20-year-old eyes."

Tim often said, "God is still in charge of our climate, contrary to the warmists that think they are God and can control it."

"Ninety five percent of families are dysfunctional, and the other 5% are in denial"—unknown author.

Tim often told this story in his talks. "A monk in a cloister's cell was only allowed two words a year. The first year, he said, "hard bed." The second year, "rotten food." The third year, "I quit." The Cardinal replied, "I'm not surprised; you have done nothing but complain since you got here."

The first casualty of war is the truth.—many authors.

While in a restaurant in Yellowknife, one of Tim's search and rescue crew asked the waitress if she had any scruples? She said she didn't know but would ask the chef.

Tim said publicly many times that Canada did not need a military. If anyone attacked Canada, the USA would immediately come to our aid. Our military should primarily be peacekeepers. "Who would you rather have as a world superpower, the USA, China or Russia?"

If every Chinese citizen were to have a knitted pair of socks, there wouldn't be enough sheep in the world to produce enough wool to knit them.

During the "Hole in the Ozone" crisis in the 1980s, Tim and a few other climatologists were summoned to the parliament in Ottawa to face the politicians and answer their questions. Tim assured them there were no holes in the ozone and stated why. (chloro-flouro-carbons [CFCs] are three times heavier than air, so how do they reach the ozone?)
One of the politicians said to Tim, "Sir, Galileo would be ashamed of you." Tim's answer, "To be mentioned in the same sentence as Galileo is the greatest honour I could have."

"It is not merely of some importance, but of fundamental importance, that justice should not only be done but be manifestly and undoubtedly be seen to be done." Lord Chief Justice Gordon Hewart

Tim said the only honest sport left was professional wrestling.

"The first generation accumulates the wealth, the second maintains it, and the third squanders it." Author unknown.

"A politician sees the light at the end of the tunnel and orders more tunnel." Tim

"I refuse to join a club that would have me as a member." Groucho Marx.

Tim said of a colleague who was so negative that he would have complained about having to go and pick up his lottery win.

"It's better to have loved a short man than never to have loved a tall."

After a speech in Banff, Alberta, an audience member asked Tim what his motive or agenda was. Tim was taken aback but managed to answer. "The truth. I don't want anyone saying they weren't told that Anthropogenic Global Warming is a hoax."

Unctuous is an adjective—a word Tim loved.
    —she sees through his unctuous manners | an unctuous smile: sycophantic, ingratiating, obsequious, fawning, servile, self-abasing, grovelling, subservient, wheedling, cajoling, crawling, cringing, Uriah Heepish, humble, toadying, hypocritical.

Eco-grief or eco-anxiety. Anyone who is treated for mental trauma related to 'climate change.' The fear tactics are working according to Tim.

"A job is marginally better than daytime TV." Jim Pastore and others.

Everything Reminds Me of Tim

"He is so lazy; he walks backwards." Tim

"Don't just do something; stand there." Tim

"Everyone loves success; except others' success. Unknown

"If someone asks you for the truth, run for the hills. The last thing they want to hear is the truth." Tim

A retiree's acceptance speech at an RCAF Search and Rescue Squadron stood up and said, "I'm speechless." and sat down again.

"We're turning on our legacy and calling it evil." Heather McDonald on the falling of the Western countries.

Always tell the truth. You have to remember your lies. Good advice. Tim and I were both reminded of this when we were children, so we, in turn, reminded our boys.

Twenty six percent of Americans still think the sun goes around the Earth. Many authors.

"Gravity is a myth; the earth sucks." A.V. Roe and others.

The paradigm shift happened when an astronaut took a photo of the earth from outer space. Year? The sixties or seventies? This started the environmental movement.

"A flat tax of 10% would solve so many revenue problems." Many have said this, Tim, as well.

"If you have to do something you don't like, make a game of it." Tim's advice to our whole family.

Following one of Tim's many media interviews, one journalist told Tim. "Don't ever think the story is about you; it is the story and only the story that's most important."

The Precautionary Principle. "Shouldn't we act just in case?" Tim refuted this and said "a bad plan is worse than no plan."

Tim often ended his talks with: "The mind can only absorb what the behind can endure."

"There is no consensus in Science. Consensus is a political term." Michael Crichton, in his book *State of Fear*.

"Speed up, slow down or get the hell out of the way." Lee Iacocca, CEO of Chrysler

"Give me $10 and I will tell you how to become a millionaire." Bob Sharpe

No yes-or-no answer to this question. "Have you stopped beating your wife?"

"I'm not a racist; I hate everybody." W.C. Fields

Tim said the barbecue was invented by women so that men would do the cooking.

Everything Reminds Me of Tim

Sayings that WOKE won't allow anymore.
1) It's not whether you win or lose; it's how you play the game.
2) Sticks and stones may break my bones, but names will never hurt me.
3) Imitation is the sincerest form of flattery.
4) Honesty is the best policy.

"Disgruntled! I don't even remember being gruntled." Tim.

Impressionist paintings were the result of painting the polluted skies from volcanic dust—much sulphur in the atmosphere.

"Money is the root of all evil." No. "The love of money is the root of all evil." Bible

Everyone has their price. Not Tim. He told me many times he would do everything he did in his life with or without being paid.

"There is no such thing as bad publicity." Phineas T. Barnum, showman and circus owner

We loved Tim's definition of a nymphomaniac. "Someone who other men meet with amazing regularity, and I never do."

Tim resented the phone. He often said it was the most significant invasion of privacy. He also said if he were ever to kill anyone, it would be Alexander Graham Bell.

Tim would never wear rings. In 1962, he broke his ring finger while playing soccer. There wasn't a ring cutter in Summerside PEI, at that time, so they had to file off the ring, causing excruciating pain. Poor man! I had his wedding ring cut to fit my right ring finger. I wear it all the time.

I often told Tim he would give the shirt off his back. His comment was, "I've run out of shirts."

Many years ago, Barbara Frum of the CBC 10 PM news would prerecord her interviews with Tim. If she didn't like his answers to her questions, she would say, "No, we'll deep-six this one," and hang up the phone.

"I'm not going to get married again. I'm just going to find a woman I hate and buy her a house." Rod Stewart

"Just because you are paranoid doesn't mean no one is out to get you." —Joseph Heller, author of *Catch 22*

Tim said, "Dentists drilled through your tooth right down to your wallet."

Tim hated lint pickers. You know who you are. The wives who pick lint from their husband's clothes in public.

"I don't discuss my wife with anyone because they may be more knowledgeable than me on that subject."
—Alexis de Tocqueville

America is great because she is good. She will cease to be great when she ceases to be good." Alexis de Tocqueville, quoted later by president Eisenhower.

Tim was often called a "Don Quixote." Tilting at windmills (attacking imaginary enemies).

One of Tim's favourite paintings is by Frances M. Hopkins, Canoes in a Fog, 1869. We have it hanging in our condo, kindly gifted to Tim by Andy Stewart, our computer guy. Hopkins usually painted herself in her paintings even though she was not there.

"The Media lurches from one crisis to another." Tim

"When I die, I want to go to Hell. There, I will be warm forever, and there won't be any mosquitos." Tim

A greeting in many third-world countries is, "Have you eaten today?"

"I remember once I thought I was wrong, but I was right." Many quoted this.

Tim often told me I had two speeds: "dead slow and frenetic."

Tim didn't like the comment, "It doesn't take a rocket scientist." He said it should be, "It doesn't take a farmer." He said farmers are more intelligent and knowledgable than any rocket scientist.

"The only thing necessary for the triumph of evil is for the good men to do nothing." Edmund Burke

"A farmer's wife not only has to worry about the weather, but she also has to worry about her husband's reaction to the weather." Tim

The only church closed on Sundays is in the business district of London, England.

Scientists were determined to define what made us different from the animal kingdom. They said humans lie. They found animals could lie as well. They said animals could not add. They found they could add. The concluding argument was that humans could think about death—animals cannot, apparently.

Everything Reminds Me of Tim

A lawyer, an accountant and farmer won a lottery worth millions of dollars. Each one stated what they would do with their share. The lawyer said he would buy real estate to build his capital worth. The accountant said he would work for the lawyer with all the real estate and double his money. The farmer said "I will continue farming until the money is all gone." Tim quoted this many times when he talked to the farmers. It always received much laughter and applause.

"That's the last millennial party I'm ever attending." Tim in the year 2000

To steal ideas from one person is plagiarism; to steal from many is research.

Environmentalists say the world is comprised of natural and unnatural beings. They consider humans to be unnatural. How can that be? Tim asked his audiences many times.

A student handed Tim his essay. At the top right-hand corner was written, Deadline Maniac. Tim considered it a compliment.

"When I get new information, I rethink. What do you do?" Tim

Tim said many times that the whole world lacked competent leadership.

A nosy neighbour is your best security.

We are led to believe that all parts of the human body are different, except the brain. They tell you that everyone's brain is the same size with the same IQ. That is not true, according to Tim.

A bumper sticker at a kiosk in Edinburgh, Scotland: "English spoken, American understood."

Virtue is its own reward.

Tim said of the guillotine, "They say all you feel is a cold piece of cold metal on the back of your neck—how do they know that?"

"Did the millions of buffalo roaming the prairies not emit methane? That may be why they have such big heads." Tim said this often with a smile.

Tim's usual greeting at the beginning of his speeches was, "Morning. (or afternoon, or evening.) Who am to decide if it is good?"

When our West Hawk Lake neighbour Bob Armstrong married, Tim asked, "Armo, why are you getting married on a Wednesday?" Armo answered. "Because if the marriage doesn't work out, I still have the weekend."

"Capitalism and altruism are incompatible; they are

philosophical opposites; they cannot co-exist in the same man or society." Ayn Rand
(These did co-exist in Tim. The one stipulation Tim made was that the Capitalists must have profit-sharing employees. There would then be no need for unions. Staff would work harder, with less abuse of sick time, and so on.)

"Patriotism is the last refuge of a scoundrel." (1775) Samuel Johnson

"This, too, shall pass away." Abraham Lincoln

Over these many years, Tim had thousands of emails and phone calls asking for advice, information and opinions. Tim was very generous with his time and knowledge. He felt his duty was to share this knowledge with as many as he could. (Marty: Many sucked him in, chewed him up and spit him out. Am I bitter? Not anymore.)

"I was born for the storm because the calm doesn't suit me." President Andrew Jackson

"Moderation in all things." Aristotle

"A rising tide lifts all boats." Used and made famous by John F. Kennedy

"What's the difference between ignorance and apathy?"
Answer: "I don't know, and I don't care."

Tim always called his Toyota Prius "my pious."

"In what career, other than academia, does your peer group decide whether you get a merit increase or a promotion?" Tim

Tim noted that one of the pitfalls of public speaking was the media questions: One had to constantly be on guard for the *gotcha* questions: They were usually designed to enhance the questioner's brilliance, or to catch you in a lie.

Tim offered to debate anyone on climate, but no-one ever came forward. They only knew how to hand out ad hominem attacks against Tim.

"Tact is the art of making a point without making an enemy." Howard Newton

If you rob Peter to pay Paul, you will have Paul's support forever.

"When people get used to preferential treatment, equal treatment seems like discrimination." Thomas Sowell

"Take my wife, please." Henny Youngman

"I don't believe in reincarnation. Of course, I didn't believe in it last time I was here either." Tim

"The word two can be spelled in three different ways (two, to and too), but no word describes that word." Tim

A couple were entertaining another couple for dinner. While the visiting wife goes to the bathroom and the hostess

Everything Reminds Me of Tim

wife is in the kitchen, the visiting husband says to the host husband, "My wife is behaving like a nun lately." The host husband says, "Come into the kitchen, and I will introduce you to the BVM (Blessed Virgin Mary)."

While Tim was in a Catholic public school in England, the boys had to go to confession every Saturday morning. Tim could not remember any sins, so he made up sins and confessed them to the priest. The following Saturday, he confessed that he had made up the sins the week before. I asked Tim how many times he got away with this. "Only once."

"Of course, I've been unfaithful, you've had a headache for four years!" Unknown.

Tim's sister Liz and I were shopping in the Dollar Store, waiting for Tim to meet us. As he walked in, the cashier said, "May I help you?" Tim said kiddingly, "I am looking for a Fabergé egg." She said, "I'm sorry, but we don't have any of those."

"Such is the irresistible nature of truth that all it asks and wants is the liberty of appearing." Thomas Paine

If someone speaks with an accent, you know they speak at least two languages fluently.

Tim managed to arrange his coffee cup on the microwave's turntable so the handles faced him when it stopped.

"The medium is the message." Marshall McLuhan (1964)

"No one is a prophet in their own land." Robert Kaplinsky

Shrouds don't have pockets. Jewish proverb

Tim thought all sewer and power lines should be under the sidewalks rather than the roads. They should also be made of PVC and placed below the frost line. Less cost, and less obstructive to install, repair or replace.

"Sarcasm is the lowest form of wit." Oscar Wilde

"If you are going through hell, keep going." Winston Churchill

"The early bird catches the worm, and the second mouse gets the cheese." Jeremy Paxman

"You always find what you are looking for in the last place you look, so why don't you look in the last place first?" Tim

Tim never gave me presents on my birthday or Christmas. He called this duty giving. He would surprise me with gifts when I least expected them, like flowers, chocolate, a book or whatever he thought would please me.

At home during his illness, including early dementia, he patiently waited for the digital clock to turn 123.45 or 234.56. He would call me to see it a few seconds before it appeared so I could share his joy. It took so little to make him happy.

Question? How many Torontonians does it take to change a lightbulb?

Answer. Only one. They hold the bulb while the whole world rotates around it.

Marty has so many relatives that everyone south of Regina, Saskatchewan is related to her.

Being famous means more people know you than you know.

Tim's mother, Marjorie, often said, "If I die and find out there is no heaven, when I've been good all these years, I will be furious."

Tim once asked a used car salesman, "How can you sell a lemon with a straight face?" The Salesman said, "I tell them it's a good lemon."

Tim, "How do you make a jam sandwich? You get two pieces of bread and jam them together."

A pro-golfer makes the best of his bad shots.

"It should be won't power, not will power." Tim

"You should accomplish something daily, even if it's only making your bed." Tim

"If social workers were successful, wouldn't they eventually put themselves out of a job?" Tim.

"Everyone told me that life begins at 40. On my 40th birthday, I waited up all night to see what happened. Nothing happened." Tim

Everything Reminds Me of Tim

A historian once said, "Canada has too much geography and too little history." Tim disagreed and said, "Canada has plenty of both."

Tim spent his entire career trying to determine the effects of climate on the 'human condition.'

If you take away people's religion, it has to be replaced with something. This is now Environmentalism. Tim

After many years of marriage, I realized Tim never guffawed, and I reminded him of that. He said I guffawed enough for both of us. Ha, ha, ha, ha, ha!

The only good thing about getting old is you can say what you like, and no one will hit you.

One of Tim's colleagues was known to say: "The university would be a great place to work if it wasn't for all the students. You open the door, and they go everywhere."

"We've got to do away with career politicians." Tim

"Nothing focuses the mind like the threat of a hanging." Samuel Johnson and Mark Twain

Have you heard of the woman with many bruises on her chest? It's where they were hitting her with a ten-foot pole.

Tim reminded me often of what my mom used to say. "Martha, you can't be ecstatic every day."
In Britain, there was a three-wheeled car that was much cheaper to purchase, and even cheaper if you chose one that didn't have a reverse gear. The only door was in the front. A neighbour built a small garage to house this

precious new car. After work he planned to come home and park in his small, brand-new garage. He drove in but could not open the front door, nor back out to get out of this car. He sat there for hours until his wife found him, in a state of utter frustration.

"Lies, damnable lies and statistics." Mark Twain

"You cannot wake a man that is pretending to be asleep."

Bumper sticker: Save the planet, kill yourself.

Have you heard about the wife who didn't know her husband drank until he came home sober?

"If we are planning for global warming and it gets colder, do we add CO_2?" Tim

It's not about going green, it's about going without." Mark Steyn

"The environmentalists put on the cloak of self-righteousness and no one can penetrate it." Tim

This is what I saw as I passed Tim's office in our condo. He was on the landline phone talking to some media or someone who required Tim's undivided attention. He would not use a cordless or cell phone in case it malfunctioned.

CHAPTER THIRTY-FIVE
The Last Eleven Weeks

IN JULY 2022, Tim fell and injured his left elbow. After many falls, I could not get him back to bed this time. I called 911 at Tim's request. He knew this was the beginning of the end, and so did I. The emergency department admitted him to a ward shortly after arriving at the hospital.

The last 11 weeks of Tim's life were in the Royal Jubilee Hospital in Victoria, British Columbia. I found this time the most difficult. Not physically but mentally and emotionally.

His left elbow was so sore he could not move it for the entire 11 weeks. There was no fracture. The doctors finally diagnosed it as gout. He could not use his iPad, read, or use his cell phone. The TV on the wall by his bed was not working. I ached for him to have some mental stimulation of some sort. I know how much he missed his iPad and books. I watched him deteriorate inch by inch, knowing there was no way back. Trying to eat or do anything took a lot of work without his left arm. He could not butter his toast, peel an egg, remove the lids from the food containers, or remove the plastic wrap on some dishes. The staff were always too busy, so they didn't get to him before the food was cold. The family and I tried to time our visits at mealtime to help him.

His dementia took its toll. On one of my many visits, he would be loving and my soulmate again. On another day, he would be hostile towards me for abandoning him when there was nothing wrong with him (he thought). He could not seem to see himself as being ill.

Another day, he would accuse me of having boyfriends and entertaining them in our home. Once, he told our son I had divorced him and married one of my boyfriends. Another day, he was worried about how my car was running or if I would be driving in rush-hour traffic. He was like himself then. I didn't know I could cry so hard or for so long, usually on my way home from my visits.

On that last fatal day on September 24, I heard the death rattle in his lungs when I arrived. Before I came, the nurse said Tim had screamed for help when he had never done that before. I knew what that meant. He could not use the urinal. At that point, he knew it was over. He was in and out of consciousness. He was trying to tell me he loved me but could not get it out because his throat was too dry. I sat there for hours, holding his hand and crying. I wanted to die with him, so help me! My soulmate, my rock, my best friend, the love of my life. Oh, God! He died at 2:40 PM. He was finally at peace. God bless him! His brain never let him rest until now. I am so honoured to have been loved by this man.

I love you, Tim.

Timothy Ball Obituary

BALL, Timothy Francis, November 5, 1938-September 24, 2022.

Predeceased by his son, Douglas, aged 8 in 1970. Survived by his wife of 61 years, Marty, son David (Crystal), grandchildren, Devon and Ainsley, son Tim (Leann), step-grandaughter Carly (Aaron Lo), and step-great-grandchildren, Liam and Nash.

Tim came to Canada from England in 1957 at the age of 17. He worked in Toronto and Sudbury until 1960 when he joined the RCAF as an Aircrew Radio Operator. He was trained in Winnipeg, where he met and married Marty, who was a student nurse at St. Boniface Hospital. Tim became interested in the climate while on Search and Rescue in the north out of Winnipeg. He got out of the Airforce in September 1968 and went to University. He received his BA Honours at the University of Winnipeg, (United College), and his Masters (Climatology) at the University of Manitoba. He taught as a lecturer at the University of Winnipeg in 1972 and completed his PhD, (Climatology) at Queen Mary College at the University of London, England. Tim spent the better part of his career trying to convince the world that 'Anthropogenic Global Warming' was a man-made hoax. He fought lawsuits, death threats, website hackings, lies and attacks, too numerous to mention. A sense of humour unequaled. Generous to a fault. There will be no public celebrations. No charitable donations and/or flowers, please. Just share a moment with the ones you love.

Marty Ball, et al

Indispensable Advice

…inscribed on a beer mug that Tim had on his desk for many years. Unknown origin….

Sometime when you're feeling important,
Sometime when your ego's in bloom,
Sometime when you take it for granted
You're the best-qualified person in the room,
Sometime when you feel that you're going
Would leave an unfillable hole,
Just follow this simple instruction
And see how it humbles your soul:

Take a bucket and fill it with water,
Put your hand in it up to your wrist;
Pull it out and hole that's remaining
Is a measure of how you'll be missed.
The moral of this quaint example
(as quoted by poets anon.)
Be proud of yourself but remember
There is **NO INDISPENSABLE ONE**.

—Author unknown

CHAPTER THIRTY-SIX
Curriculum Vitae—Dr Tim Ball

Education

BA Honours, University of Winnipeg
MA University of Manitoba
PhD Doctor of Science, Queen Mary College, University of London, England.

Career History

1960 to 1962 Aircrew, Navigation, Electronics, 415 Squadron, Summerside, PEI
1962 to 1964 Operations Officer, Operational Training Unit, Summerside, PEI
1964 to 1968 Operations Officer and Aircrew, 111 Search and Rescue Unit, Winnipeg, Manitoba
1971 to 1982 Instructor/Lecturer, University of Winnipeg
1977 to 1978 Acting Dean of Students
1978 to 1988 Associate Professor, University of Winnipeg
1988 to 1996 Professor, University of Winnipeg
1996 to 2018 Environmental Consultant, Public Speaker, Columnist

Profile

Extensive science background in climatology, especially the reconstruction of past climates and the impact of climate change on human history and the human condition. One of the first climatology PhDs in the world.

Additional experience in water resources, sustainable development, pollution prevention, environmental regulations, and the impact of government policy on business and economics. Chair of provincial boards on water management, environmental issues and sustainable development. Extensive public speaking experience and presentations to professional societies, business conferences, public forums, and various public, private and non-profit organizations. Hundreds of public educational talks on science and the environment in the last fifty years.

Heavily involved throughout his career in local and national committees related to climate, water and river management, and hazardous waste.

A regular contributing writer for The Country Guide and research/author of numerous papers on climate, long-range weather patterns, impacts of climate change on sustainable agriculture, ecosystems, historical climatology, air quality, untapped energy resources, silting and flooding problems, bird migration patterns, historical sites development.

Research Fellow for the George Morris Centre at the University of Guelph, Ontario

Comprehensive involvement in education at all levels, from kindergarten to senior citizens. Curriculum consulting and development. Non-credit courses for seniors on science, environment, sustainable development, water, and geopolitics. Organizer and participant for in-service and professional development for teachers. Board member, Agriculture in the Classroom, in British Columbia.

Books

Ball, Timothy. *The Deliberate Corruption of Climate Science*, Stairway Press, 2014.
Ball, Timothy. *Global Warming, The Biggest Deception in History*. Self-published 2015.
Ball, Timothy co-authoured with Dr Stuart and Mary Houston *The Eighteenth-Century Naturalists of The Hudson Bay*. Published by McGill-Queen's University Press, foreword written by Judith Beattie, Keeper of the Archives, Winnipeg. 2005

Contributions and/or Assistance

Books One and Two of Peter C. Newman's Trilogy of The Hudson Bay Company
The Company of Adventures
Caesars of the Wilderness

The Secret Voyage of Sir Francis Drake by Sam Bawlf

Slaying the Sky Dragon—Parts 1 and 2

The documentary video—*The Great Global Warming Swindle* by Martin Durkin

The Green Gospel, Sheila Zilinsky

Career Achievements

- Founder and Director, Rupert's Land Research Centre 1980-1996
- Former Member, Manitoba Water Commission 1980-1996
- Past President, Manitoba Social Science Teachers Association
- Past Editor, Manitoba Social Science Teachers Journal
- Past Chairman, Canadian Committee on Climatic Fluctuation and Man
- Former Board Member, The Forks Development Heritage Advisory Board
- Former Board Member, Western Canada Pictorial Index
- Former Chair, City of Winnipeg's Advisory Committee on Hazardous Waste
- Technical Advisor to the Canadian Cattlemen's Association
- Former Chair Assiniboine River Management Advisory Board
- Seventeen years as Columnist Country Guide agricultural magazine, 1990-2007
- Columnist—Ontario Landowners Magazine
- Winner of Queen's Diamond Jubilee Medal

Queen Elizabeth II
Diamond Jubilee Medal

Médaille du Jubilé de Diamant
de la Reine Elizabeth II

Tim Ball

By Command of Her Majesty The Queen, the Diamond Jubilee Medal is presented to you in commemoration of the sixtieth anniversary of Her Majesty's Accession to the Throne and in recognition of your contributions to Canada.

Par ordre de Sa Majesté la Reine, la Médaille du jubilé de diamant vous est présentée en commémoration du soixantième anniversaire de l'accession de Sa Majesté au Trône et en reconnaissance de votre contribution au service du Canada.

Governor General of Canada *Gouverneur général du Canada*

1952 – 2012

Awards

- Clifford Robson Award for Teaching Excellence, University of Winnipeg
- Atchison Award for Community Service, University of Winnipeg
- Humboldt Award, Geography Department, University of Winnipeg
- Graduate Fellowship, University of Manitoba
- Research Fellow for the George Morris Centre
- Rotary Club, Paul Harris Fellow

List of Publications for which he Wrote Regular Columns

Country Guide: 1990-2007 Monthly column titled Weather Talk. Approximately 144 articles. Tim was dismissed. "We are going in a different direction" was their reasoning. What is more appropriate information for farmers than a weather column?

Canada Free Press: Tim wrote weekly, approximately 200 articles 1990-2007
This ended when Tim was sued by Andrew Weaver of the University of Victoria, the leader of the Green Party of BC.

Watts Up with That: Tim wrote many articles for this website. Thank you so much, Anthony Watts. About 160 articles.

Landowners Magazine: December 16, 2013 to March 2017. Approximately 80 articles.

Climate Science International: Tim wrote for and advised Tom Harris over many years. Tom wrote a chapter in this book. He was a great friend and supporter of Tim.

Friends of Science: Tim helped set up this group in Calgary, making strides in getting the media to give them some attention. Not easy to do as they were labelled as being paid by the oil industry and are still struggling to this day. Many members are retired geologists. One very astute and brilliant member was Albert Jacobs. A lovely man in every way. He died in 2019 and is very much missed.

The Frontier Centre for Public Policy: Tim wrote for and helped the CEO, Peter Holle, for many years.

These are other websites, TV programs and radio programs that Tim did regularly.

Technocracy News
Erskine Radio by Night: Erskine Payton
Coast to Coast: George Noory
Freedom Free for All: Josh Steffler
Radio America Greg Columbus
Victoria Taft Radio Show
I Spy Radio: Karla Davenport
CFAX Joe Easingwood
CFAX Ian Jessop

Everything Reminds Me of Tim

The National Gallery bought the *Voice of Fire* painting for $1.76 million in 1967.
(How much would that be in today's dollars?)

Tim said then: "How do they know if it is upside down?"

$1,760,000 in 1967 is worth $16,163,861.08 today

Source: https://www.in2013dollars.com/

Tim and Marty, 1988

Requiescat in Pace, Tim

Was, a song by Ken Coffman

Days I was down, he loaned a light
A fitful flicker 'gainst the velvet night
But now's no time for glib clichés
Or mentioning the big man's mysterious ways

Flowers bloom and fade away
Seeds sown for another day
We don't only walk the Earth sun-kissed
Things we do should be worth the risk

Life cut short, soul's rent, heart's broke
But while we had him, he laughed and joked
We're here and gone—that's the grand plan
But the way we end is not the measure of the man

Was is a sad word, a bad word, a loss
Casting a shadow on life's shiny gloss

It hurts to say he *was* my colleague, my friend
It should be *is*, unfinished—no end

I won't believe his life was wasted
…won't insult the joys he tasted
We're here and gone—that's the grand plan
The way we end is not the measure of the man

Should be *is*, unfinished…no end